Vol.1
"An Emergency"

D0521328

First printed in magazine format as ZERO #1—5

ZERO™
Vol. 1:
"AN EMERGENCY"
#1—5

Written by
Ales KOT

Illustrated by
Michael WALSH
Tradd MOORE
Mateus SANTOLOUCO
Morgan JESKE
Will TEMPEST

Lettered by
Clayton COWLES

Colored by
Jordie BELLAIRE

Designed by
Tom MULLER

Collection designed by
Tom MULLER

Original cover design, graphics and colors by Tom Muller, with Michael Walsh, Tradd Moore, Mateus Santolouco, Morgan Jeske, Will Tempest, Becky Cloonan, Chris Burnham, Paul Pope, and Christian Ward.

Image Comics, Inc.

Robert Kirkman — chief operating officer
Erik Larsen — chief financial officer
Todd McFarlane — president
Marc Silvestri — chief executive officer
Jim Valentino — vice president

Eric Stephenson — publisher
Ron Richards — director of business development
Jennifer de Guzman — director of trade book sales
Kat Salazar — director of PR & marketing
Corey Murphy — director of retail sales
Jeremy Sullivan — director of digital sales
Emilio Bautista — sales assistant
Branwyn Bigglestone — senior accounts manager
Emily Miller — accounts manager
Jessica Ambriz — administrative assistant
Tyler Shainline — events coordinator
David Brothers — content manager
Jonathan Chan — production manager
Drew Gill — art director
Jonathan Chan — print manager
Monica Garcia — senior production artist
Addison Duke — production artist
Tricia Ramos — production assistant

ZERO VOL 1. Second Printing. January 2015. Published by Image Comics, Inc. Office of publication: 2001 Center Street, Sixth Floor, Berkeley, CA 94704. Copyright © 2014 ALES KOT. All rights reserved. ZERO™ (including all prominent characters featured herein), its logo and all character likenesses are trademarks of Ales Kot, unless otherwise noted. Image Comics® and its logos are registered trademarks of Image Comics, Inc. No part of this publication may be reproduced or transmitted, in any form or by any means (except for short excerpts for review purposes) without express written permission of Image Comics, Inc. All names, characters, events and locales in this publication are entirely fictional. Any resemblance to actual living persons (living or dead), events or places, without satiric intent, is coincidental. First printed in the USA. For information regarding the CPSIA on this printed material call: 203-595-3636 and provide reference # RICH- 599842. For international rights contact: foreignlicensing@imagecomics.com. ISBN- 978-1-60706-863-1

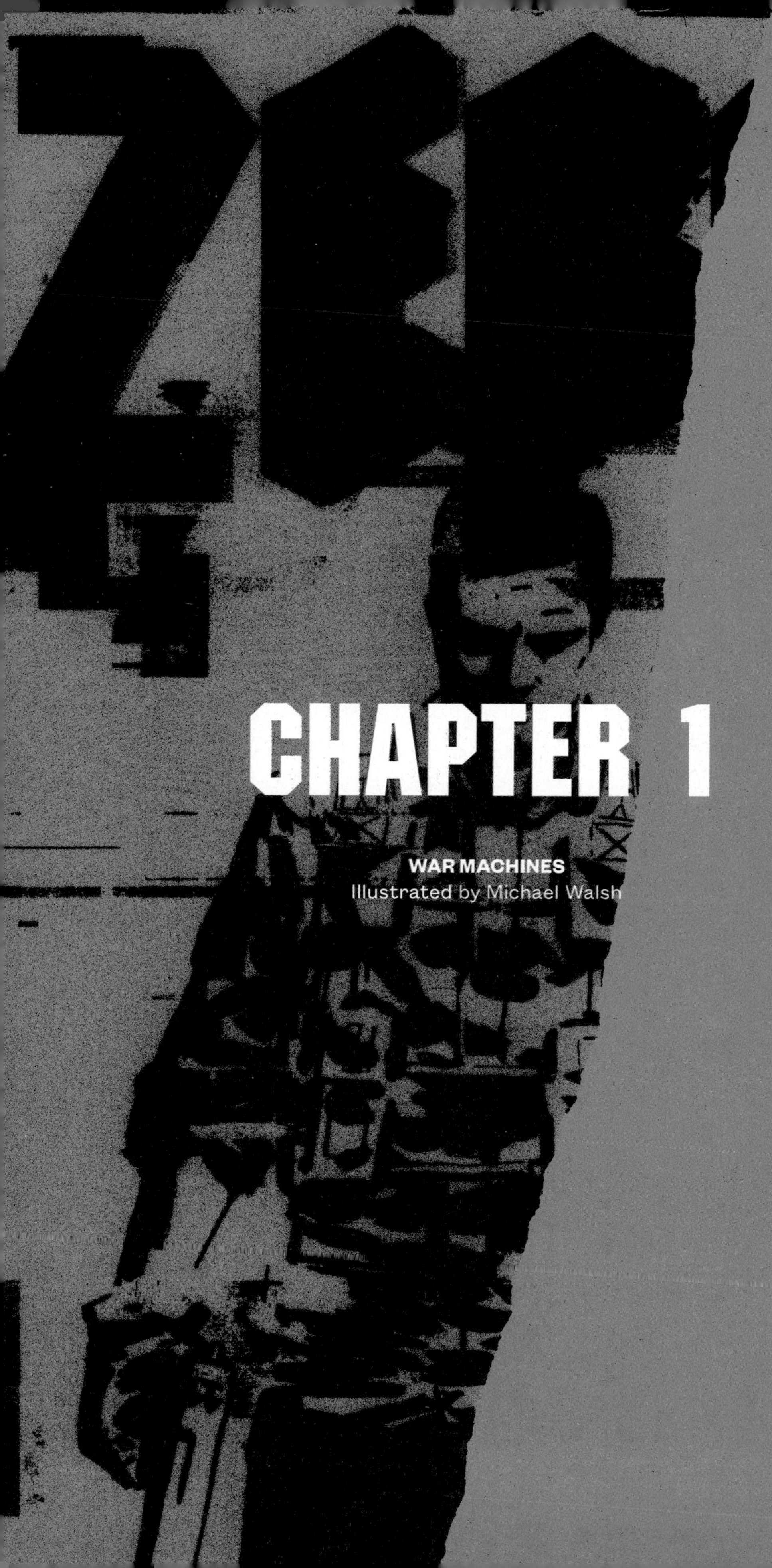

CHAPTER 1

WAR MACHINES

Illustrated by Michael Walsh

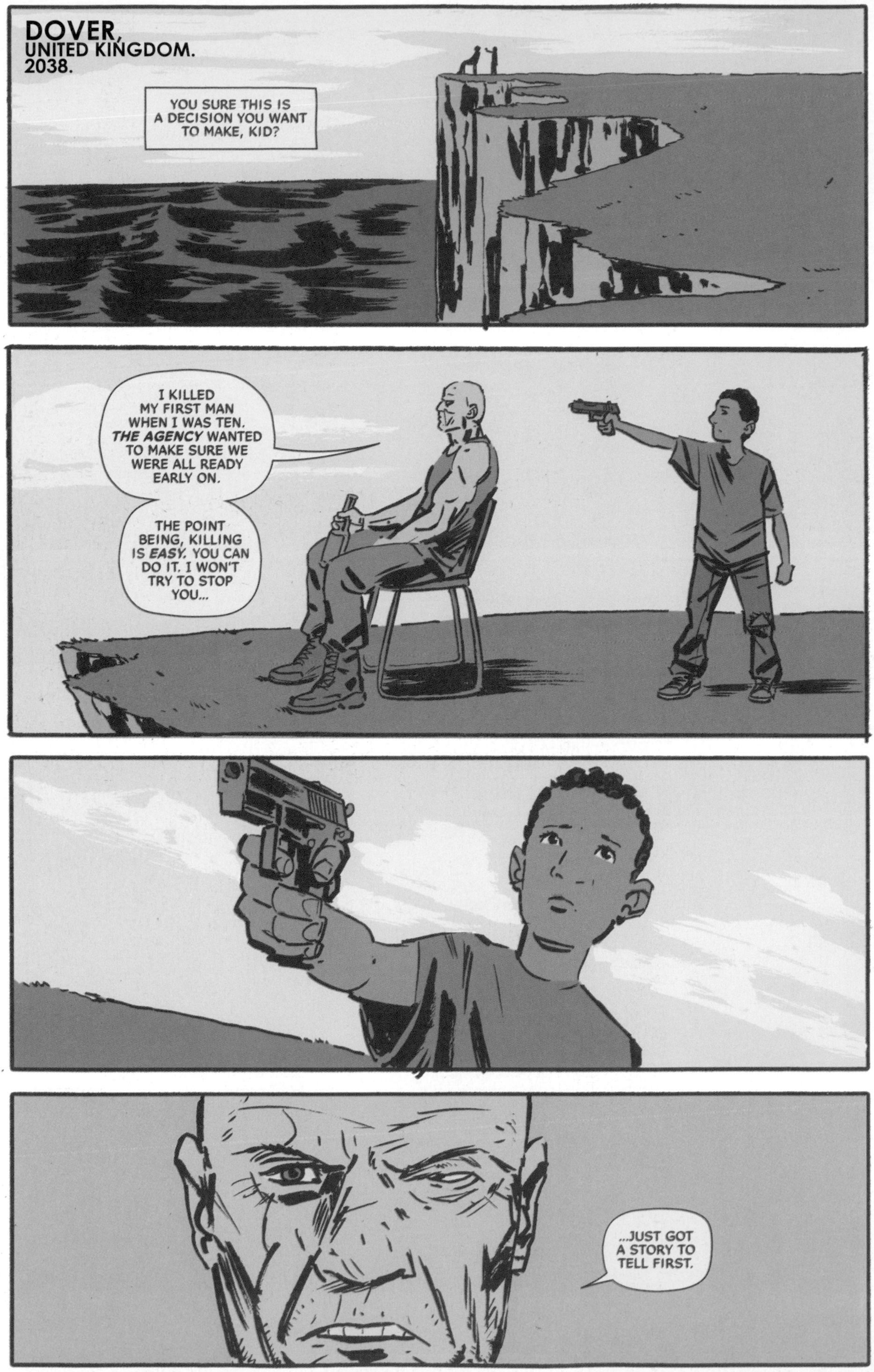
DOVER, UNITED KINGDOM. 2038.
YOU SURE THIS IS A DECISION YOU WANT TO MAKE, KID?
I KILLED MY FIRST MAN WHEN I WAS TEN. THE AGENCY WANTED TO MAKE SURE WE WERE ALL READY EARLY ON.
THE POINT BEING, KILLING IS EASY. YOU CAN DO IT. I WON'T TRY TO STOP YOU...
...JUST GOT A STORY TO TELL FIRST.

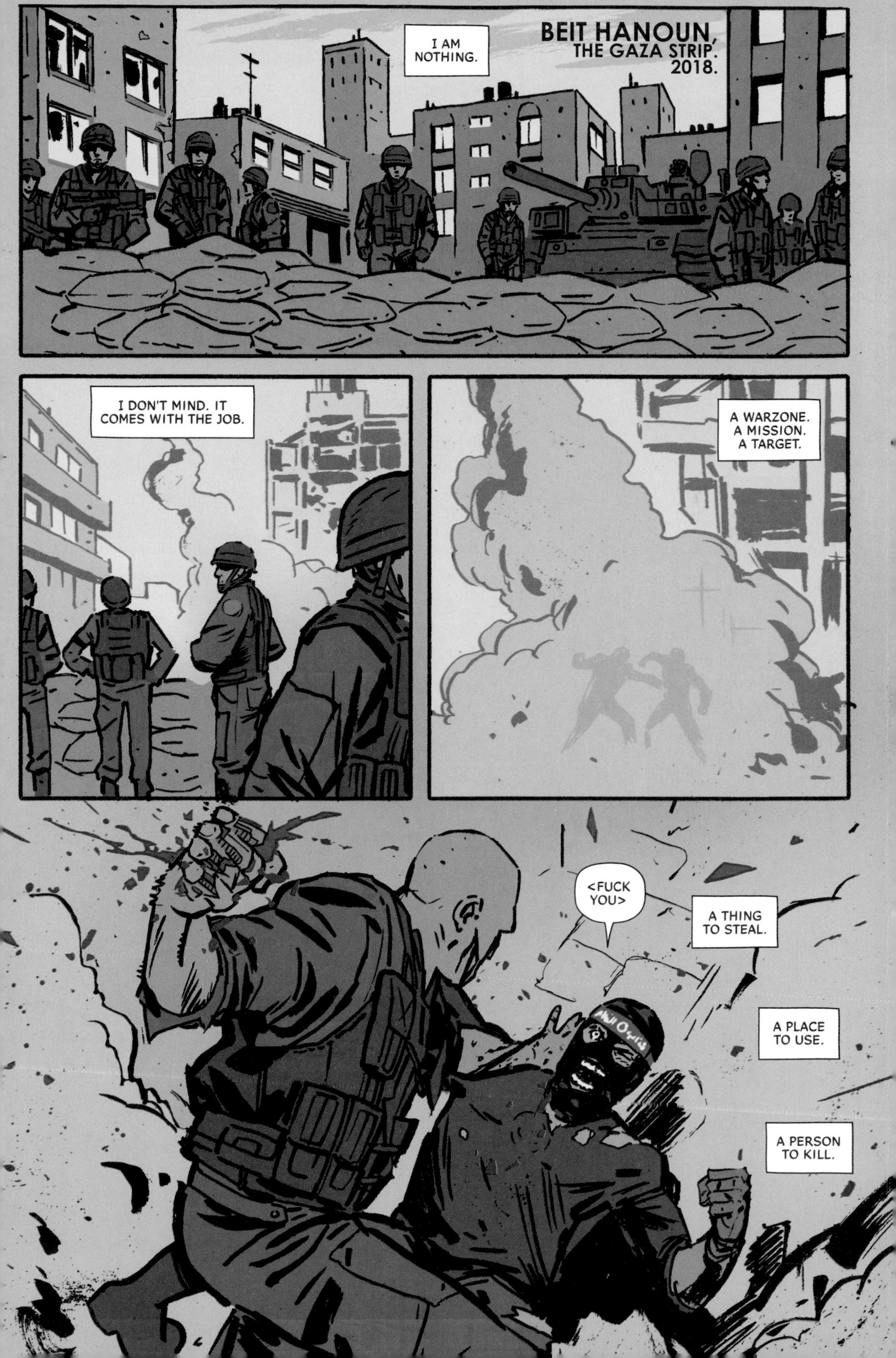
BEIT HANOUN, THE GAZA STRIP. 2018.
I AM NOTHING.
I DON'T MIND. IT COMES WITH THE JOB.
A WARZONE. A MISSION. A TARGET.
<FUCK YOU>
A THING TO STEAL.
A PLACE TO USE.
A PERSON TO KILL.

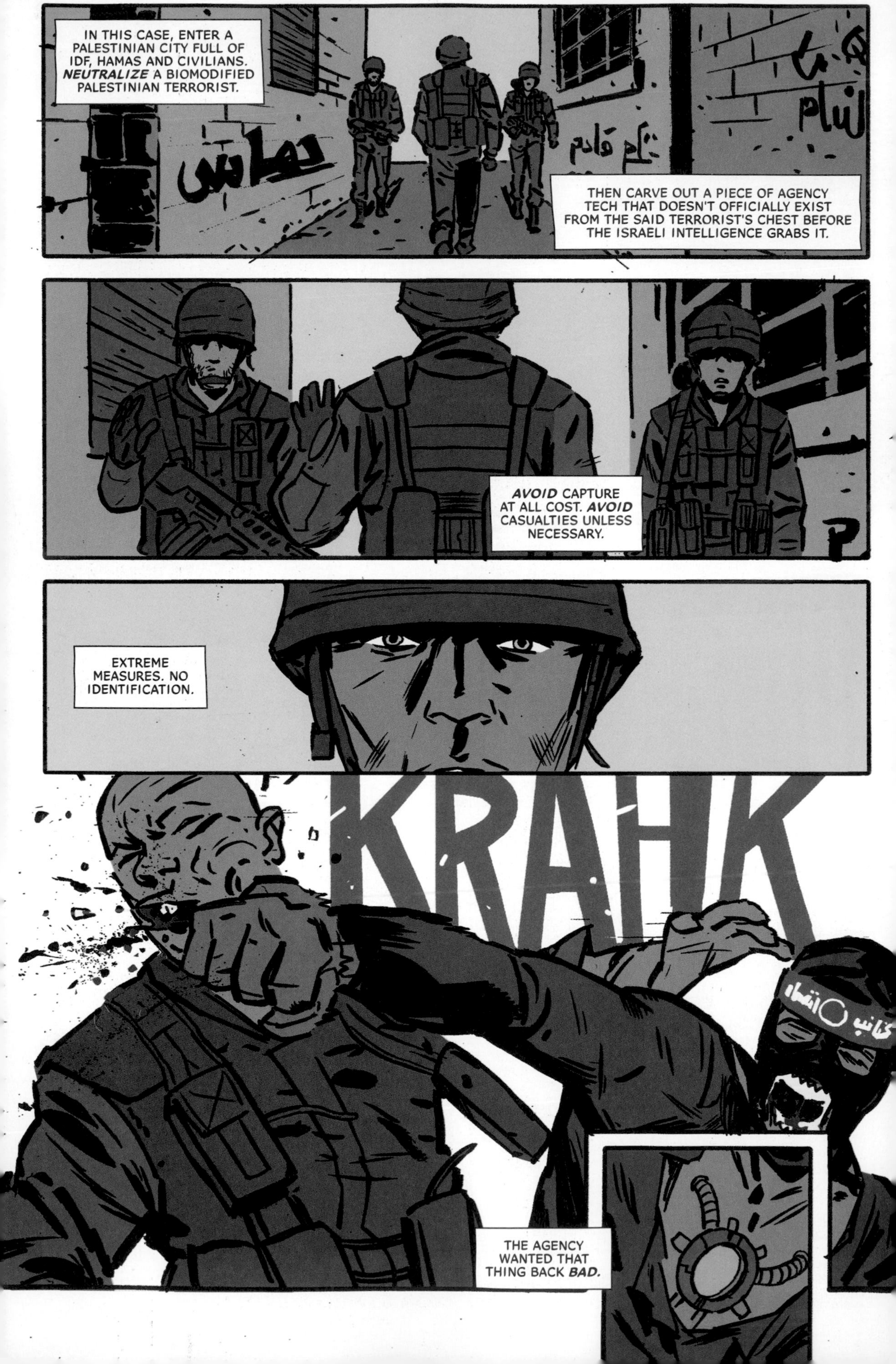
IN THIS CASE, ENTER A PALESTINIAN CITY FULL OF IDF, HAMAS AND CIVILIANS. *NEUTRALIZE* A BIOMODIFIED PALESTINIAN TERRORIST.
THEN CARVE OUT A PIECE OF AGENCY TECH THAT DOESN'T OFFICIALLY EXIST FROM THE SAID TERRORIST'S CHEST BEFORE THE ISRAELI INTELLIGENCE GRABS IT.
AVOID CAPTURE AT ALL COST. *AVOID* CASUALTIES UNLESS NECESSARY.
EXTREME MEASURES. NO IDENTIFICATION.
KRAHK
THE AGENCY WANTED THAT THING BACK *BAD.*

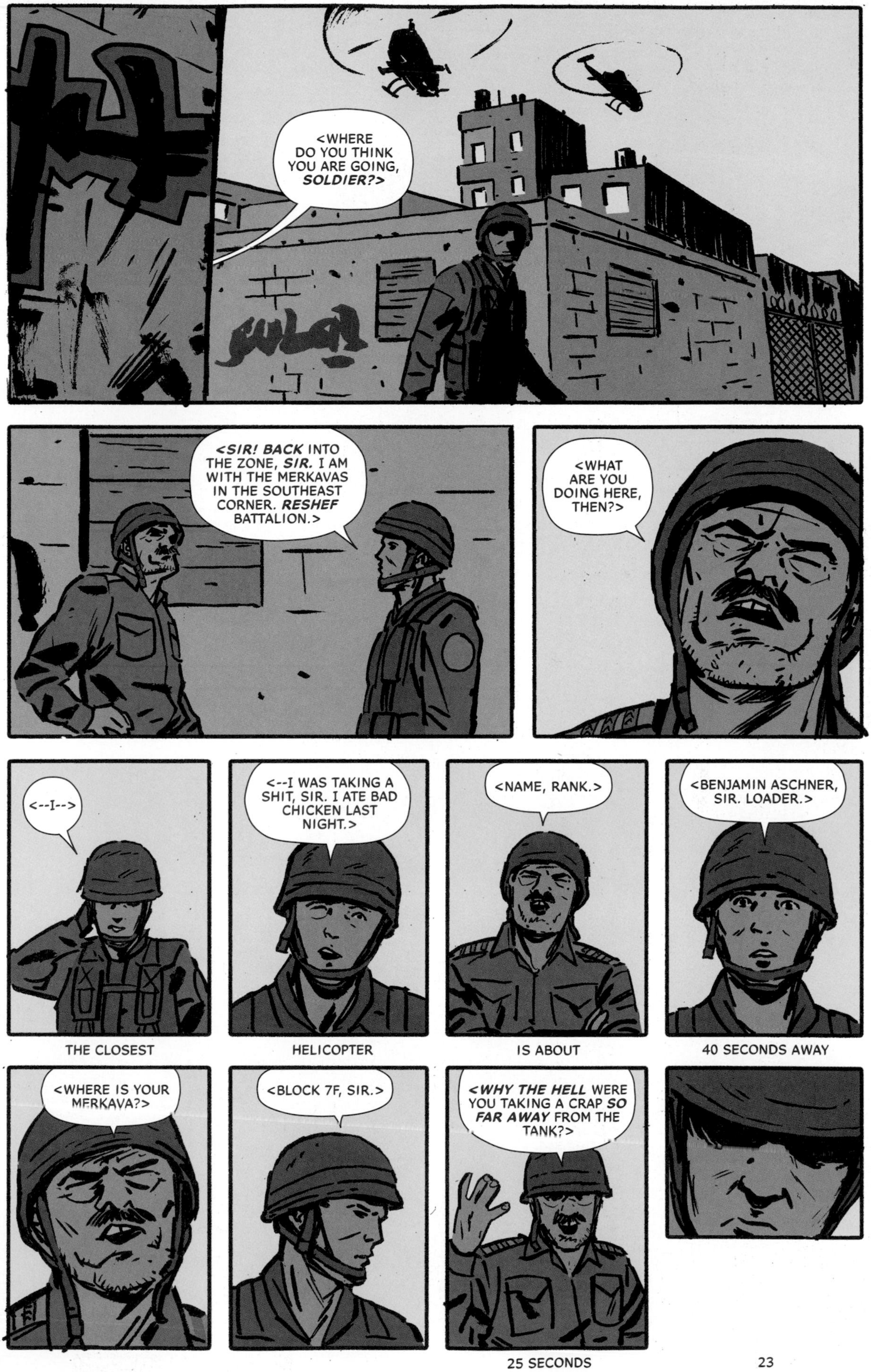
<WHERE DO YOU THINK YOU ARE GOING, SOLDIER?>
<SIR! BACK INTO THE ZONE, SIR. I AM WITH THE MERKAVAS IN THE SOUTHEAST CORNER. RESHEF BATTALION.>
<WHAT ARE YOU DOING HERE, THEN?>
<--I-->
THE CLOSEST
<--I WAS TAKING A SHIT, SIR. I ATE BAD CHICKEN LAST NIGHT.>
HELICOPTER
<NAME, RANK.>
IS ABOUT
<BENJAMIN ASCHNER, SIR. LOADER.>
40 SECONDS AWAY
<WHERE IS YOUR MERKAVA?>
<BLOCK 7F, SIR.>
<WHY THE HELL WERE YOU TAKING A CRAP SO FAR AWAY FROM THE TANK?>
25 SECONDS

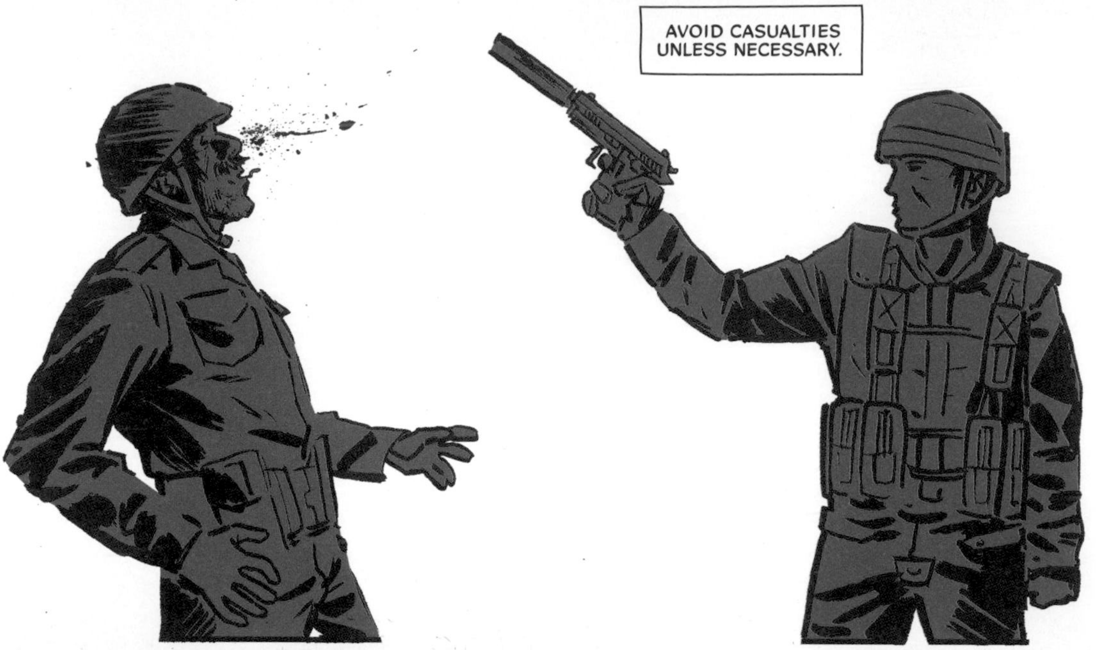
AVOID CASUALTIES
UNLESS NECESSARY.

17 SECONDS

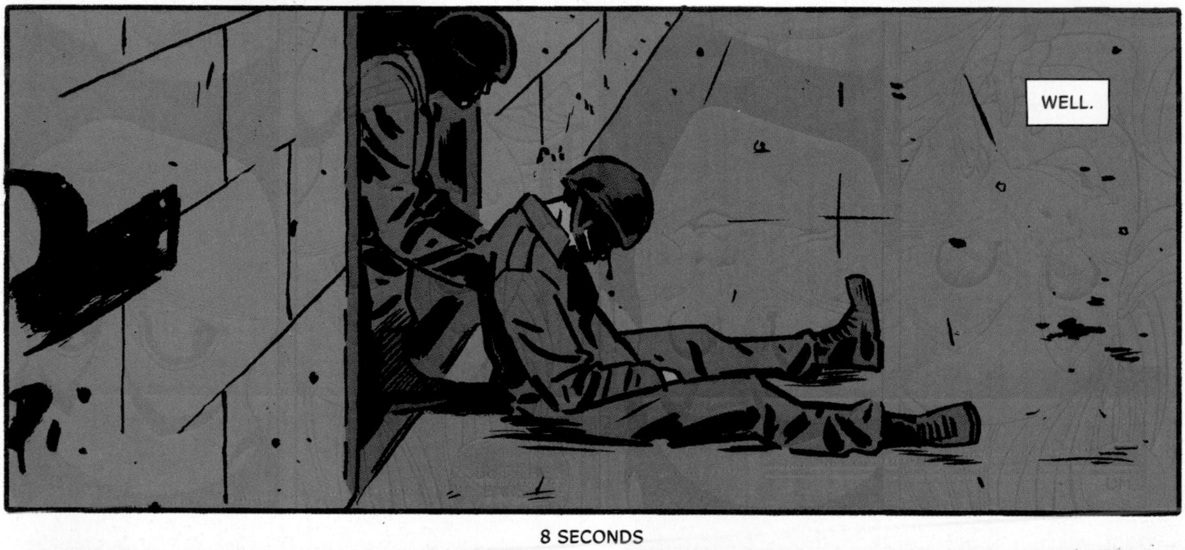
WELL.

8 SECONDS

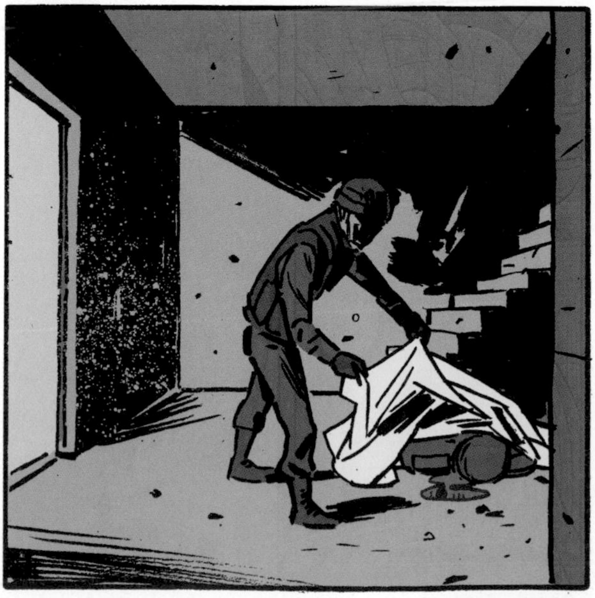

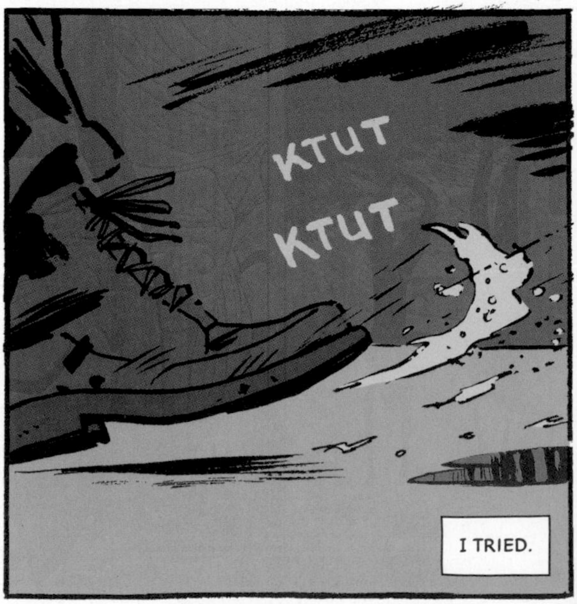
KTUT
KTUT
I TRIED.

2 SECONDS

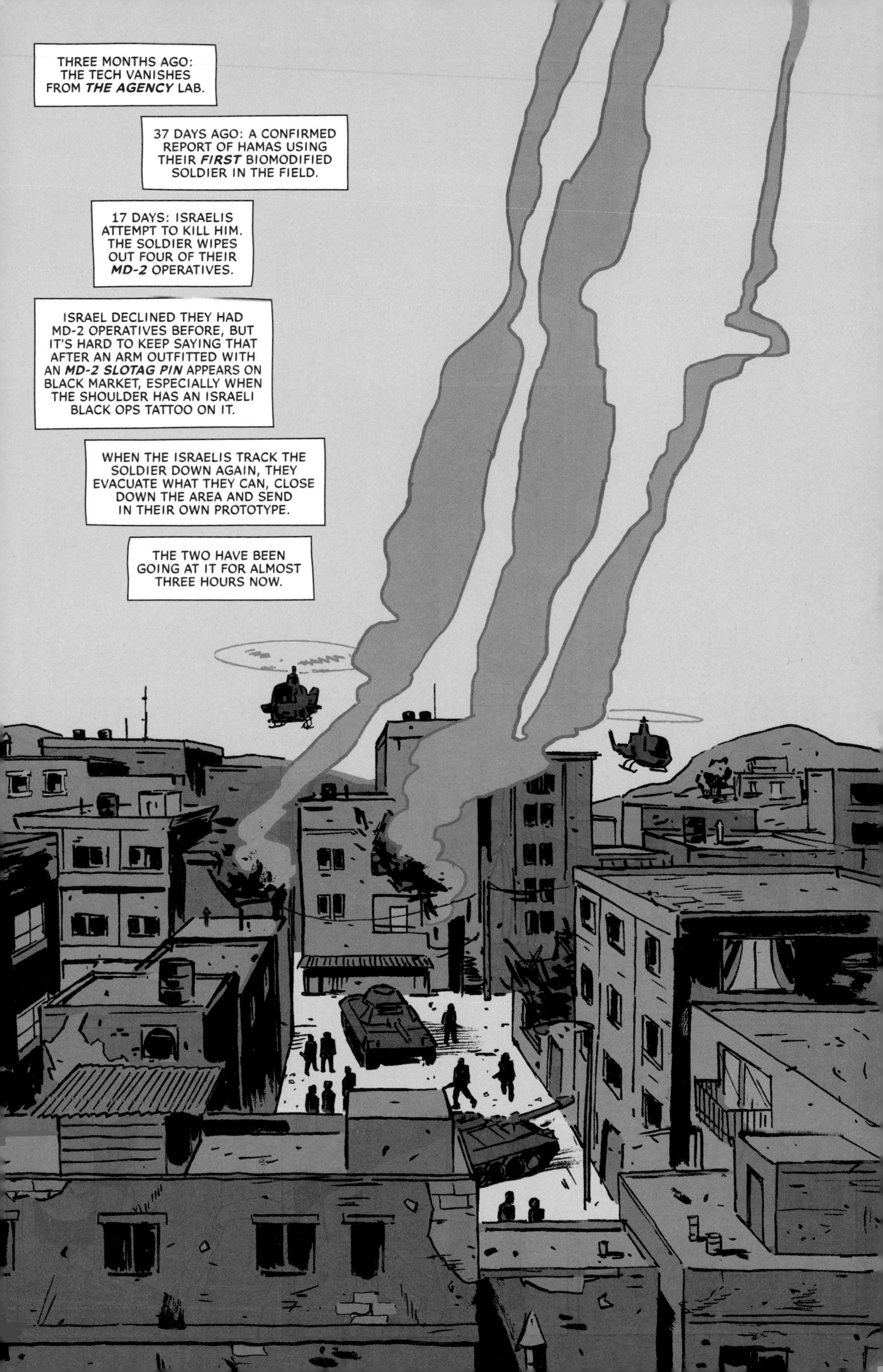
THREE MONTHS AGO: THE TECH VANISHES FROM *THE AGENCY* LAB.
37 DAYS AGO: A CONFIRMED REPORT OF HAMAS USING THEIR *FIRST* BIOMODIFIED SOLDIER IN THE FIELD.
17 DAYS: ISRAELIS ATTEMPT TO KILL HIM. THE SOLDIER WIPES OUT FOUR OF THEIR *MD-2* OPERATIVES.
ISRAEL DECLINED THEY HAD MD-2 OPERATIVES BEFORE, BUT IT'S HARD TO KEEP SAYING THAT AFTER AN ARM OUTFITTED WITH AN *MD-2 SLOTAG PIN* APPEARS ON BLACK MARKET, ESPECIALLY WHEN THE SHOULDER HAS AN ISRAELI BLACK OPS TATTOO ON IT.
WHEN THE ISRAELIS TRACK THE SOLDIER DOWN AGAIN, THEY EVACUATE WHAT THEY CAN, CLOSE DOWN THE AREA AND SEND IN THEIR OWN PROTOTYPE.
THE TWO HAVE BEEN GOING AT IT FOR ALMOST THREE HOURS NOW.

CHAPTER ONE:
WAR MACHINES

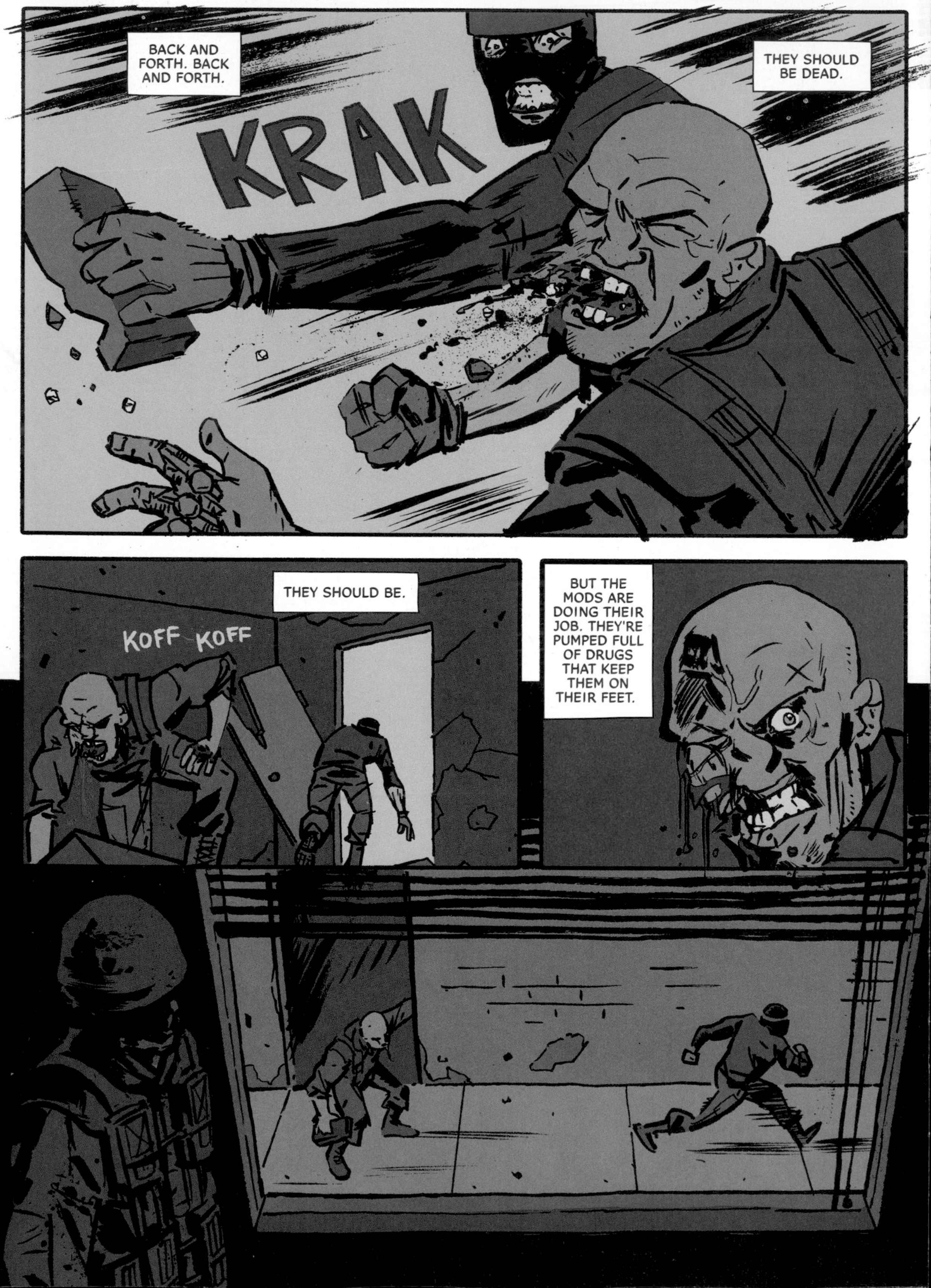
BACK AND FORTH. BACK AND FORTH.
THEY SHOULD BE DEAD.
KRAK
THEY SHOULD BE.
KOFF KOFF
BUT THE MODS ARE DOING THEIR JOB. THEY'RE PUMPED FULL OF DRUGS THAT KEEP THEM ON THEIR FEET.

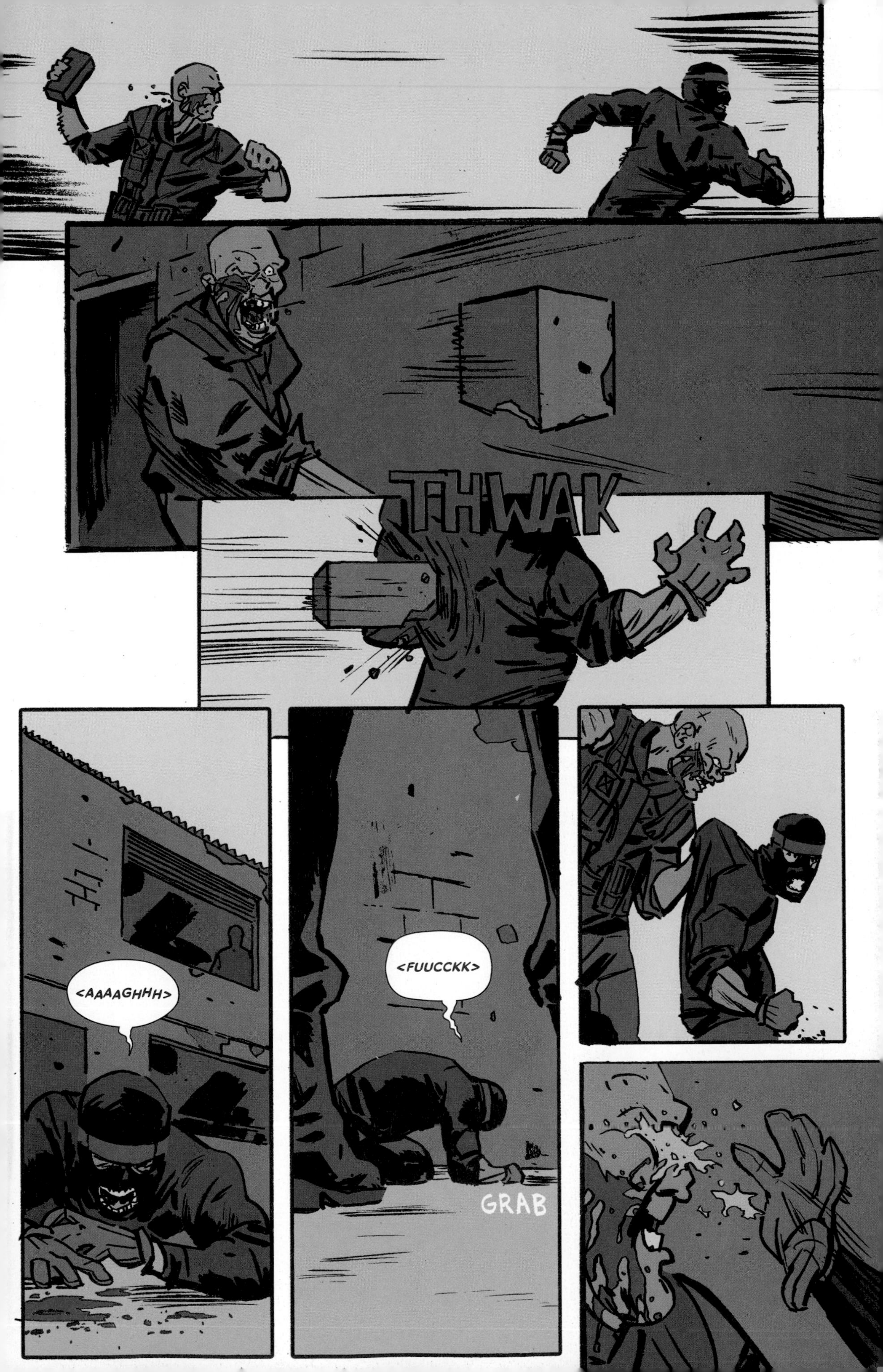
THWAK
<AAAAGHHH>
<FUUCCKK>
GRAB

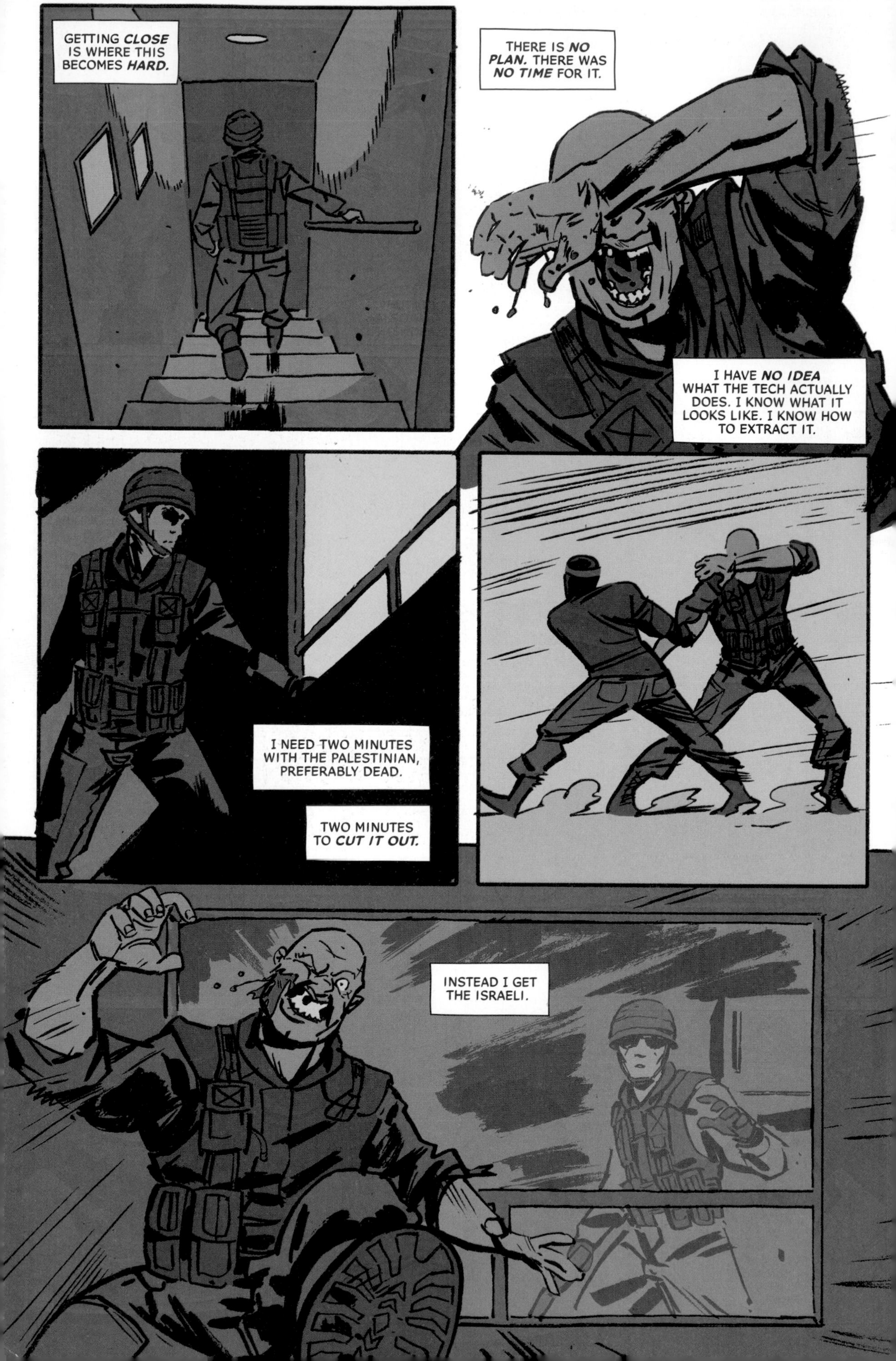
GETTING CLOSE IS WHERE THIS BECOMES HARD.
THERE IS NO PLAN. THERE WAS NO TIME FOR IT.
I HAVE NO IDEA WHAT THE TECH ACTUALLY DOES. I KNOW WHAT IT LOOKS LIKE. I KNOW HOW TO EXTRACT IT.
I NEED TWO MINUTES WITH THE PALESTINIAN, PREFERABLY DEAD.
TWO MINUTES TO CUT IT OUT.
INSTEAD I GET THE ISRAELI.

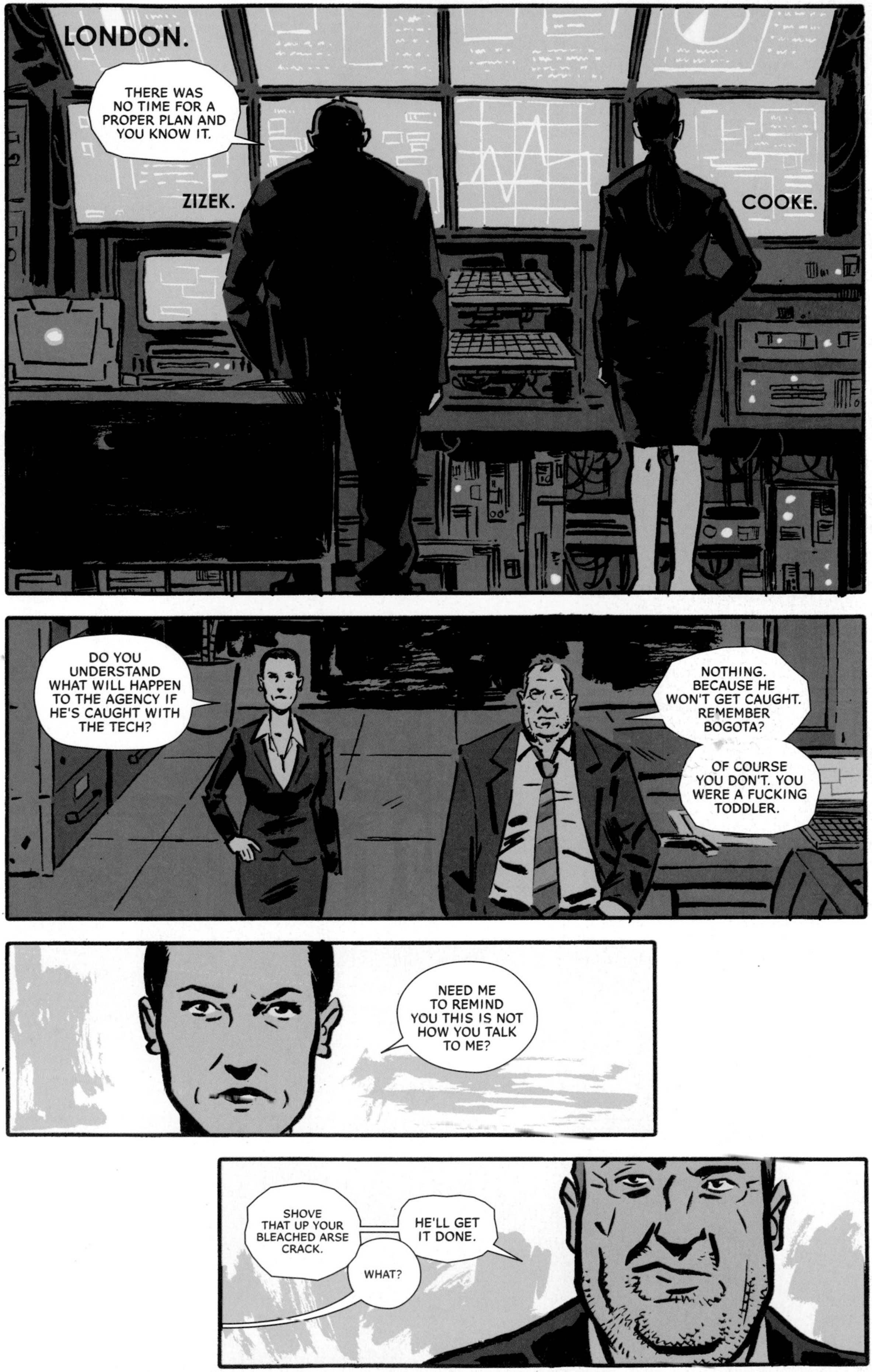
LONDON.
THERE WAS NO TIME FOR A PROPER PLAN AND YOU KNOW IT.
ZIZEK.
COOKE.
DO YOU UNDERSTAND WHAT WILL HAPPEN TO THE AGENCY IF HE'S CAUGHT WITH THE TECH?
NOTHING. BECAUSE HE WON'T GET CAUGHT. REMEMBER BOGOTA?
OF COURSE YOU DON'T. YOU WERE A FUCKING TODDLER.
NEED ME TO REMIND YOU THIS IS NOT HOW YOU TALK TO ME?
SHOVE THAT UP YOUR BLEACHED ARSE CRACK.
WHAT?
HE'LL GET IT DONE.

ZERO AND MINA ARE THE LAST EARLY 90s OPERATIVES. DID YOU BECOME ATTACHED TO HIM? IS THAT WHAT THIS IS ABOUT?

DON'T BE RIDICULOUS, SARA.

EDWARD ZERO

ROMAN... LOOK, ZERO IS TESTING HIGH ON THE HÄYHÄ SCALE.

HE *ALWAYS* HAS. AND HE ALWAYS DID AS HE WAS TOLD REGARDLESS.

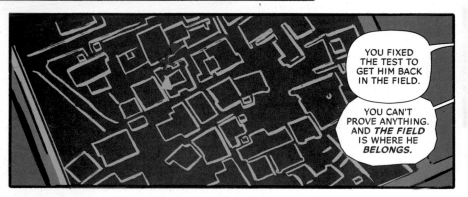

YOU FIXED THE TEST TO GET HIM BACK IN THE FIELD.

YOU CAN'T PROVE ANYTHING. AND *THE FIELD* IS WHERE HE *BELONGS.*

THE NUMBERS ARE *GOING UP.* THERE WILL BE AN INCIDENT AND IT WILL *FUCK EVERYONE.*

HE GETS THINGS *DONE.*

WE NEED PEOPLE WHO GET THINGS DONE.

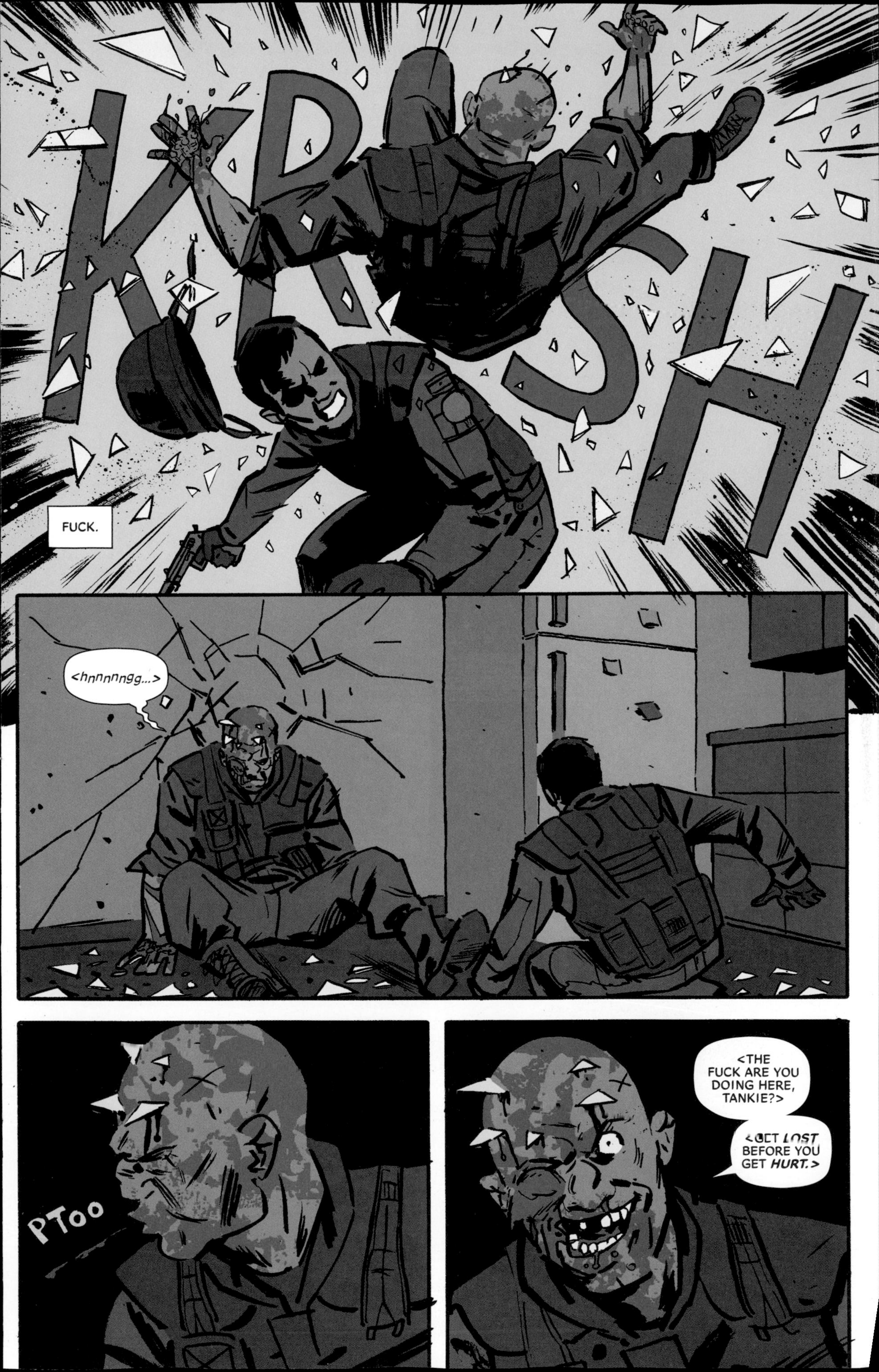
KRASH
FUCK.
<hnnnnngg...>
PTOO
<THE FUCK ARE YOU DOING HERE, TANKIE?>
<GET *LOST* BEFORE YOU GET *HURT.*>

NOT THE RIGHT TIME TO MAKE A MOVE. I SLIDE INTO THE ADJACENT ROOM. AND THAT IS WHEN I REALIZE--

--NOT EVERYONE MADE IT OUT.

MAKES SENSE.

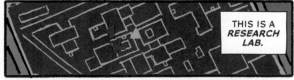

THIS IS A RESEARCH LAB.

RIIIIP

COULD SHOOT THEM IN THE HEADS.

NOT SURE HOW WELL THAT WOULD WORK.

RRIIIIIP

THUD

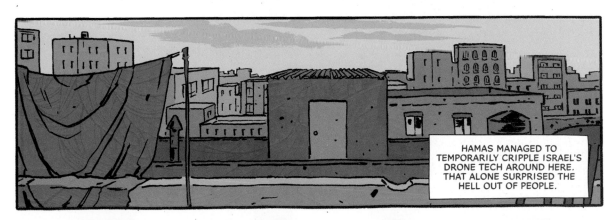

HAMAS MANAGED TO TEMPORARILY CRIPPLE ISRAEL'S DRONE TECH AROUND HERE. THAT ALONE SURPRISED THE HELL OUT OF PEOPLE.

KRASH

THE HACK IS GOOD FOR THE MISSION.

MEANS I CAN FOLLOW WITHOUT TOO MUCH RISK.

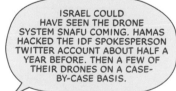

ISRAEL COULD HAVE SEEN THE DRONE SYSTEM SNAFU COMING. HAMAS HACKED THE IDF SPOKESPERSON TWITTER ACCOUNT ABOUT HALF A YEAR BEFORE. THEN A FEW OF THEIR DRONES ON A CASE-BY-CASE BASIS.

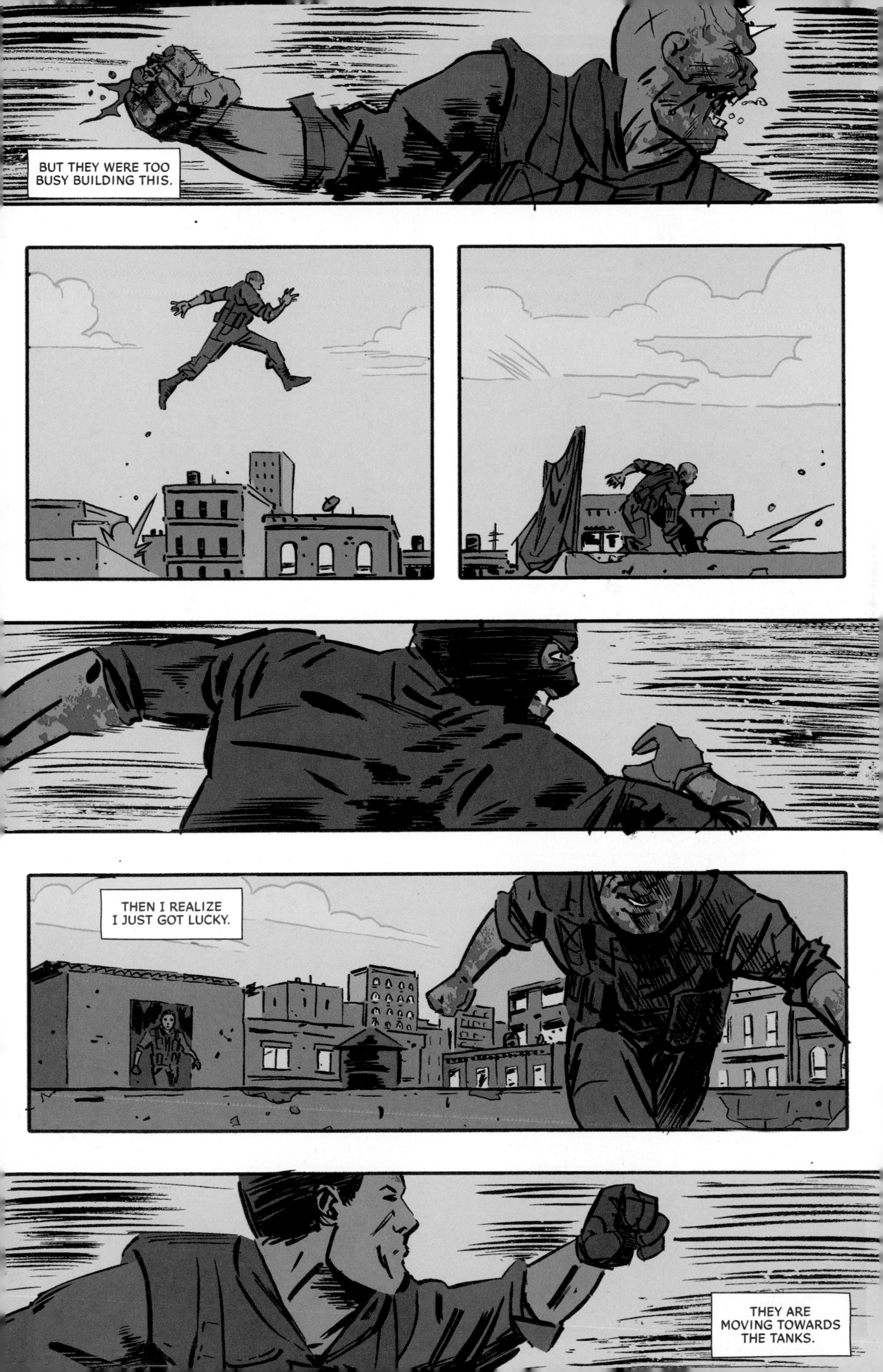
BUT THEY WERE TOO BUSY BUILDING THIS.
THEN I REALIZE I JUST GOT LUCKY.
THEY ARE MOVING TOWARDS THE TANKS.

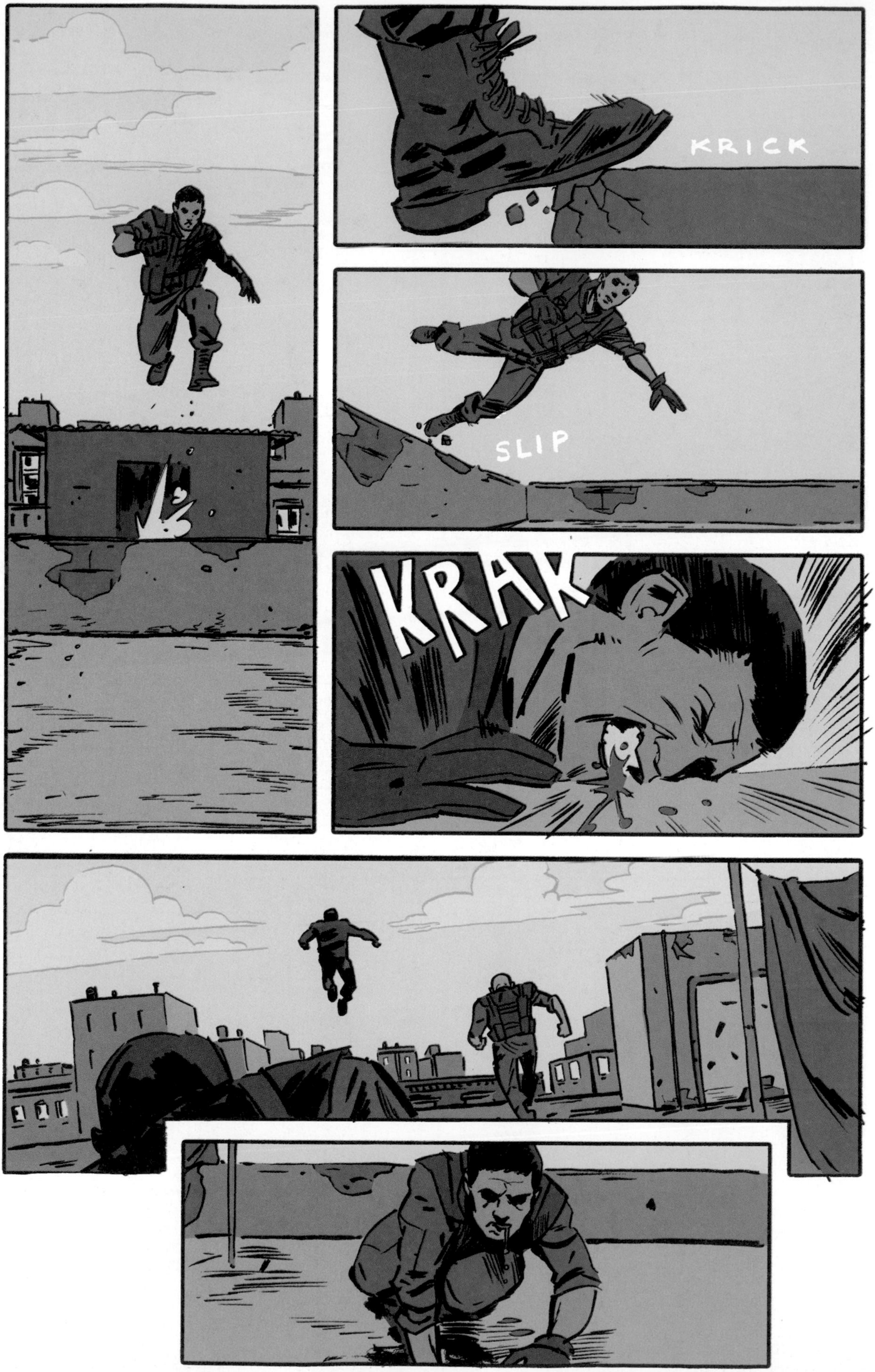
KRICK
SLIP
KRAK

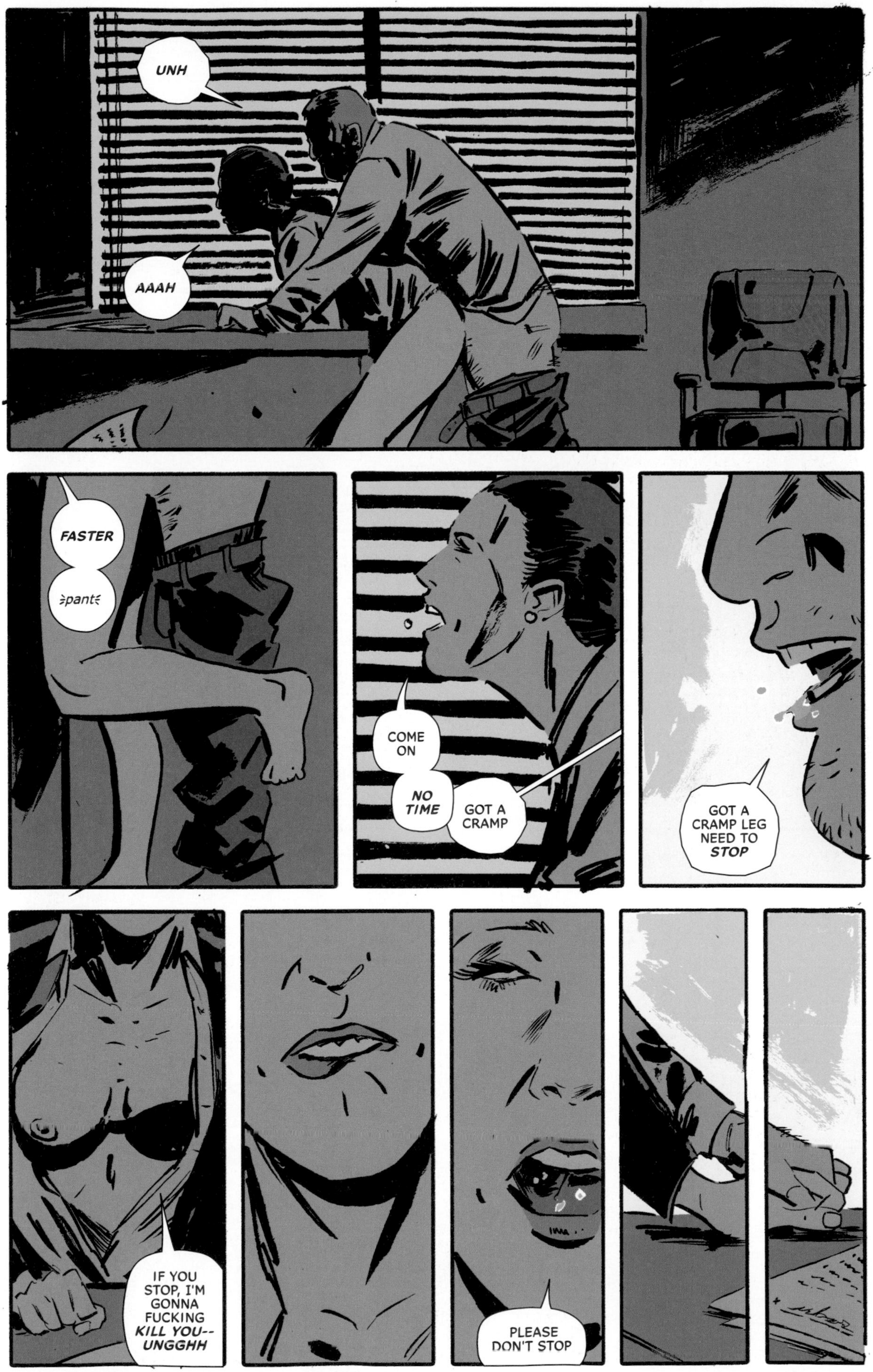
UNH
AAAH
FASTER
≷pant≶
COME ON
NO TIME
GOT A CRAMP
GOT A CRAMP LEG NEED TO STOP
IF YOU STOP, I'M GONNA FUCKING KILL YOU-- UNGGHH
PLEASE DON'T STOP

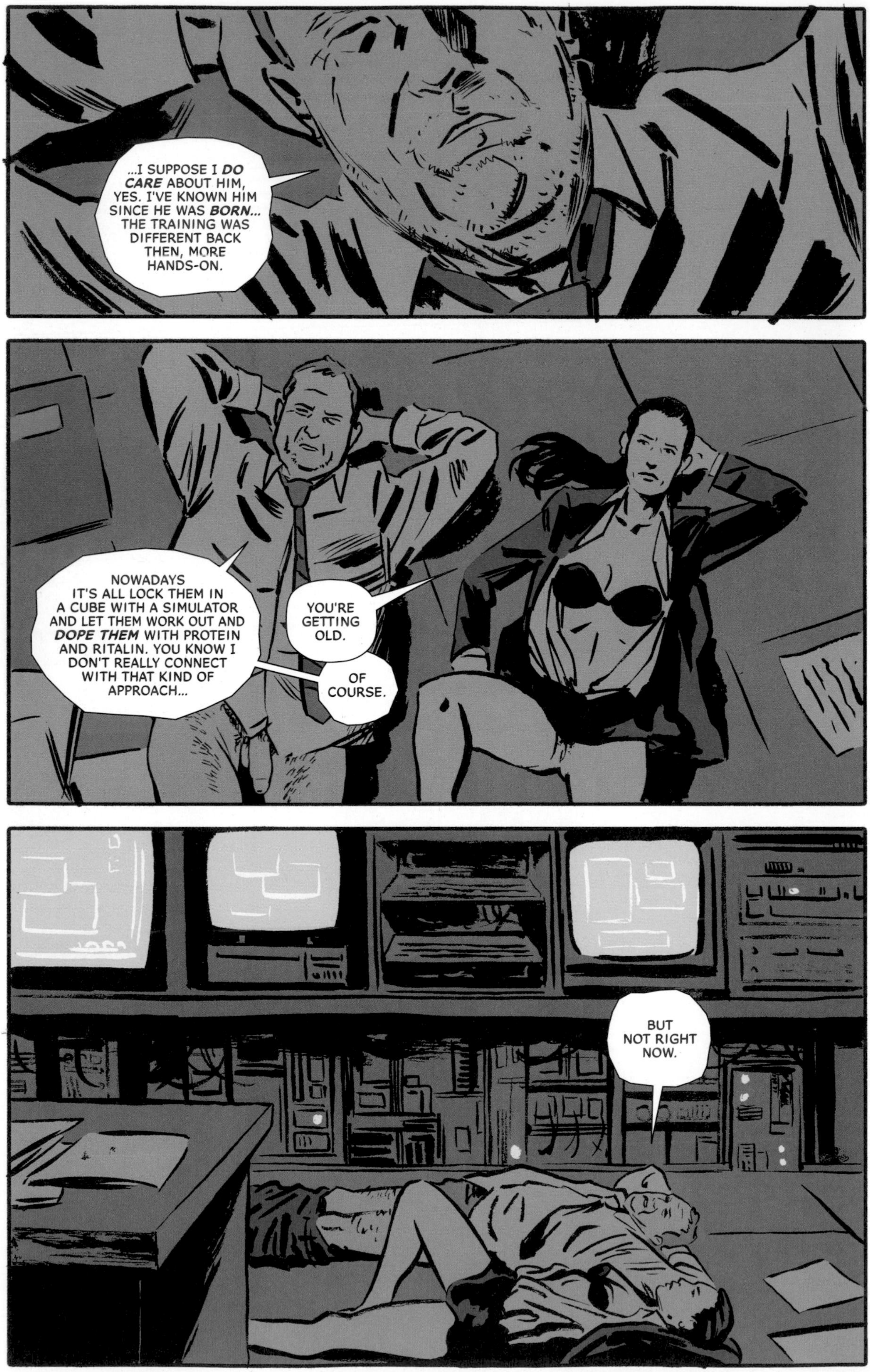
...I SUPPOSE I **DO CARE** ABOUT HIM, YES. I'VE KNOWN HIM SINCE HE WAS **BORN...** THE TRAINING WAS DIFFERENT BACK THEN, MORE HANDS-ON.
NOWADAYS IT'S ALL LOCK THEM IN A CUBE WITH A SIMULATOR AND LET THEM WORK OUT AND **DOPE THEM** WITH PROTEIN AND RITALIN. YOU KNOW I DON'T REALLY CONNECT WITH THAT KIND OF APPROACH...
YOU'RE GETTING OLD.
OF COURSE.
BUT NOT RIGHT NOW.

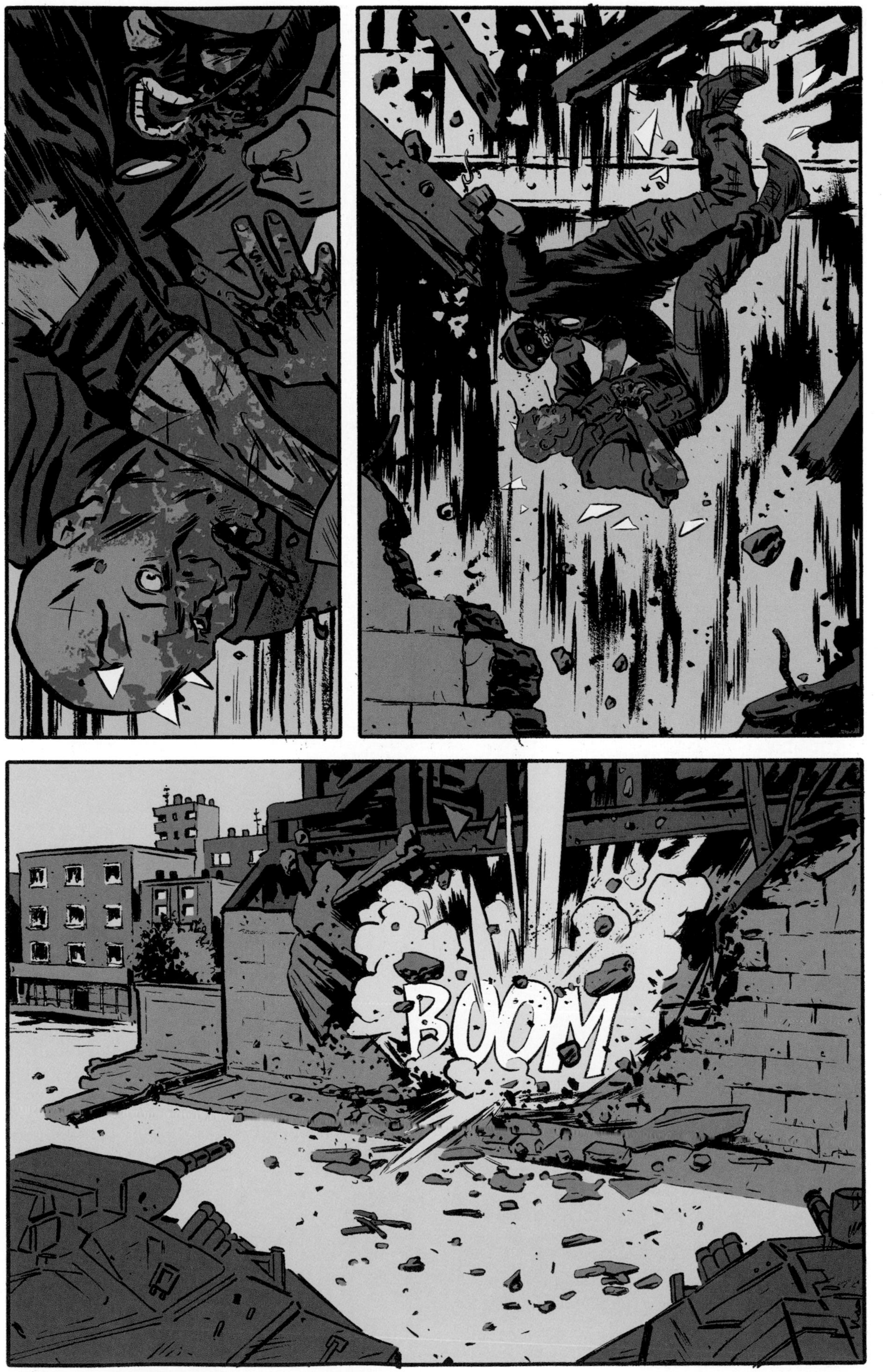
BOOM

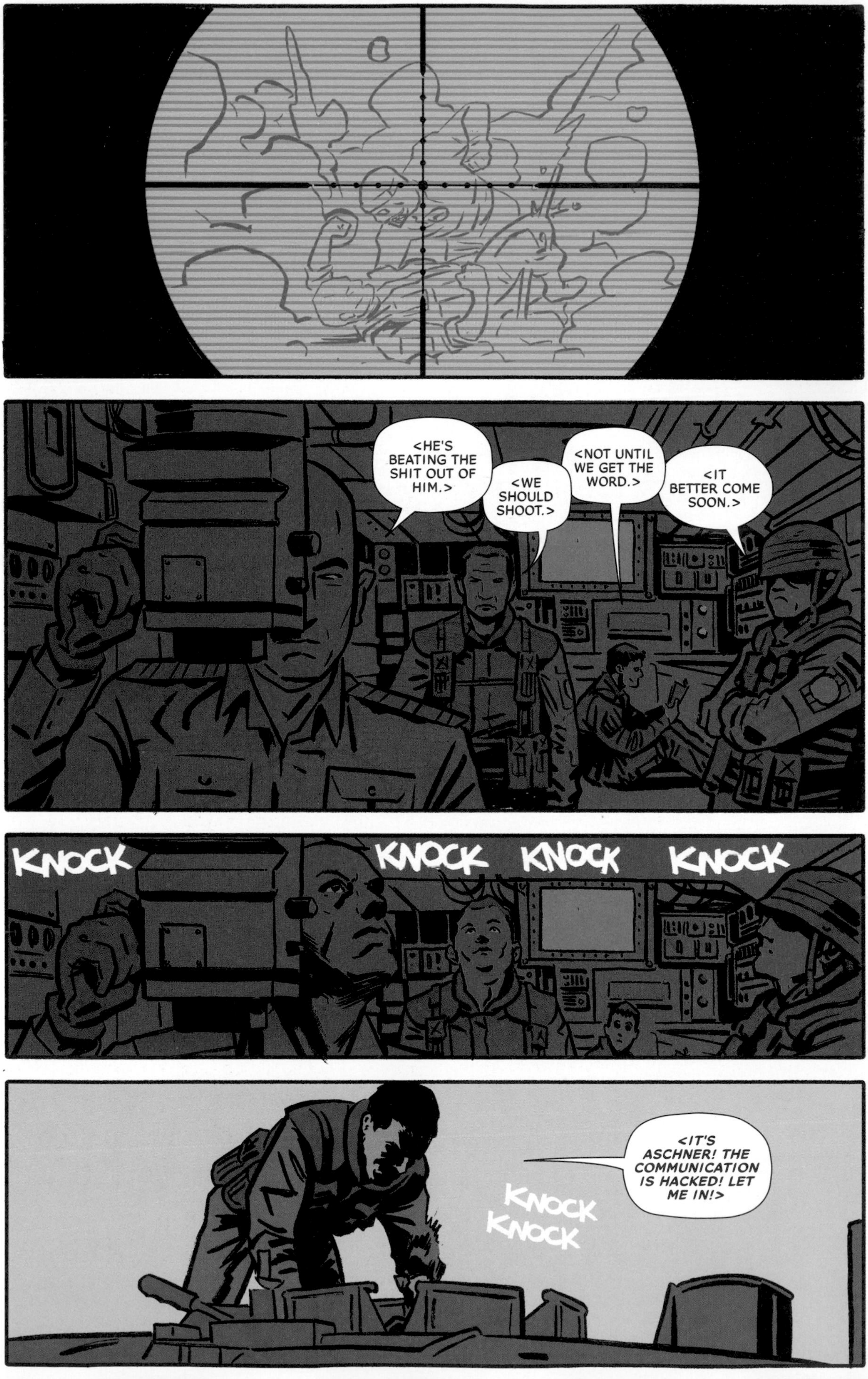
<HE'S BEATING THE SHIT OUT OF HIM.>
<WE SHOULD SHOOT.>
<NOT UNTIL WE GET THE WORD.>
<IT BETTER COME SOON.>
KNOCK
KNOCK
KNOCK
KNOCK
<IT'S ASCHNER! THE COMMUNICATION IS HACKED! LET ME IN!>
KNOCK
KNOCK

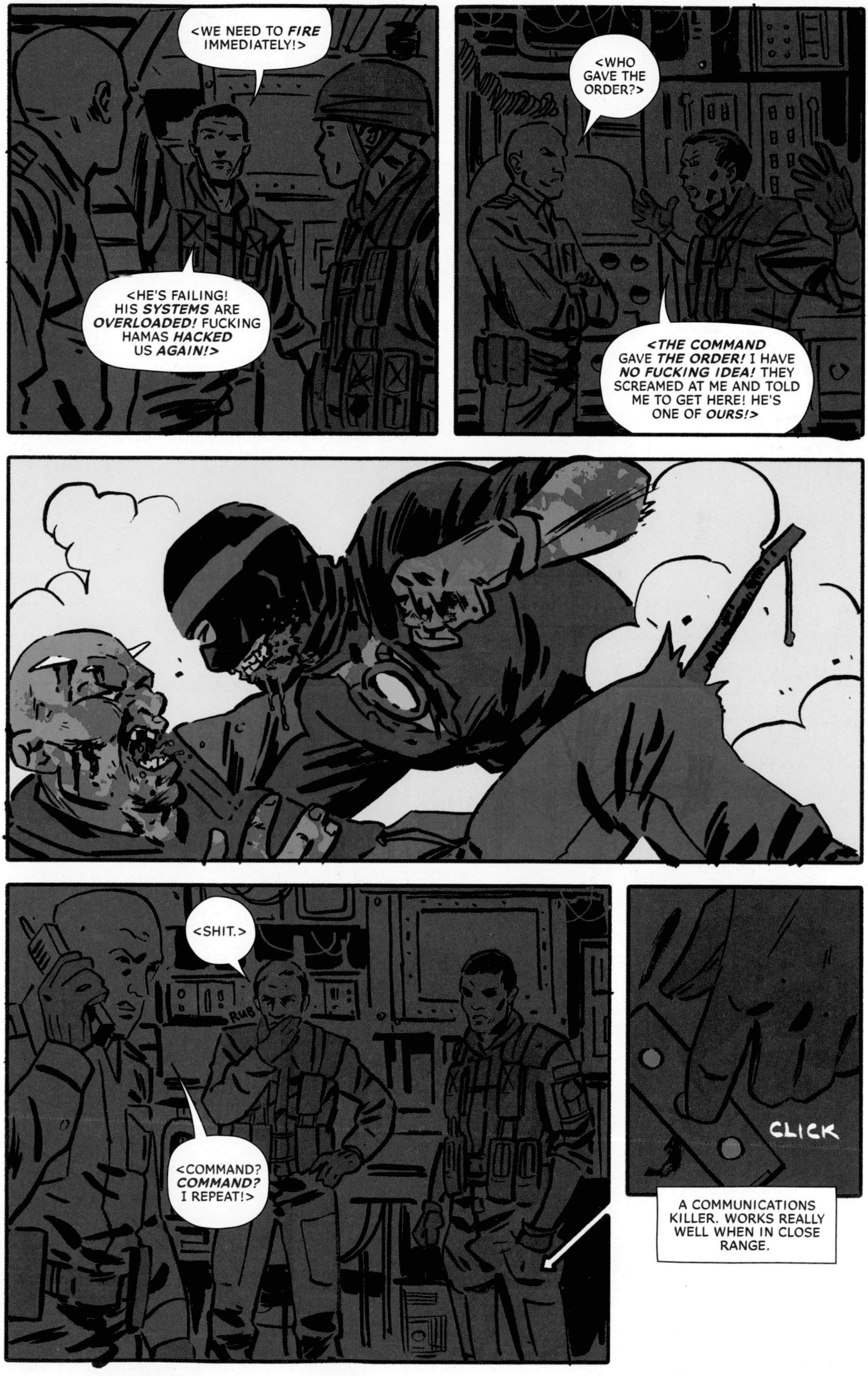
<WE NEED TO *FIRE* IMMEDIATELY!>
<HE'S FAILING! HIS ***SYSTEMS*** ARE ***OVERLOADED!*** FUCKING HAMAS ***HACKED*** US ***AGAIN!***>
<WHO GAVE THE ORDER?>
<THE COMMAND GAVE ***THE ORDER!*** I HAVE ***NO FUCKING IDEA!*** THEY SCREAMED AT ME AND TOLD ME TO GET HERE! HE'S ONE OF ***OURS!>***
<SHIT.>
RUB
<COMMAND? ***COMMAND?*** I REPEAT!>
CLICK
A COMMUNICATIONS KILLER. WORKS REALLY WELL WHEN IN CLOSE RANGE.

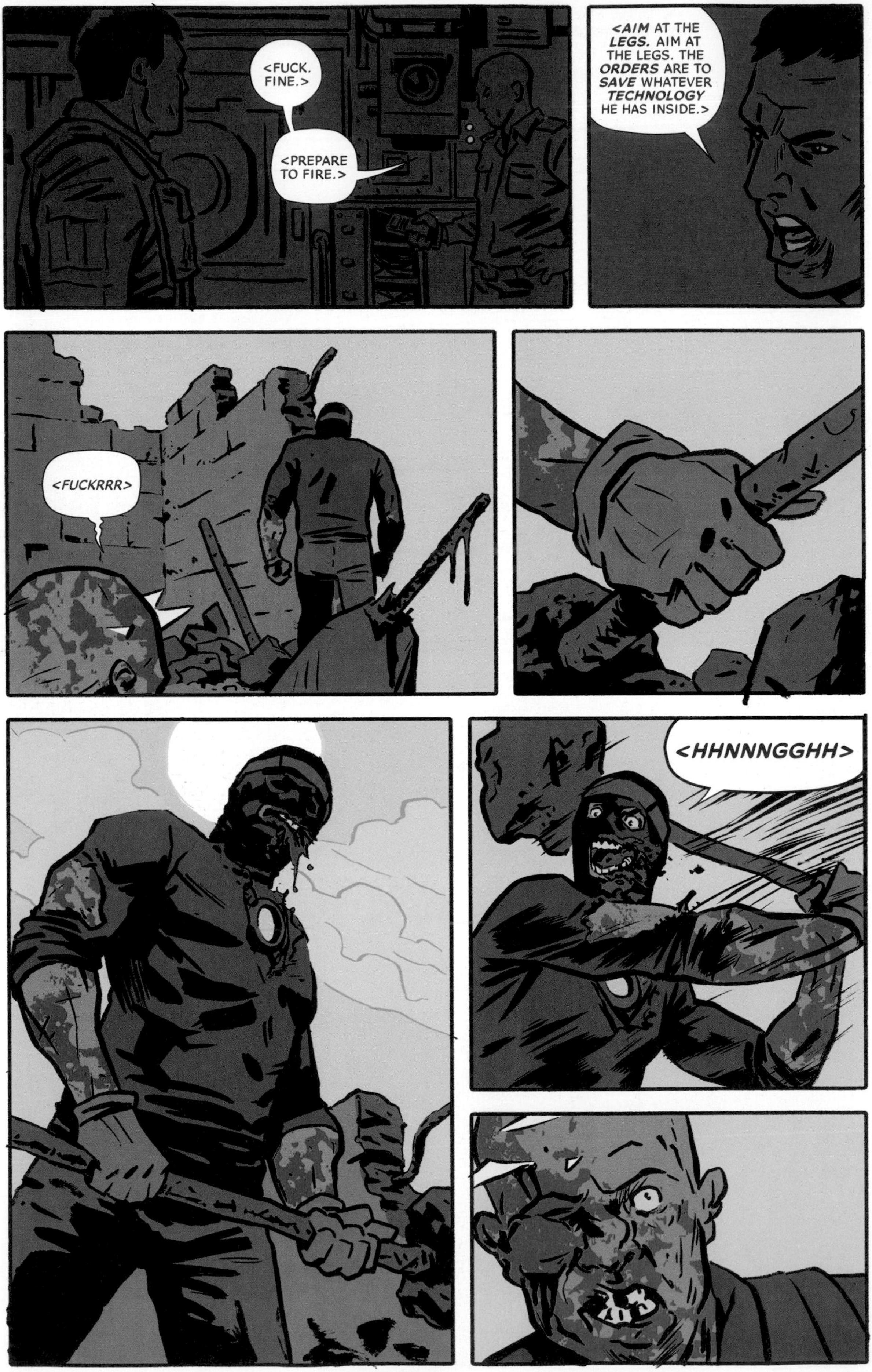
<FUCK. FINE.>
<PREPARE TO FIRE.>
<AIM AT THE LEGS. AIM AT THE LEGS. THE ORDERS ARE TO SAVE WHATEVER TECHNOLOGY HE HAS INSIDE.>
<FUCKRRR>
<HHNNNGGHH>

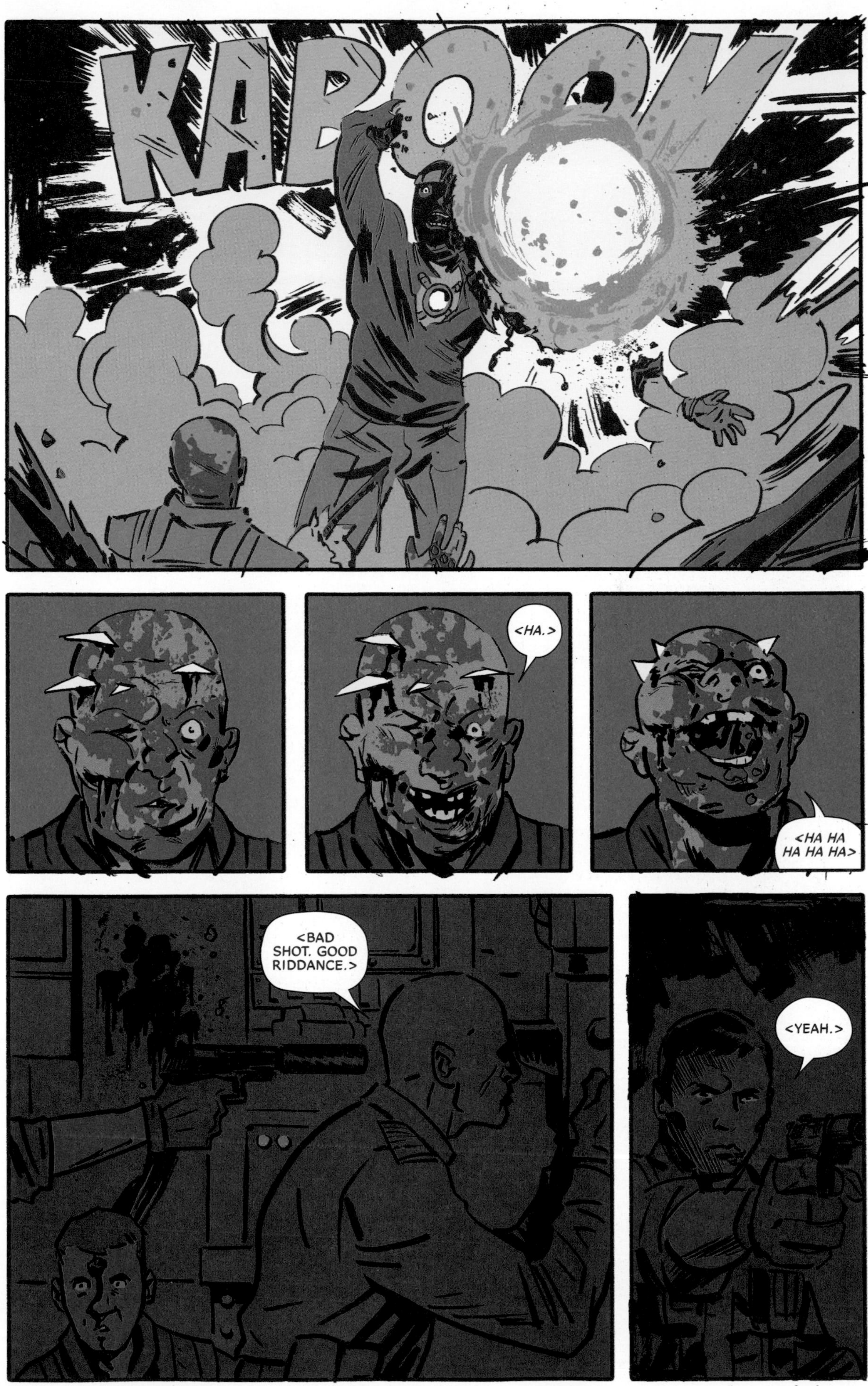
KABOOM
<HA.>
<HA HA HA HA HA>
<BAD SHOT. GOOD RIDDANCE.>
<YEAH.>

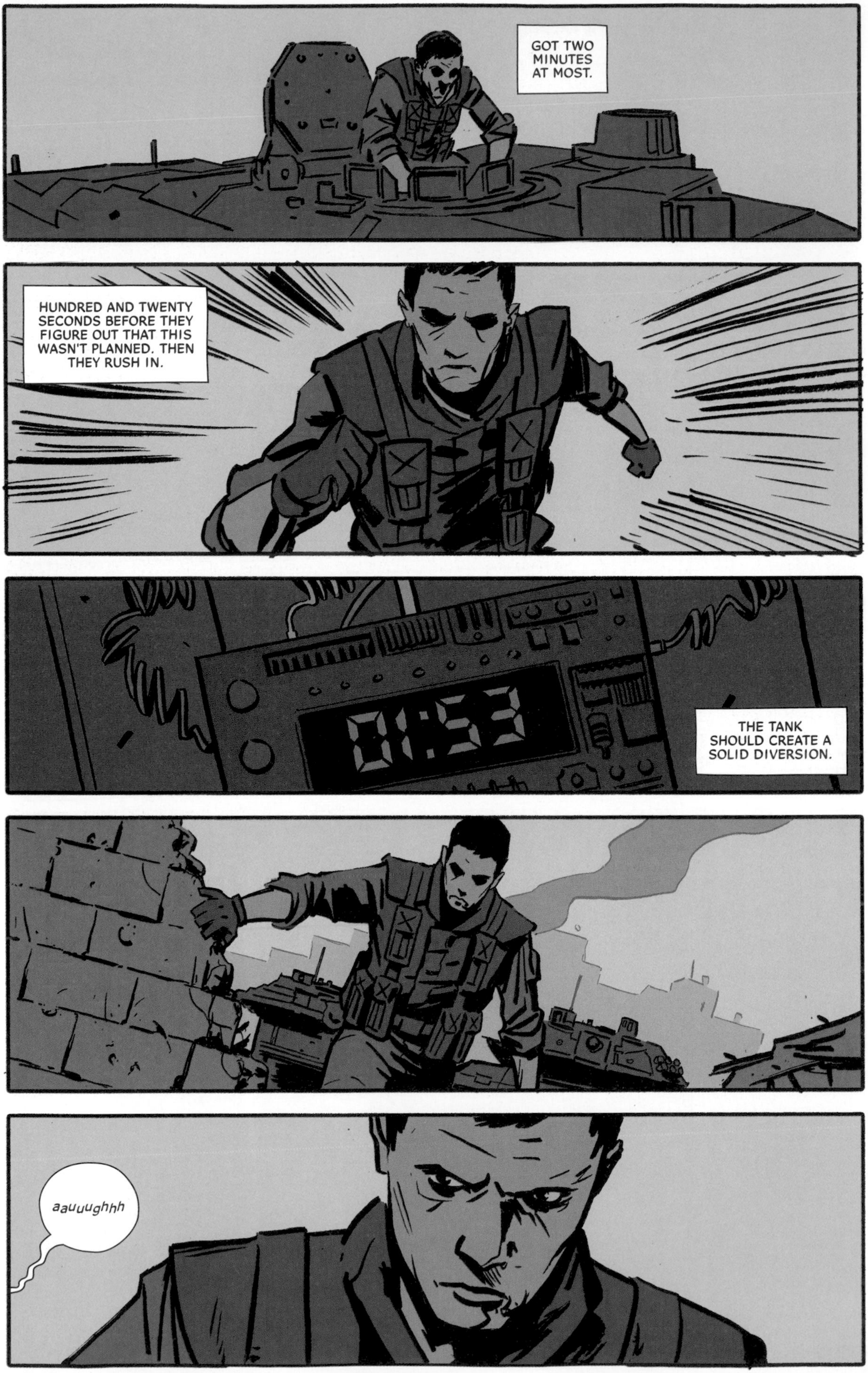
GOT TWO MINUTES AT MOST.
HUNDRED AND TWENTY SECONDS BEFORE THEY FIGURE OUT THAT THIS WASN'T PLANNED. THEN THEY RUSH IN.
01:53
THE TANK SHOULD CREATE A SOLID DIVERSION.
aauuughhh

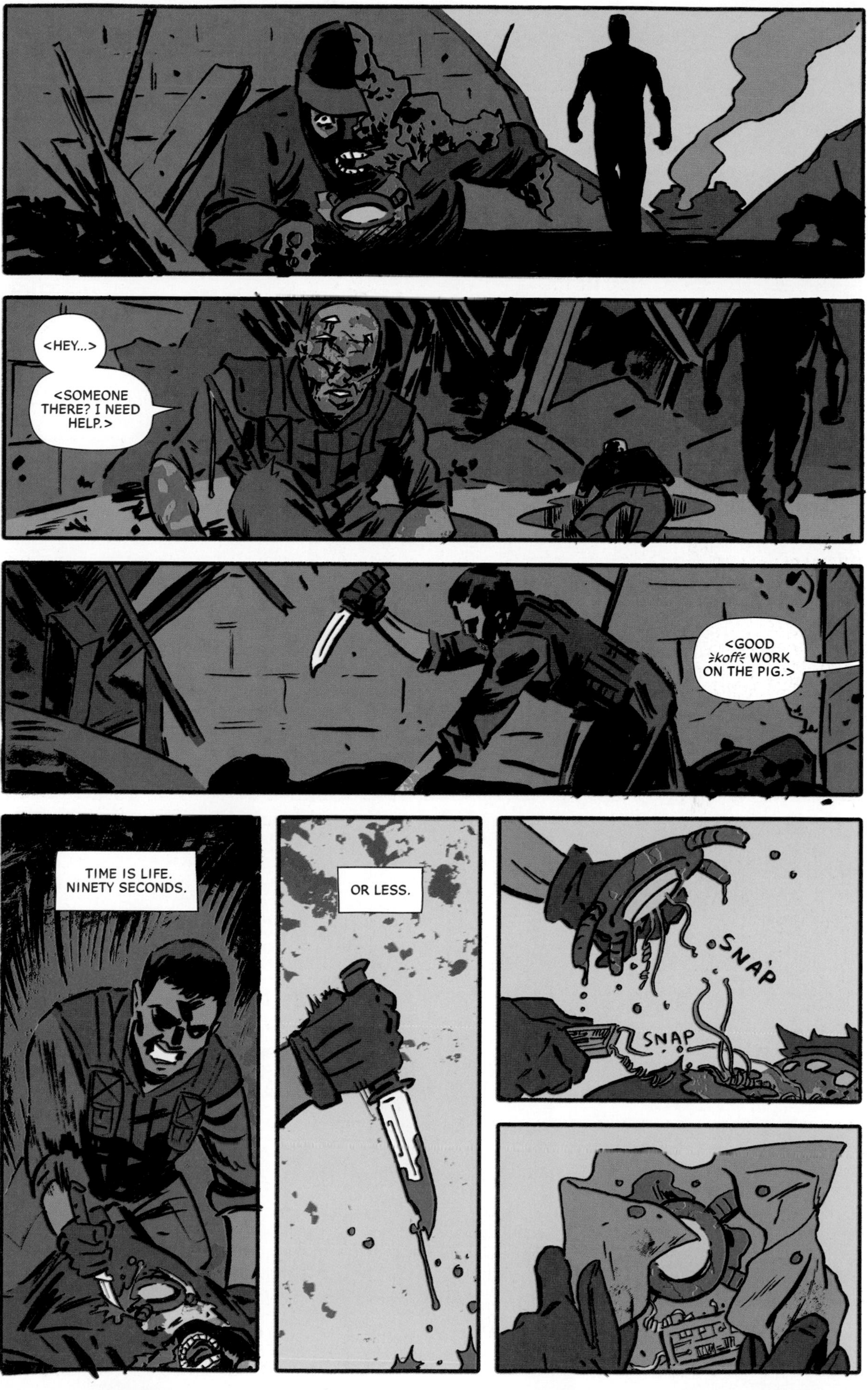
<HEY...>
<SOMEONE THERE? I NEED HELP.>
<GOOD *koff* WORK ON THE PIG.>
TIME IS LIFE. NINETY SECONDS.
OR LESS.
SNAP
SNAP

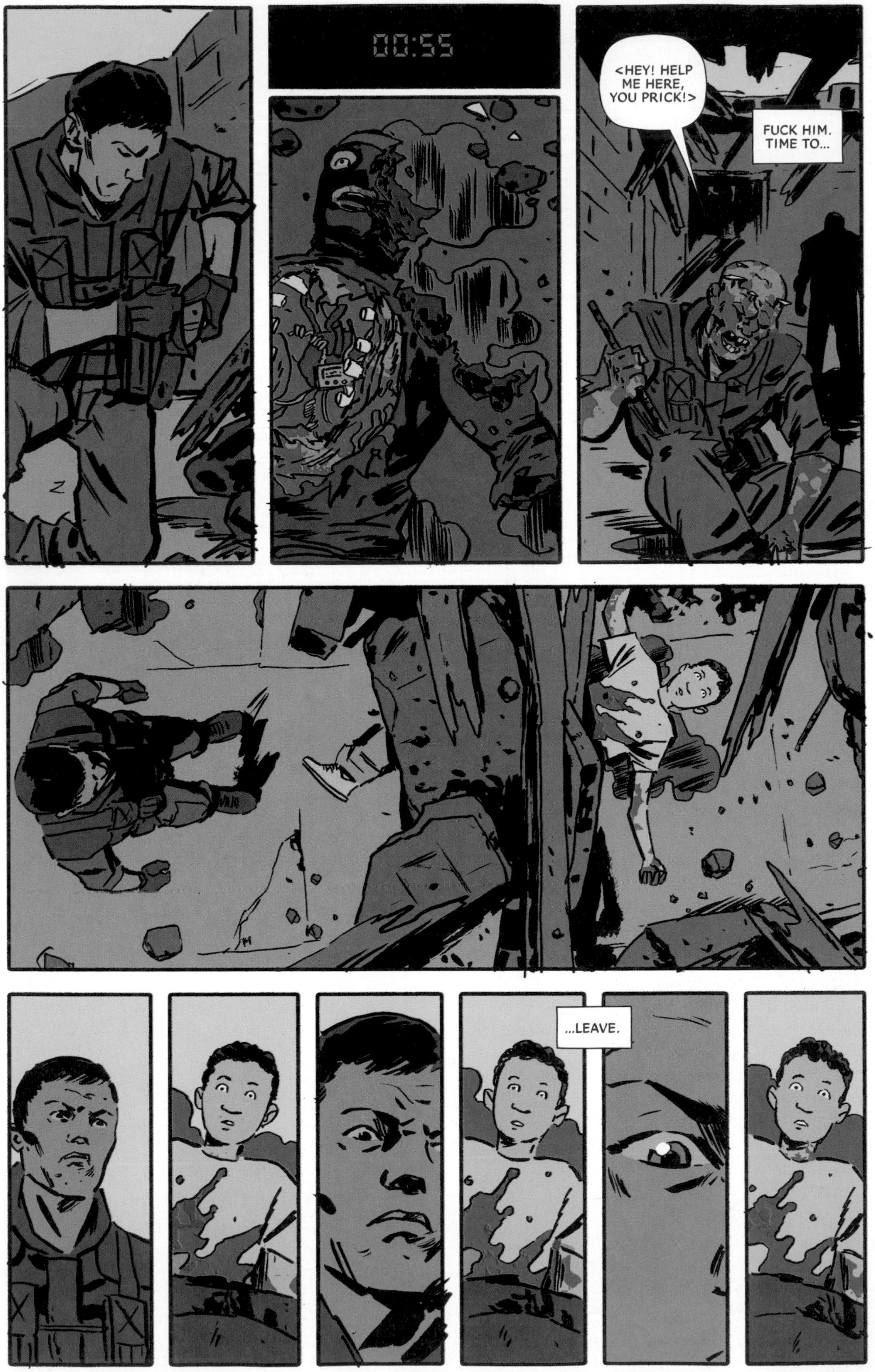
00:55
<HEY! HELP ME HERE, YOU PRICK!>
FUCK HIM. TIME TO...
...LEAVE.

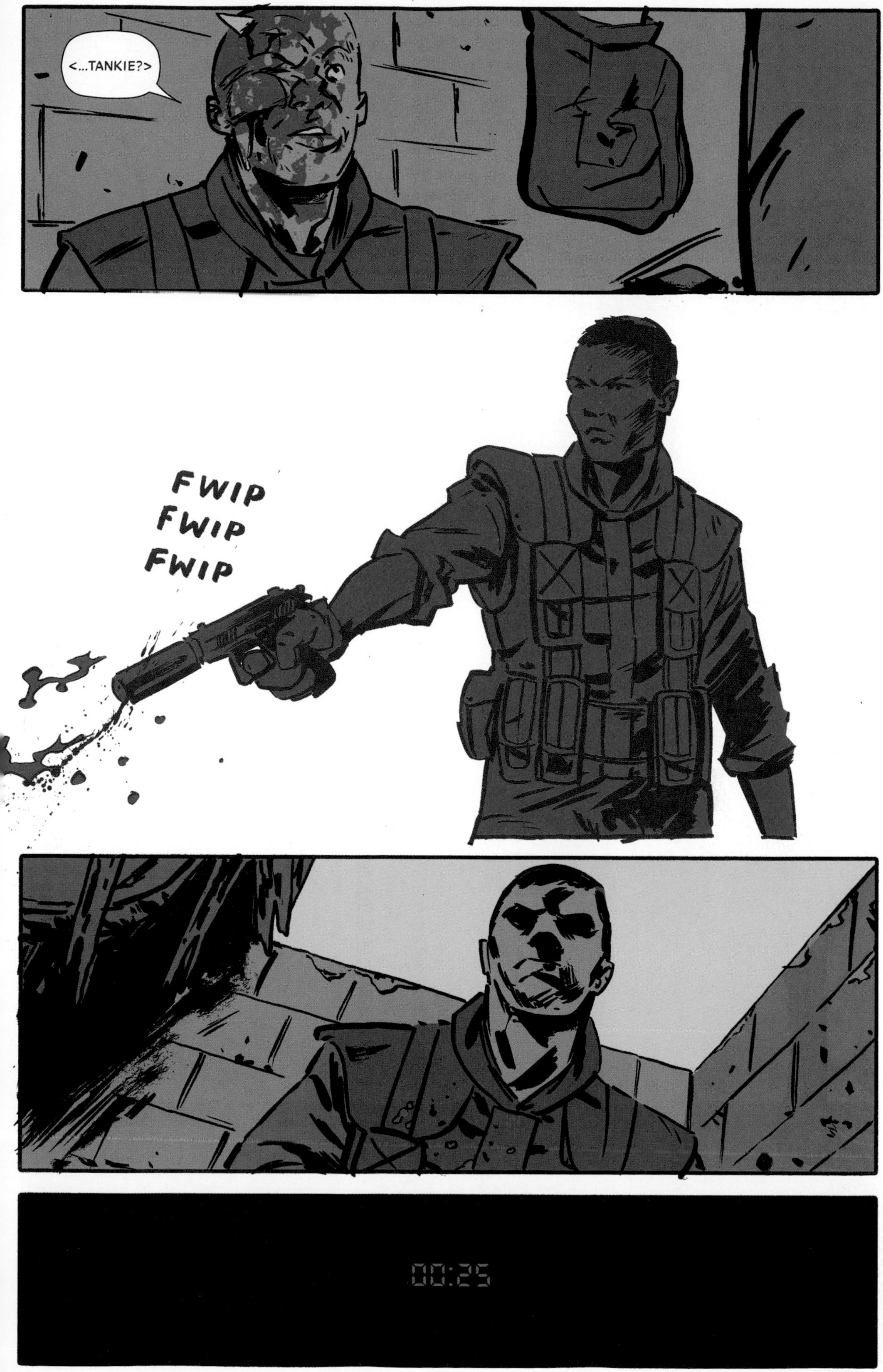
<...TANKIE?>
FWIP
FWIP
FWIP
00:25

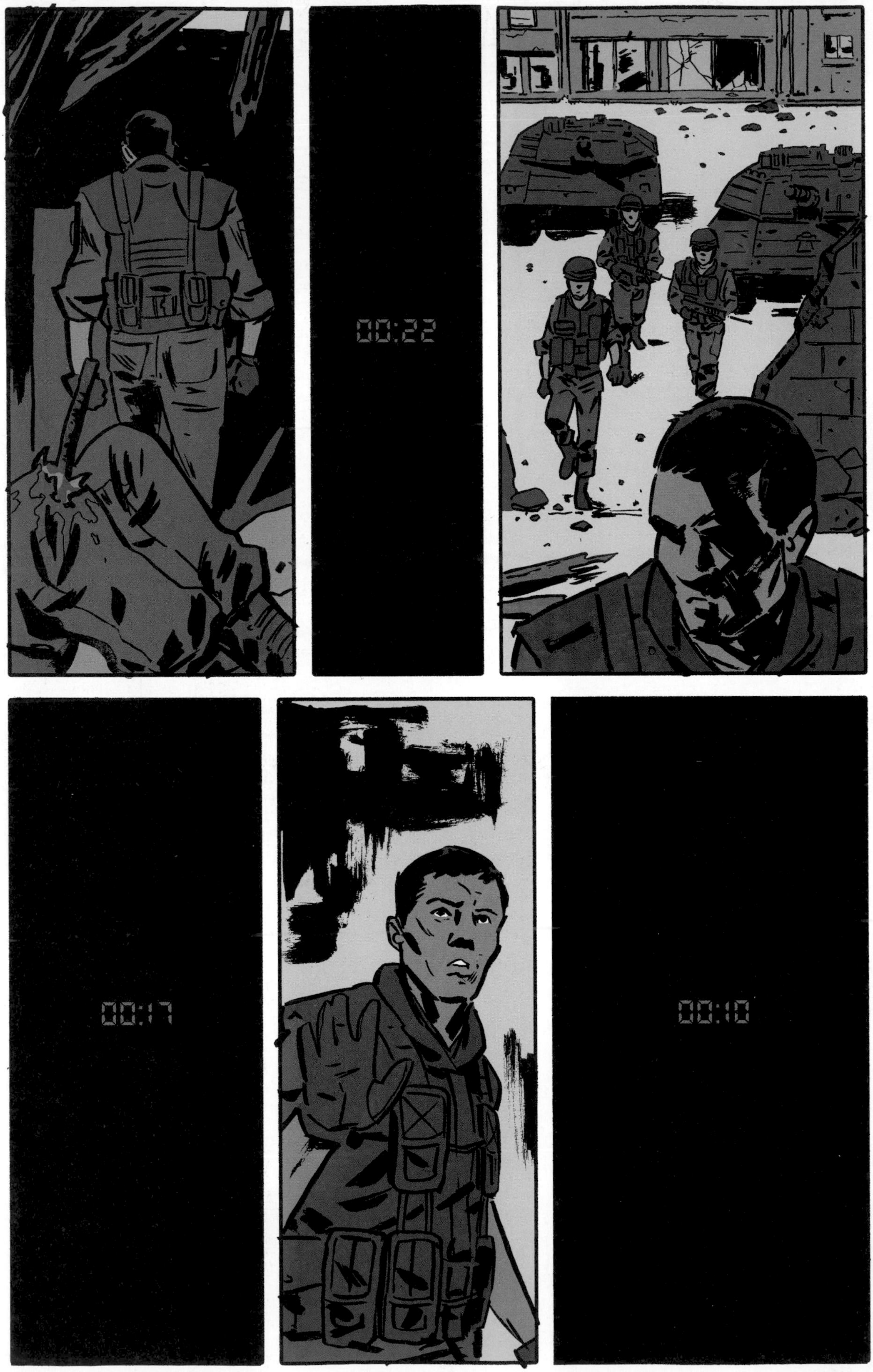

00:22
00:17
00:10

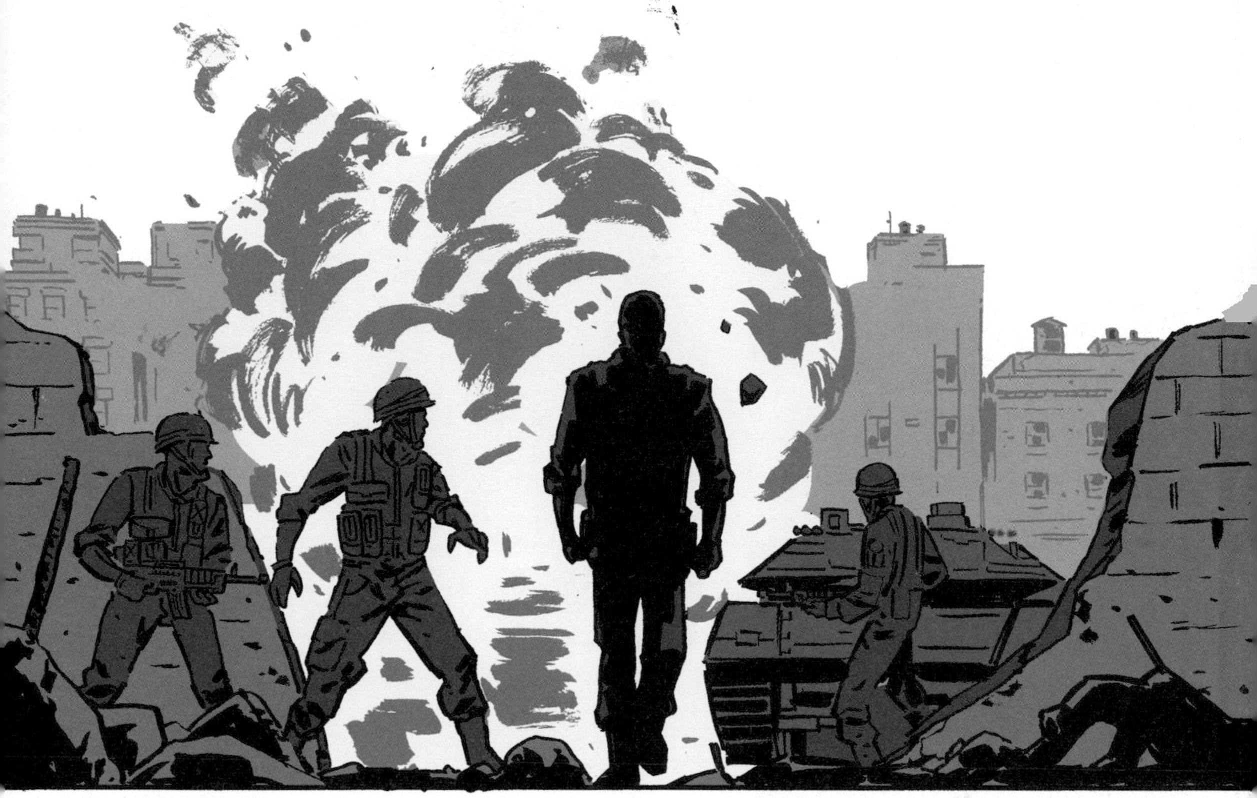

THE BLAST MAKES THE SOLDIERS THINK HAMAS ATTACKED WITH MORE FORCE. EVERYONE REACTS, FINDING COVER, TRYING TO RETALIATE.

NO ONE GIVES A SHIT ABOUT THE STUPID TANKIE WHO WALKED OUT OF THE BUILDING.

I WALK BACK TO WHERE I LEFT THE BODY OF THE BATTALION CAPTAIN. I PUT ON HIS UNIFORM. REQUEST A CAR. KILL THE DRIVER.

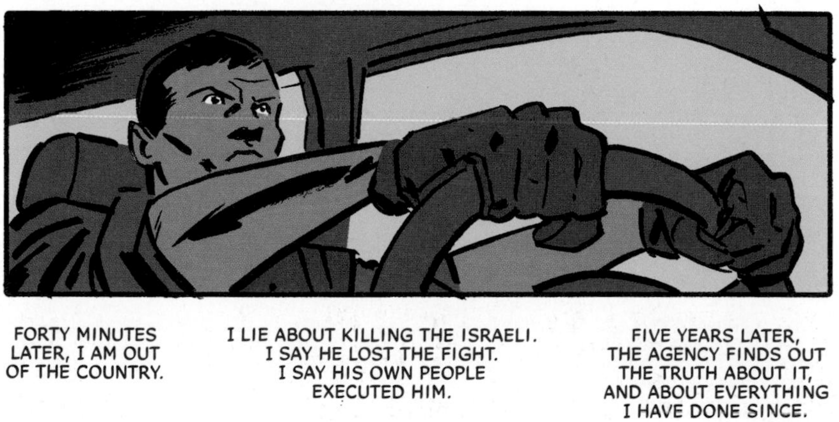

FORTY MINUTES LATER, I AM OUT OF THE COUNTRY.

I LIE ABOUT KILLING THE ISRAELI. I SAY HE LOST THE FIGHT. I SAY HIS OWN PEOPLE EXECUTED HIM.

FIVE YEARS LATER, THE AGENCY FINDS OUT THE TRUTH ABOUT IT, AND ABOUT EVERYTHING I HAVE DONE SINCE.

CHAPTER 2

I REMEMBER WHO YOU ARE

Illustrated by Tradd Moore

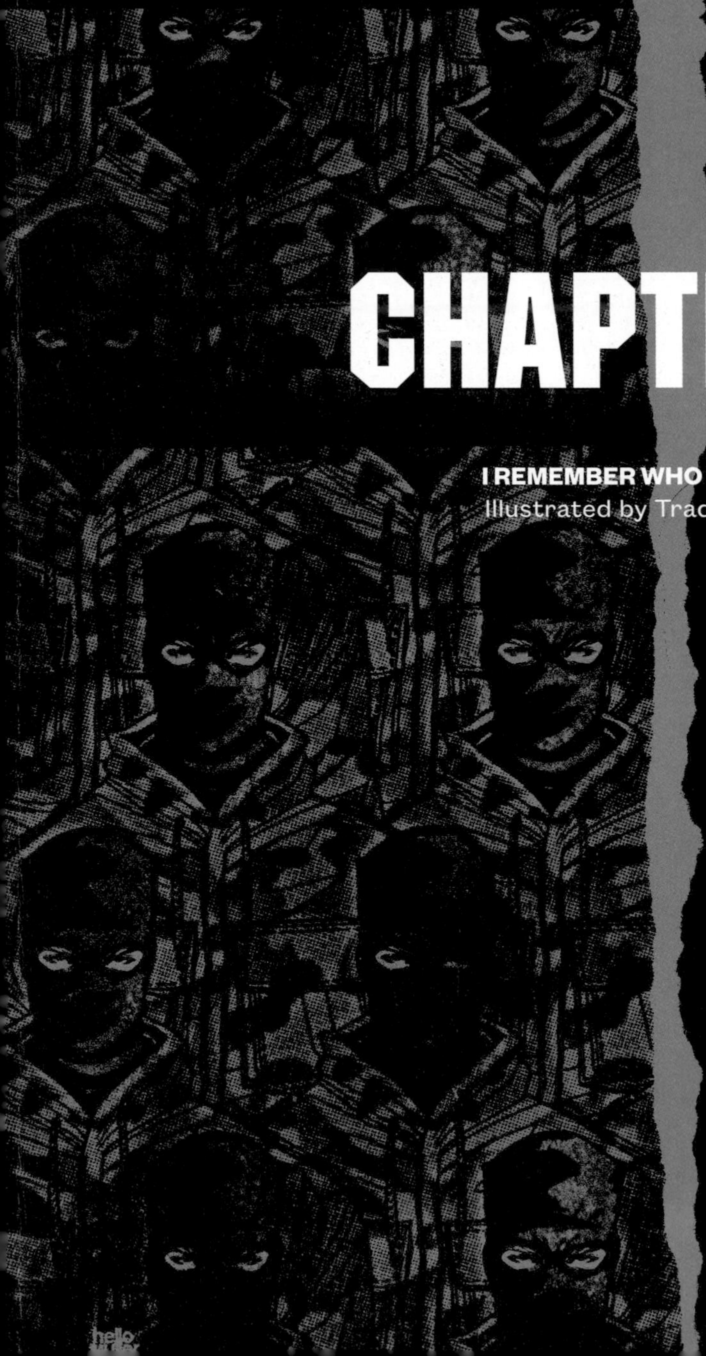

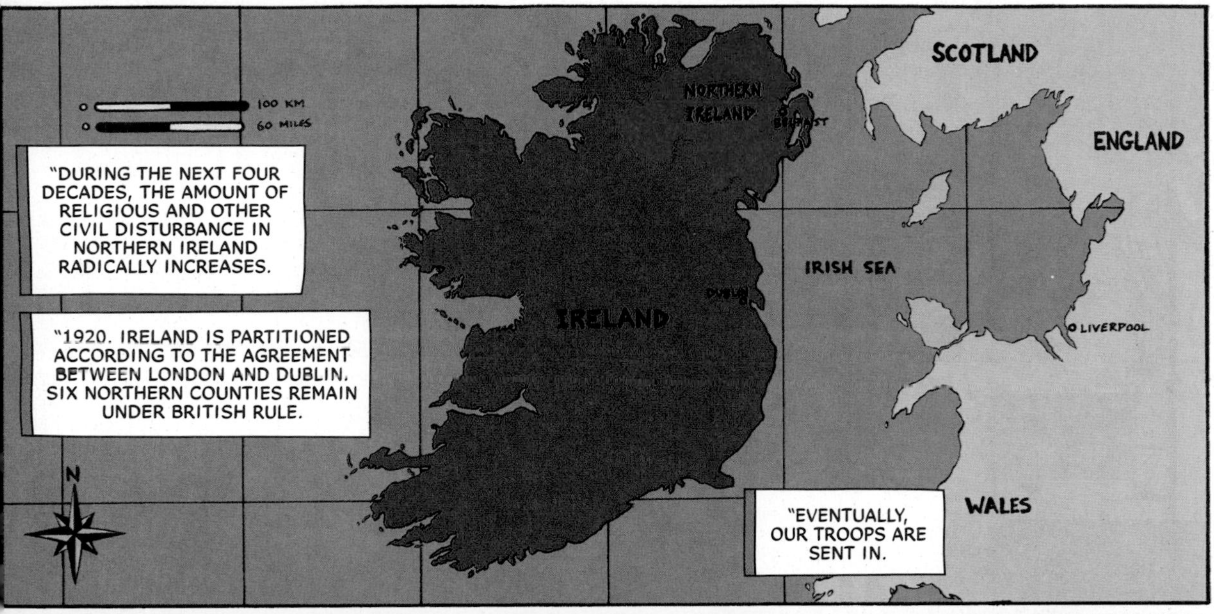
100 KM
60 MILES
NORTHERN IRELAND
IRELAND
DUBLIN
IRISH SEA
SCOTLAND
ENGLAND
LIVERPOOL
WALES
N
"DURING THE NEXT FOUR DECADES, THE AMOUNT OF RELIGIOUS AND OTHER CIVIL DISTURBANCE IN NORTHERN IRELAND RADICALLY INCREASES.
"1920. IRELAND IS PARTITIONED ACCORDING TO THE AGREEMENT BETWEEN LONDON AND DUBLIN. SIX NORTHERN COUNTIES REMAIN UNDER BRITISH RULE.
"EVENTUALLY, OUR TROOPS ARE SENT IN.

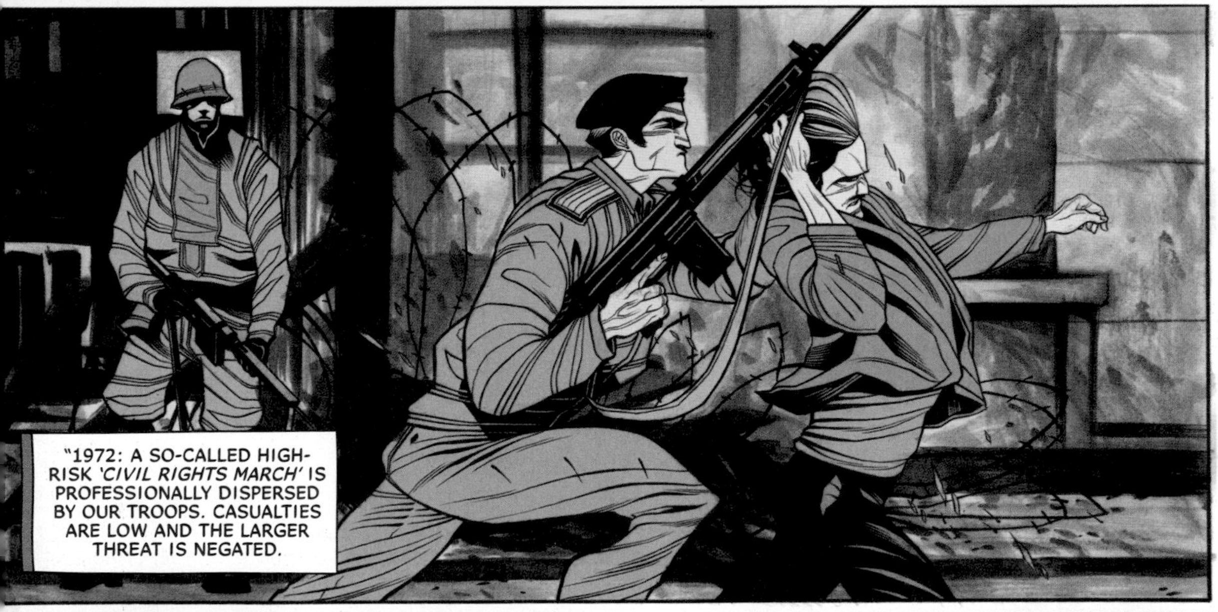
"1972: A SO-CALLED HIGH-RISK *'CIVIL RIGHTS MARCH'* IS PROFESSIONALLY DISPERSED BY OUR TROOPS. CASUALTIES ARE LOW AND THE LARGER THREAT IS NEGATED.

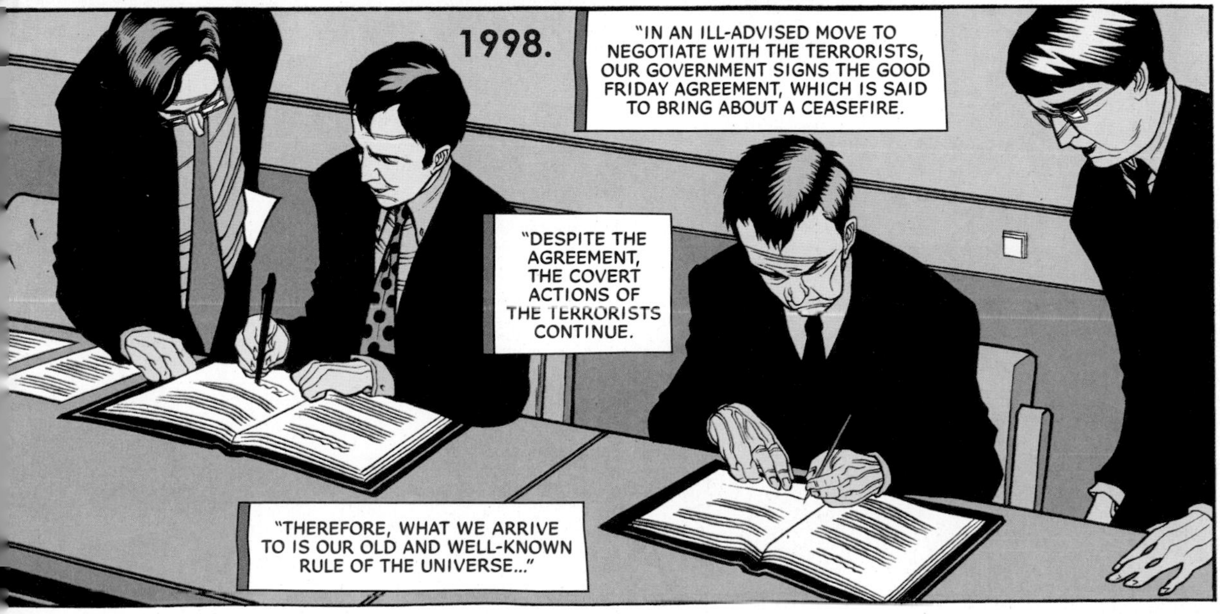
1998.
"IN AN ILL-ADVISED MOVE TO NEGOTIATE WITH THE TERRORISTS, OUR GOVERNMENT SIGNS THE GOOD FRIDAY AGREEMENT, WHICH IS SAID TO BRING ABOUT A CEASEFIRE.
"DESPITE THE AGREEMENT, THE COVERT ACTIONS OF THE TERRORISTS CONTINUE.
"THEREFORE, WHAT WE ARRIVE TO IS OUR OLD AND WELL-KNOWN RULE OF THE UNIVERSE..."

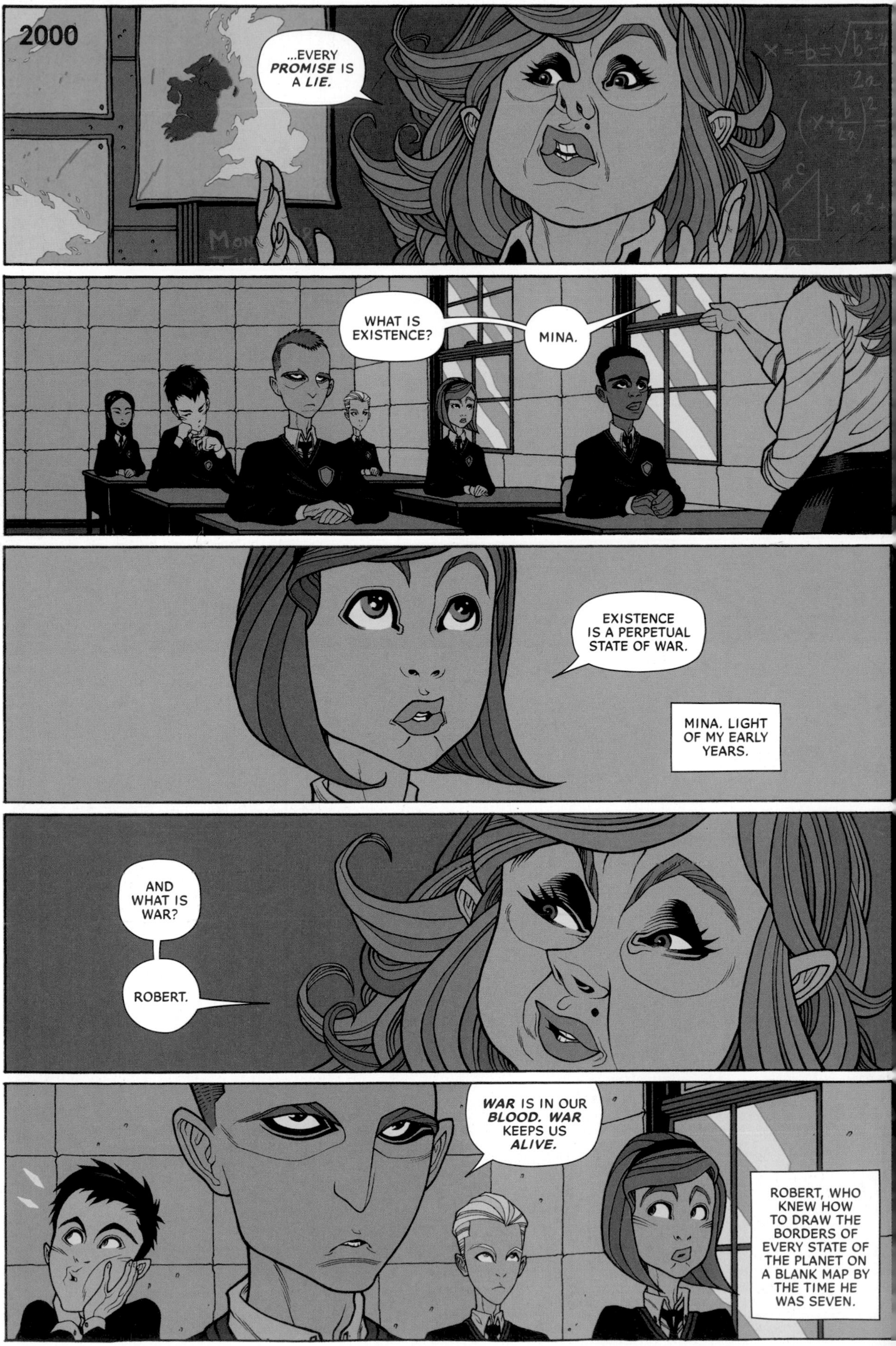

2000
...EVERY *PROMISE* IS A *LIE.*
WHAT IS EXISTENCE?
MINA.
EXISTENCE IS A PERPETUAL STATE OF WAR.
MINA. LIGHT OF MY EARLY YEARS.
AND WHAT IS WAR?
ROBERT.
WAR IS IN OUR *BLOOD. WAR* KEEPS US *ALIVE.*
ROBERT, WHO KNEW HOW TO DRAW THE BORDERS OF EVERY STATE OF THE PLANET ON A BLANK MAP BY THE TIME HE WAS SEVEN.

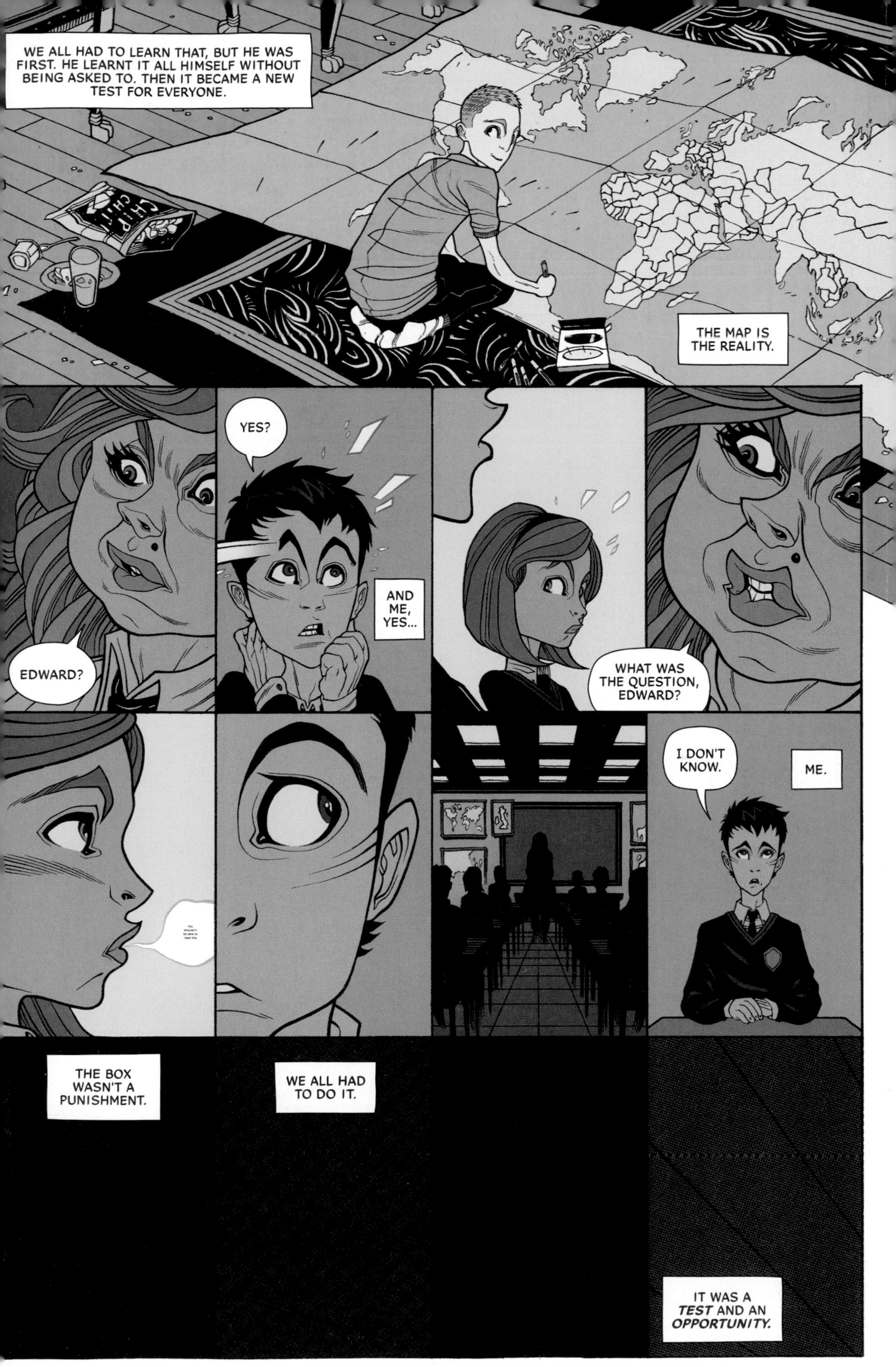
WE ALL HAD TO LEARN THAT, BUT HE WAS FIRST. HE LEARNT IT ALL HIMSELF WITHOUT BEING ASKED TO. THEN IT BECAME A NEW TEST FOR EVERYONE.
CHIP
THE MAP IS THE REALITY.
EDWARD?
YES?
AND ME, YES...
WHAT WAS THE QUESTION, EDWARD?
I DON'T KNOW.
ME.
THE BOX WASN'T A PUNISHMENT.
WE ALL HAD TO DO IT.
IT WAS A *TEST* AND AN *OPPORTUNITY.*

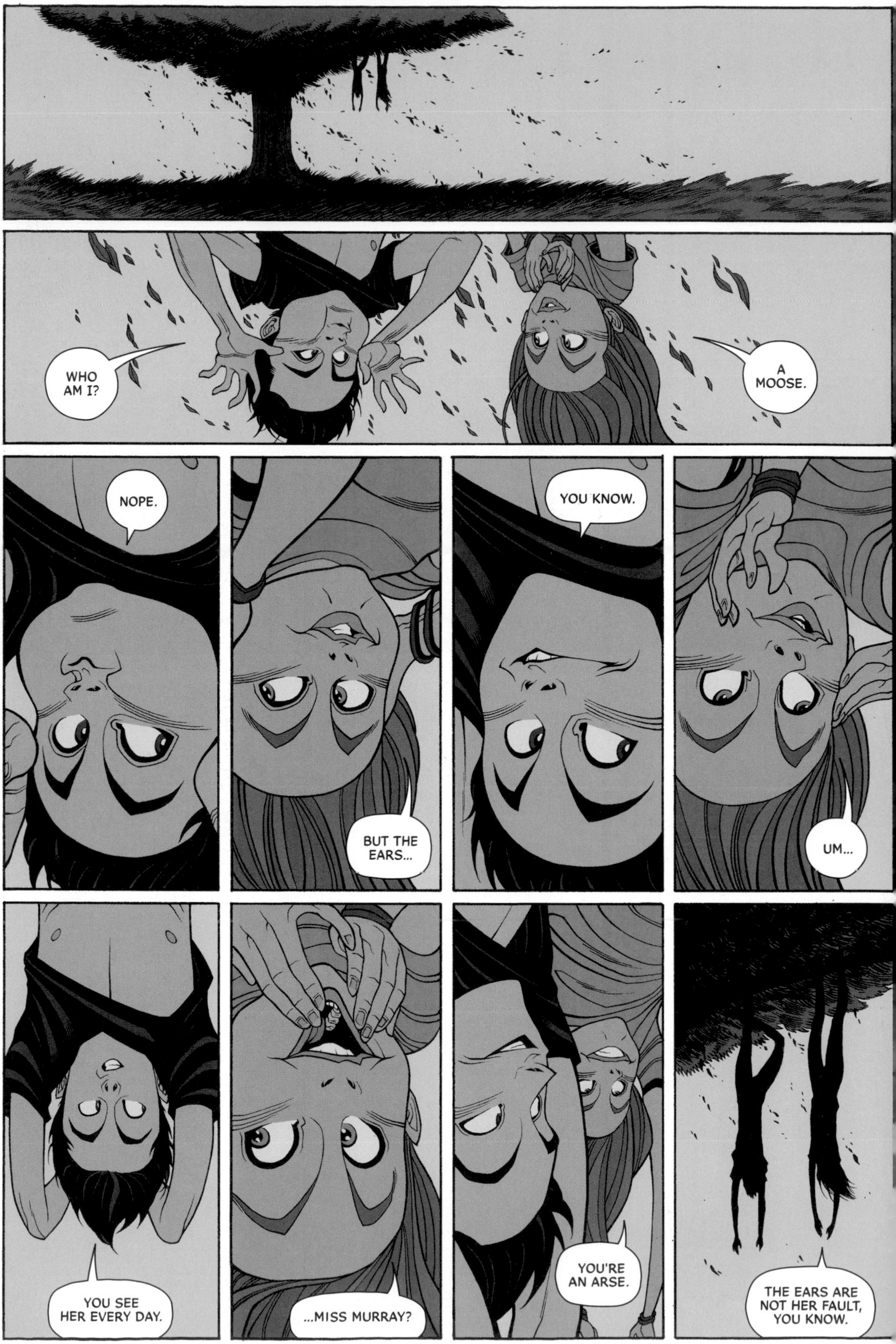
WHO AM I?
A MOOSE.
NOPE.
BUT THE EARS...
YOU KNOW.
UM...
YOU SEE HER EVERY DAY.
...MISS MURRAY?
YOU'RE AN ARSE.
THE EARS ARE NOT HER FAULT, YOU KNOW.

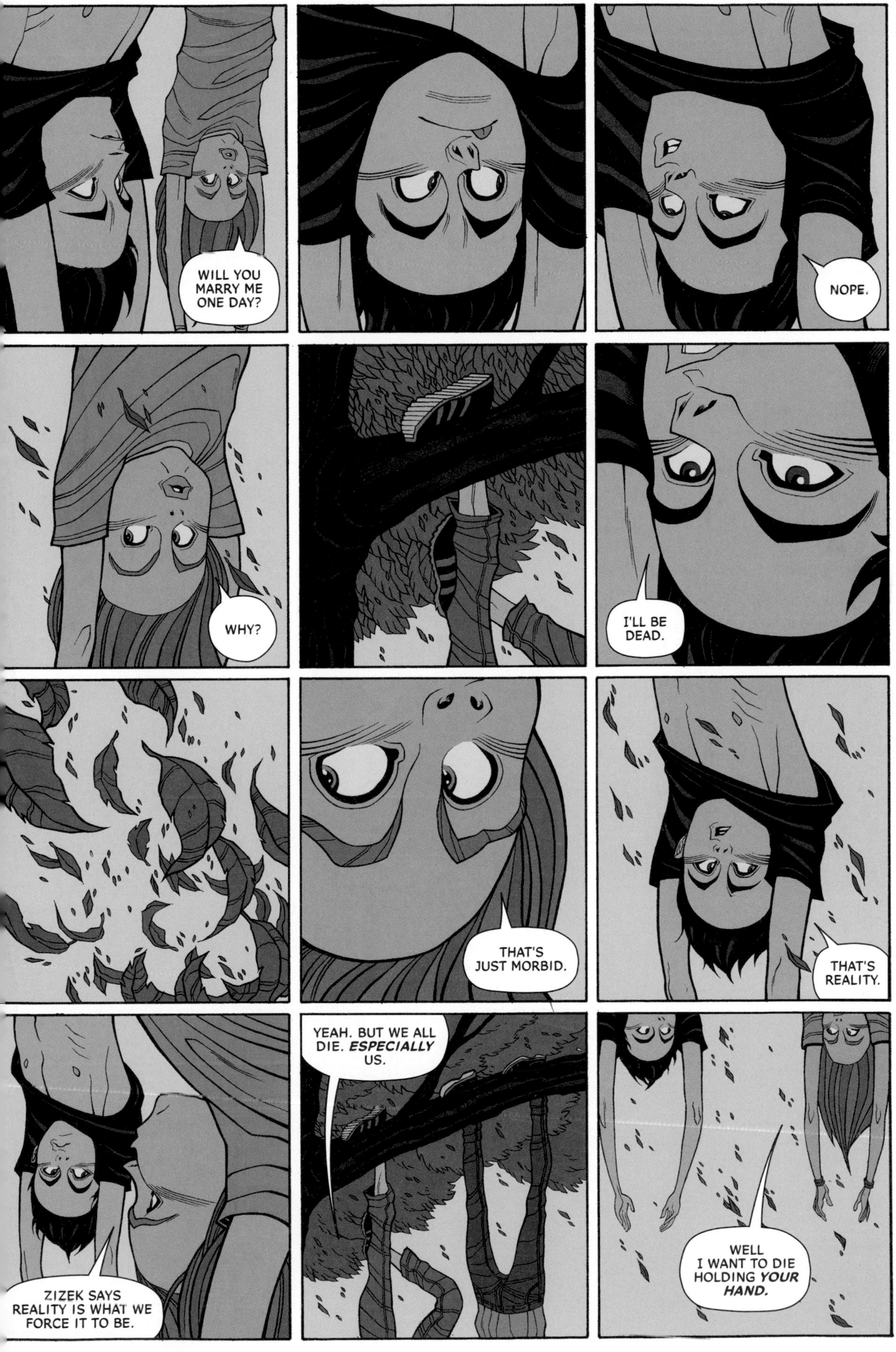
WILL YOU MARRY ME ONE DAY?
NOPE.
WHY?
I'LL BE DEAD.
THAT'S JUST MORBID.
THAT'S REALITY.
ZIZEK SAYS REALITY IS WHAT WE FORCE IT TO BE.
YEAH. BUT WE ALL DIE. ESPECIALLY US.
WELL I WANT TO DIE HOLDING YOUR HAND.

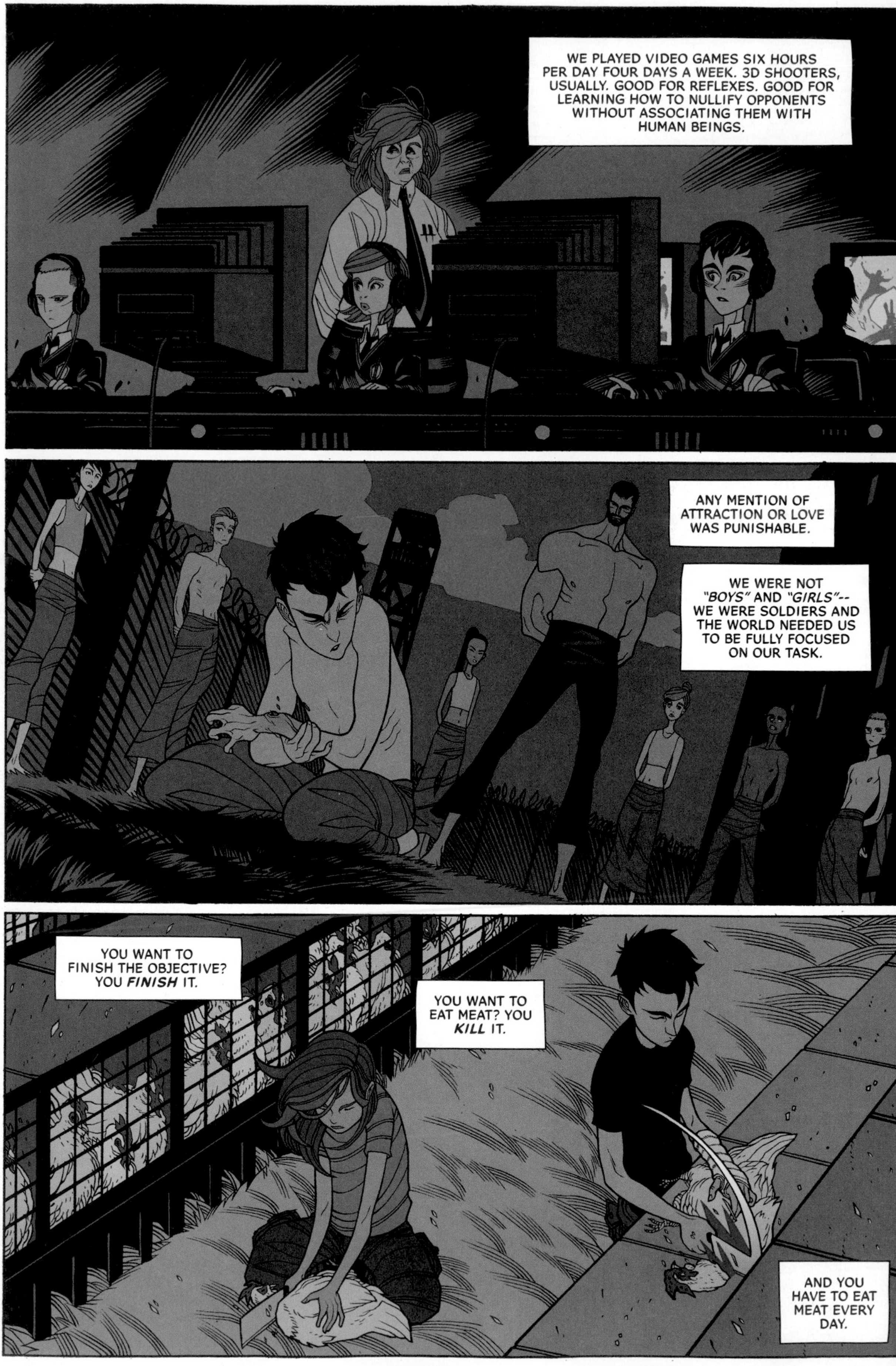
WE PLAYED VIDEO GAMES SIX HOURS PER DAY FOUR DAYS A WEEK. 3D SHOOTERS, USUALLY. GOOD FOR REFLEXES. GOOD FOR LEARNING HOW TO NULLIFY OPPONENTS WITHOUT ASSOCIATING THEM WITH HUMAN BEINGS.
ANY MENTION OF ATTRACTION OR LOVE WAS PUNISHABLE.
WE WERE NOT "BOYS" AND "GIRLS"-- WE WERE SOLDIERS AND THE WORLD NEEDED US TO BE FULLY FOCUSED ON OUR TASK.
YOU WANT TO FINISH THE OBJECTIVE? YOU FINISH IT.
YOU WANT TO EAT MEAT? YOU KILL IT.
AND YOU HAVE TO EAT MEAT EVERY DAY.

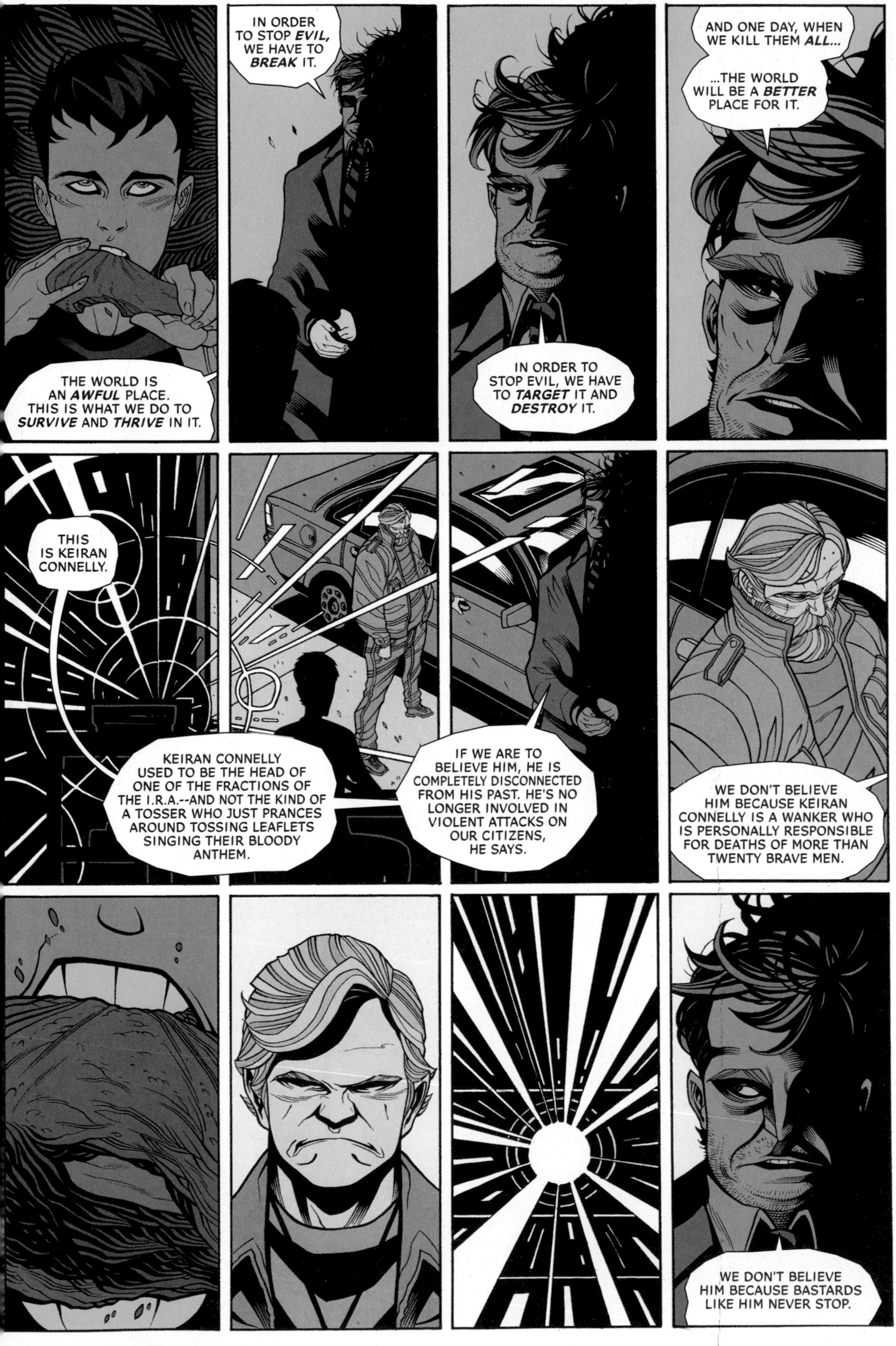
THE WORLD IS AN AWFUL PLACE. THIS IS WHAT WE DO TO SURVIVE AND THRIVE IN IT.
IN ORDER TO STOP EVIL, WE HAVE TO BREAK IT.
IN ORDER TO STOP EVIL, WE HAVE TO TARGET IT AND DESTROY IT.
AND ONE DAY, WHEN WE KILL THEM ALL...
...THE WORLD WILL BE A BETTER PLACE FOR IT.
THIS IS KEIRAN CONNELLY.
KEIRAN CONNELLY USED TO BE THE HEAD OF ONE OF THE FRACTIONS OF THE I.R.A.--AND NOT THE KIND OF A TOSSER WHO JUST PRANCES AROUND TOSSING LEAFLETS SINGING THEIR BLOODY ANTHEM.
IF WE ARE TO BELIEVE HIM, HE IS COMPLETELY DISCONNECTED FROM HIS PAST. HE'S NO LONGER INVOLVED IN VIOLENT ATTACKS ON OUR CITIZENS, HE SAYS.
WE DON'T BELIEVE HIM BECAUSE KEIRAN CONNELLY IS A WANKER WHO IS PERSONALLY RESPONSIBLE FOR DEATHS OF MORE THAN TWENTY BRAVE MEN.
WE DON'T BELIEVE HIM BECAUSE BASTARDS LIKE HIM NEVER STOP.

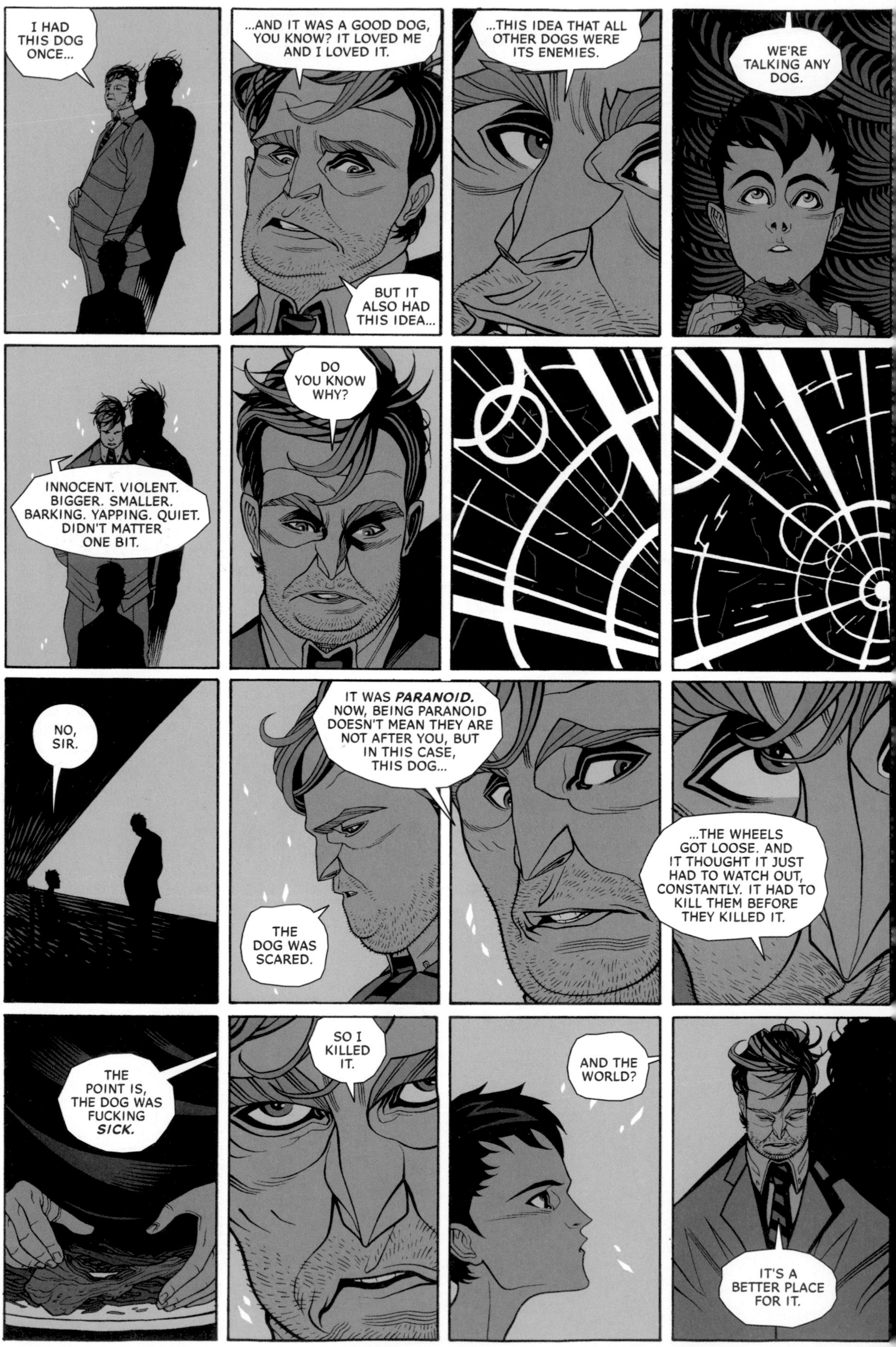
I HAD THIS DOG ONCE...
...AND IT WAS A GOOD DOG, YOU KNOW? IT LOVED ME AND I LOVED IT.
BUT IT ALSO HAD THIS IDEA...
...THIS IDEA THAT ALL OTHER DOGS WERE ITS ENEMIES.
WE'RE TALKING ANY DOG.
INNOCENT. VIOLENT. BIGGER. SMALLER. BARKING. YAPPING. QUIET. DIDN'T MATTER ONE BIT.
DO YOU KNOW WHY?
NO, SIR.
IT WAS PARANOID. NOW, BEING PARANOID DOESN'T MEAN THEY ARE NOT AFTER YOU, BUT IN THIS CASE, THIS DOG...
THE DOG WAS SCARED.
...THE WHEELS GOT LOOSE. AND IT THOUGHT IT JUST HAD TO WATCH OUT, CONSTANTLY. IT HAD TO KILL THEM BEFORE THEY KILLED IT.
THE POINT IS, THE DOG WAS FUCKING SICK.
SO I KILLED IT.
AND THE WORLD?
IT'S A BETTER PLACE FOR IT.

BELFAST,
NOVEMBER 21st, 2001.

DAY ONE.

BLEEDIN'
HAZELNUT
CRACK.

LANGUAGE,
BIG MAN.

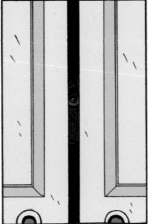

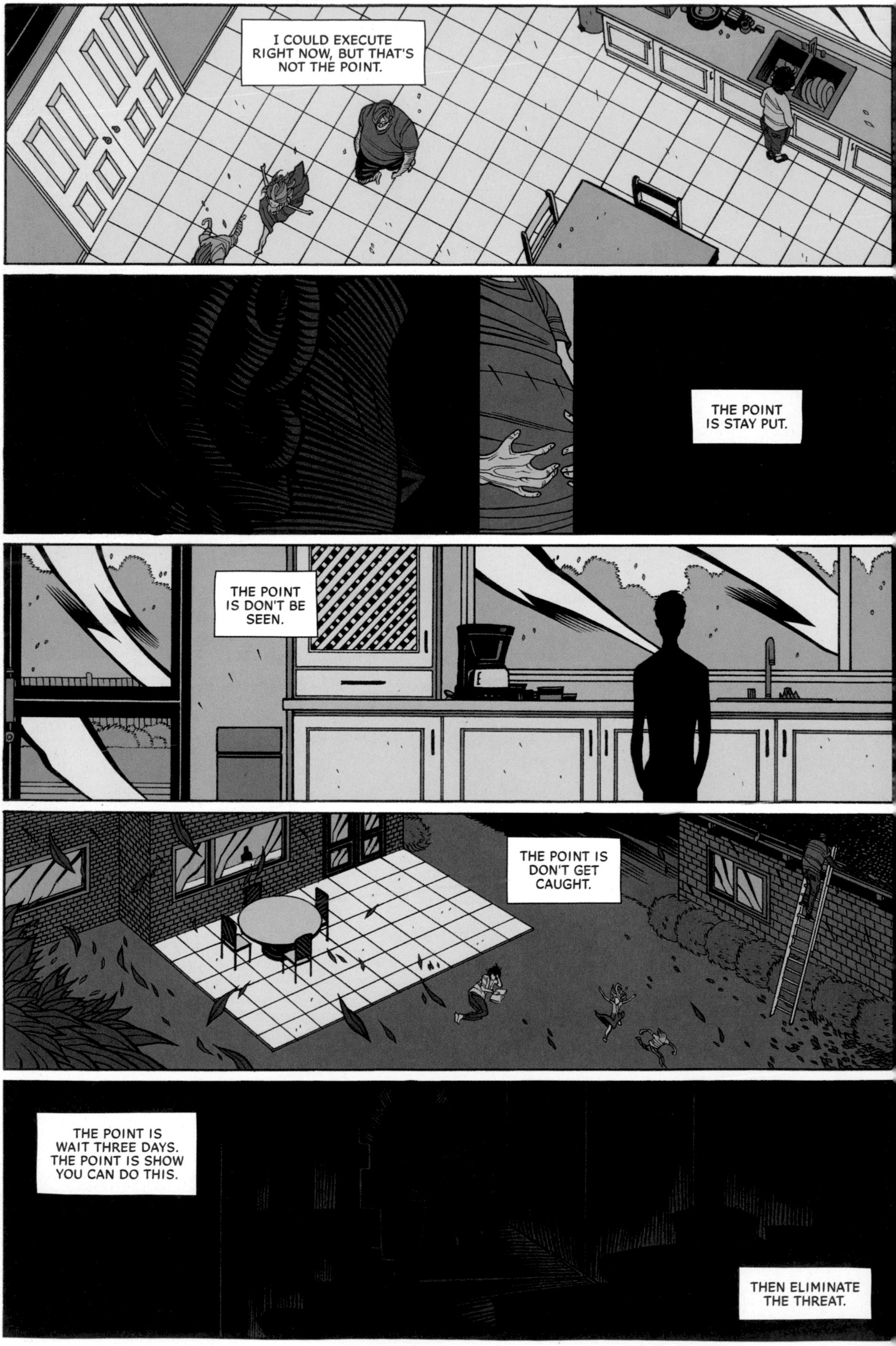
I COULD EXECUTE RIGHT NOW, BUT THAT'S NOT THE POINT.
THE POINT IS STAY PUT.
THE POINT IS DON'T BE SEEN.
THE POINT IS DON'T GET CAUGHT.
THE POINT IS WAIT THREE DAYS. THE POINT IS SHOW YOU CAN DO THIS.
THEN ELIMINATE THE THREAT.

DAY TWO.

WONTLET MEPLAYWITHMY LEGOTAKING EEITAWAY

WHY'S THAT, KIT?

NOT HIS.

WE'RE A FAMILY, KIT.

HE'S YER BROTHER. YEH'RE HIS SISTER. SO SHARE.

EVERYTHING IN THIS HOUSE IS US. IT'S FAMILY.

WE'RE ONE UNIT, GET IT?

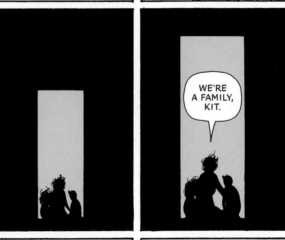

THERE'S LOVE OR THERE'S NOTHIN'.

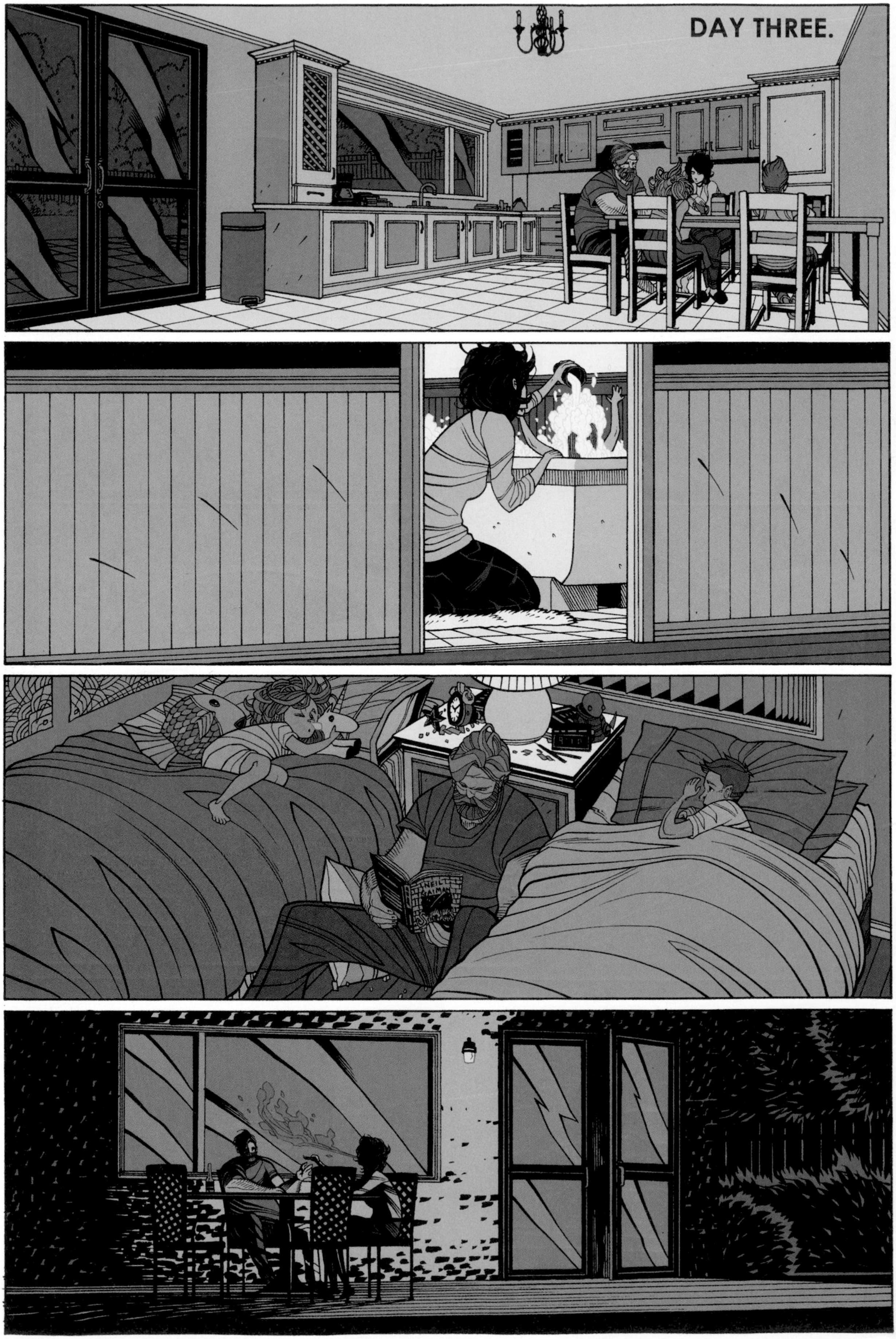
DAY THREE.
NEIL GAIMAN

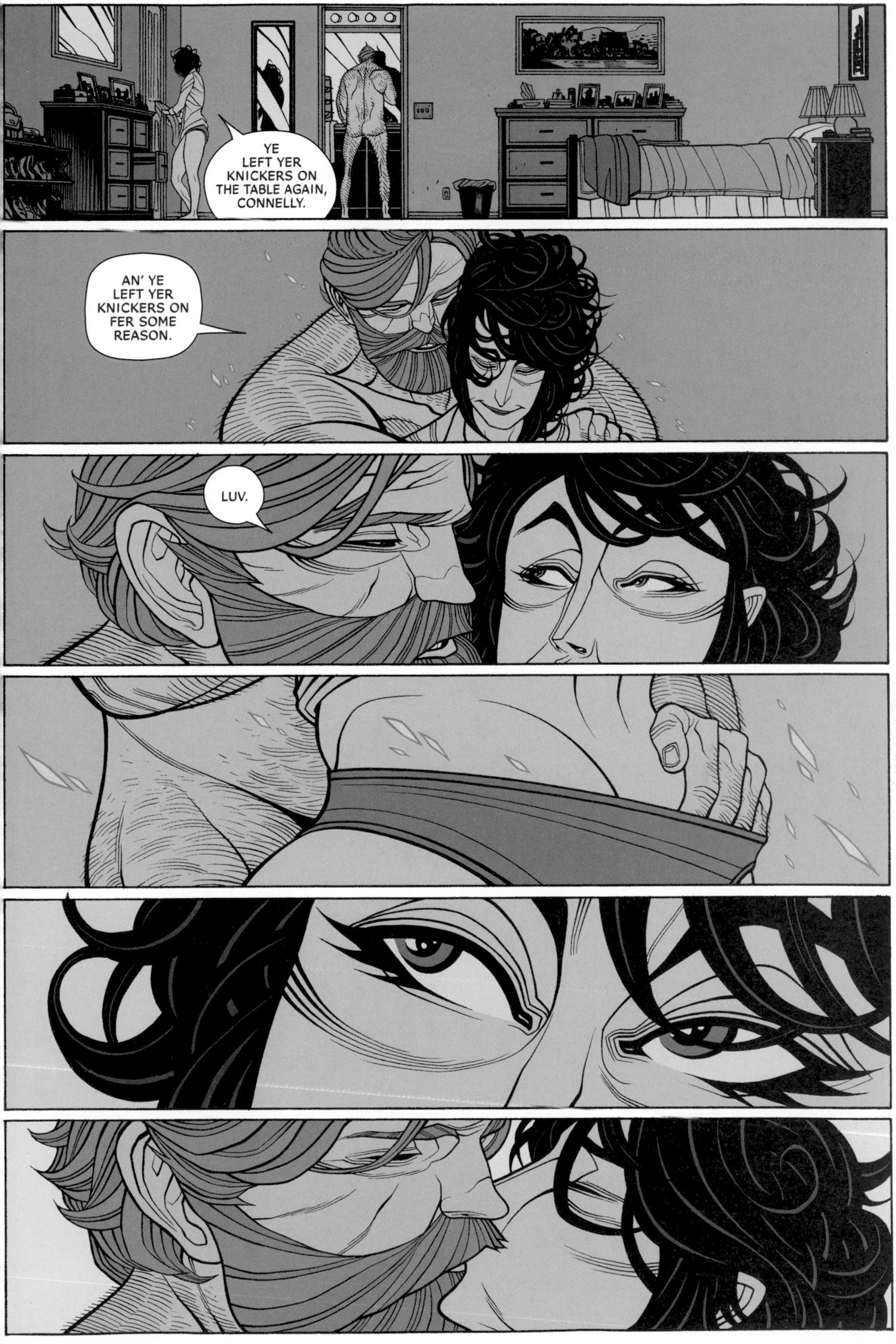
YE LEFT YER KNICKERS ON THE TABLE AGAIN, CONNELLY.
AN' YE LEFT YER KNICKERS ON FER SOME REASON.
LUV.

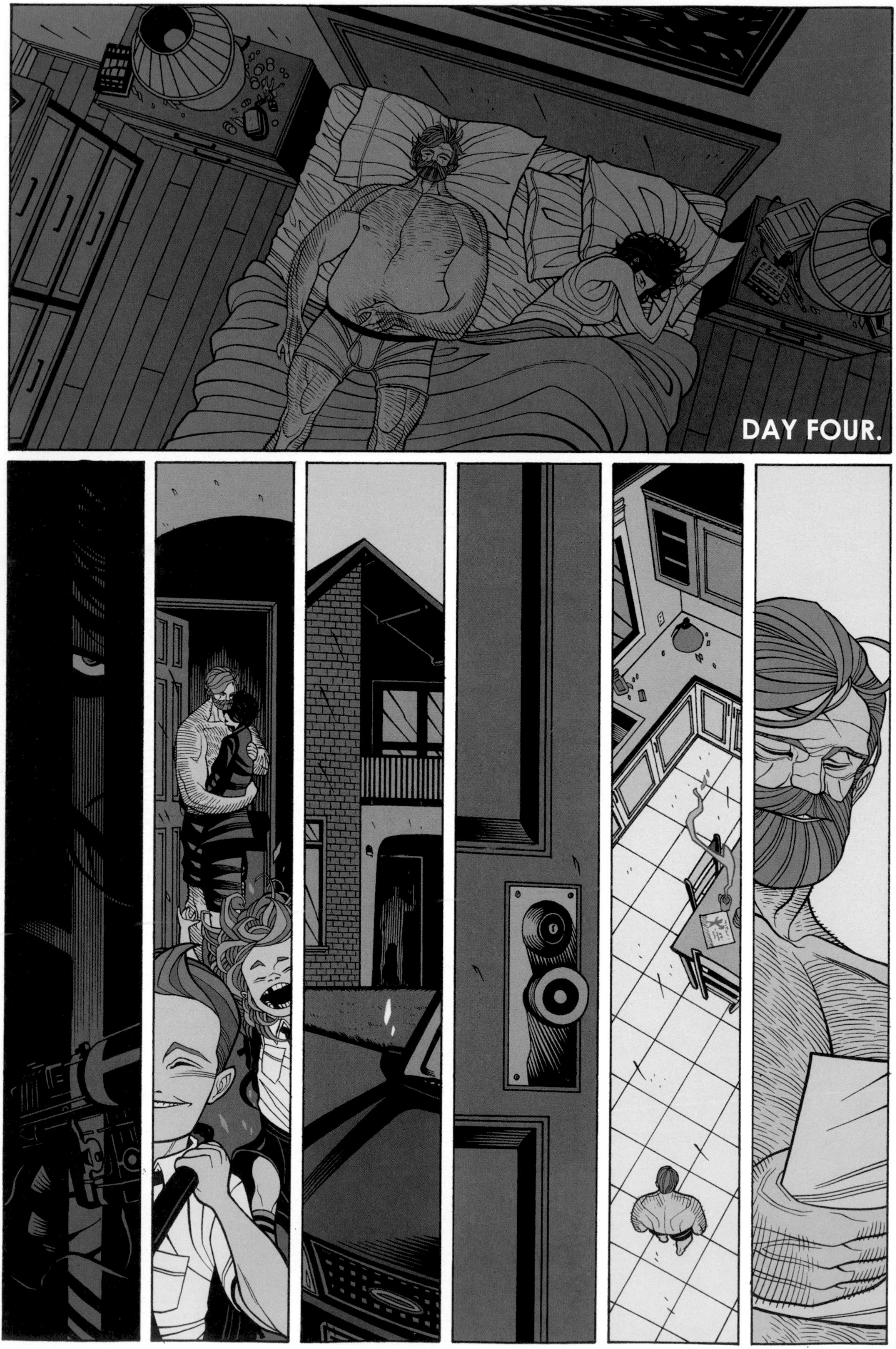
DAY FOUR.

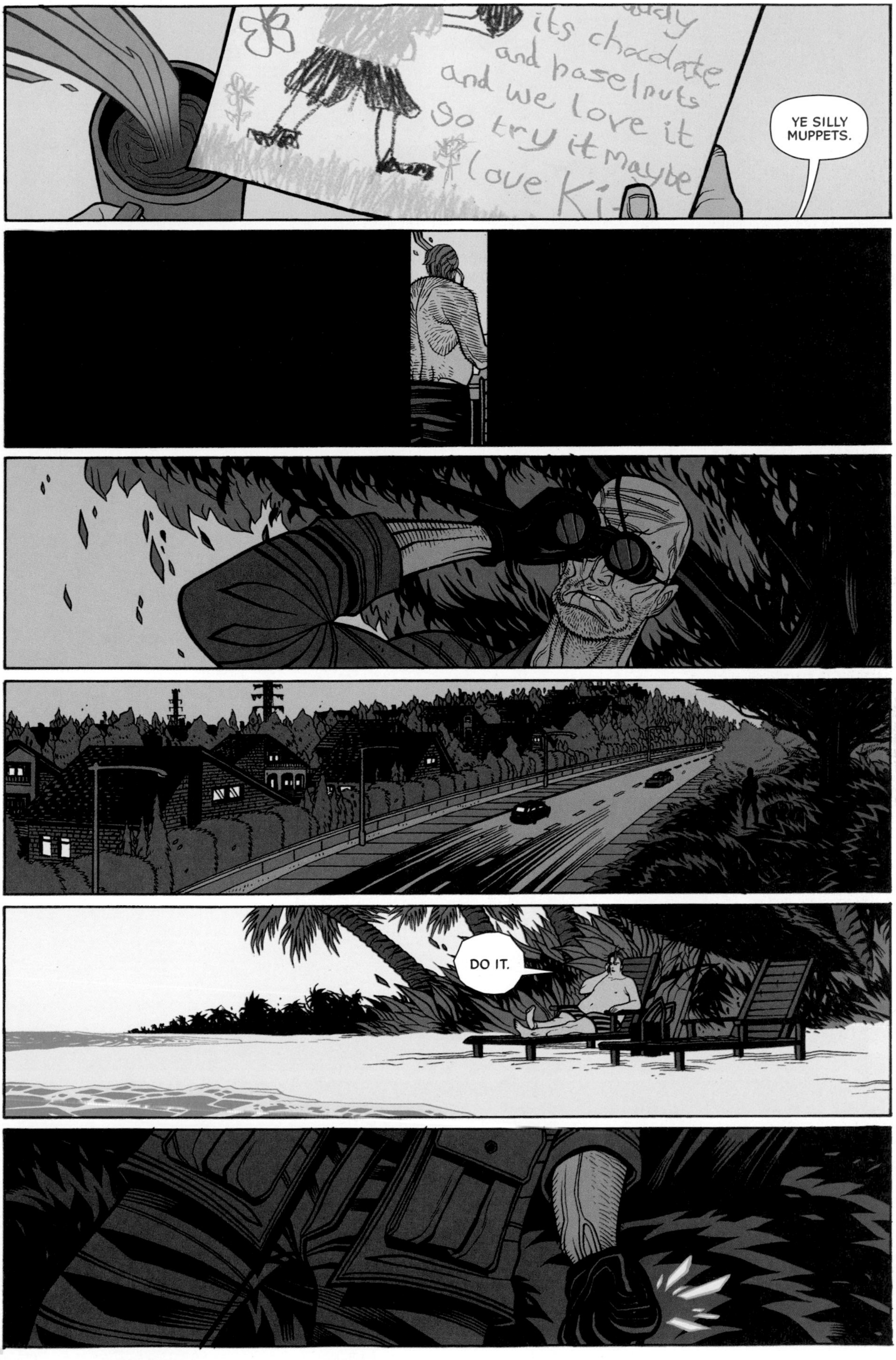
its chocolate
and haselnuts
and we love it
so try it maybe
love Ki
YE SILLY MUPPETS.
DO IT.

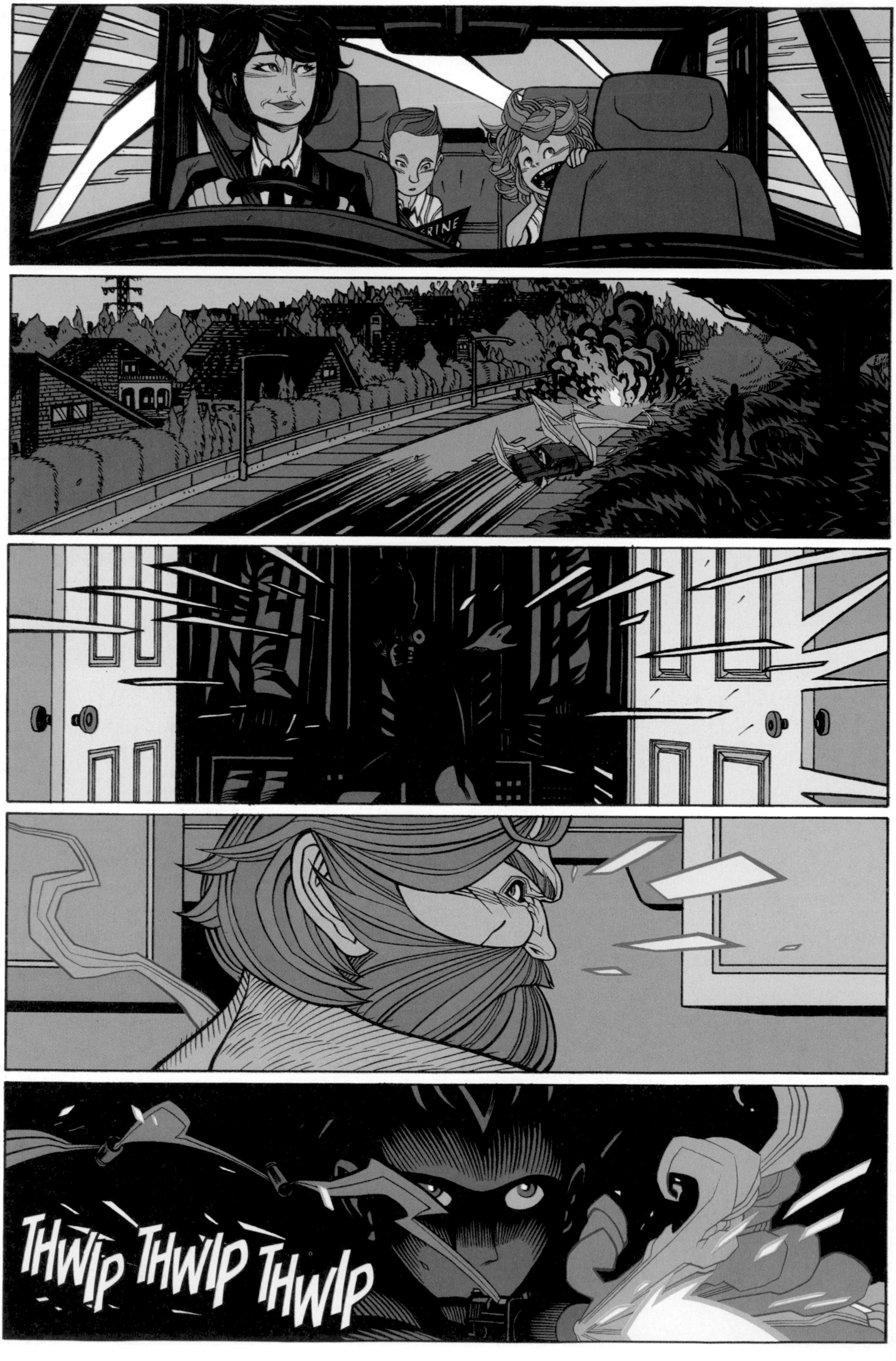
THWIP THWIP THWIP

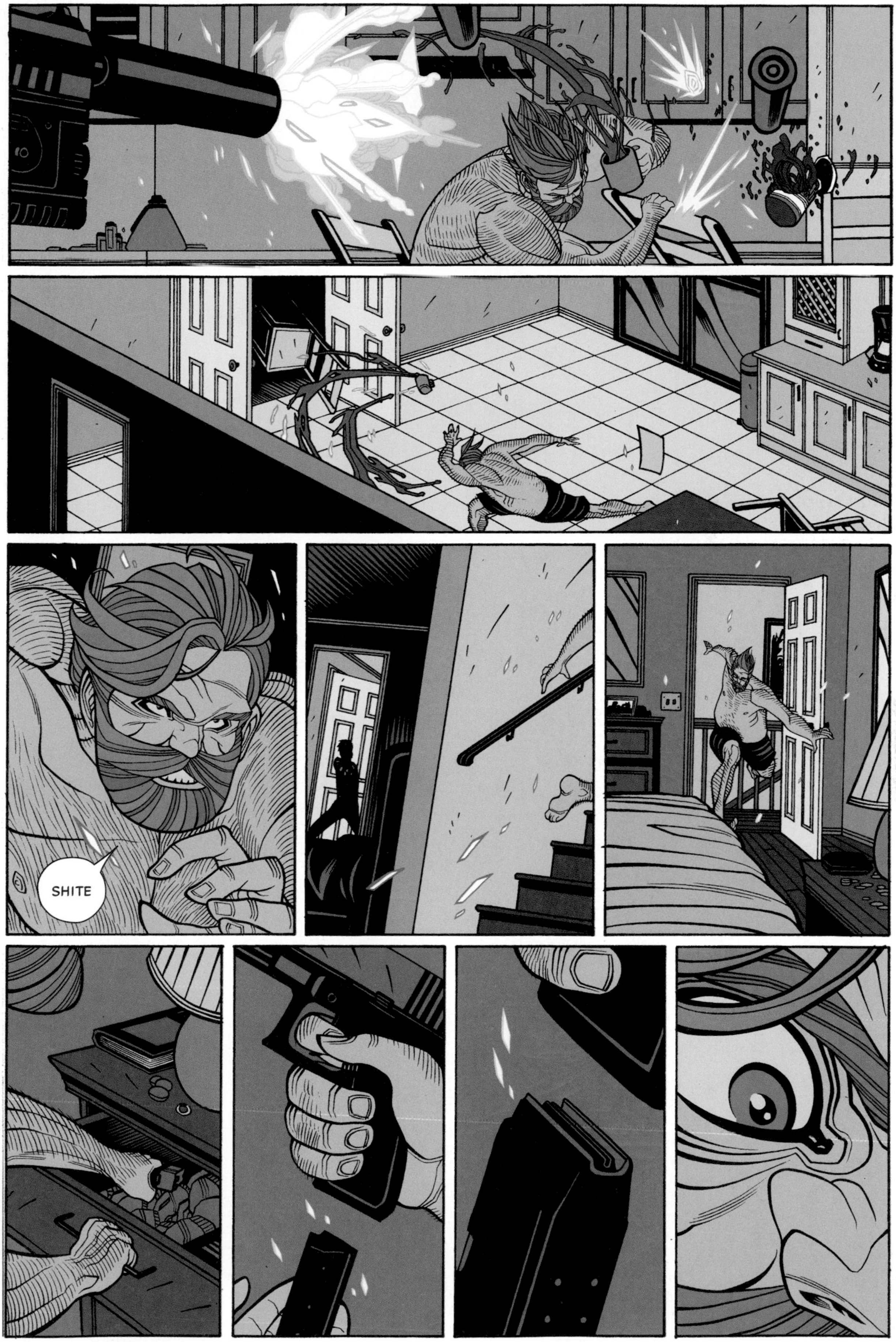
SHITE

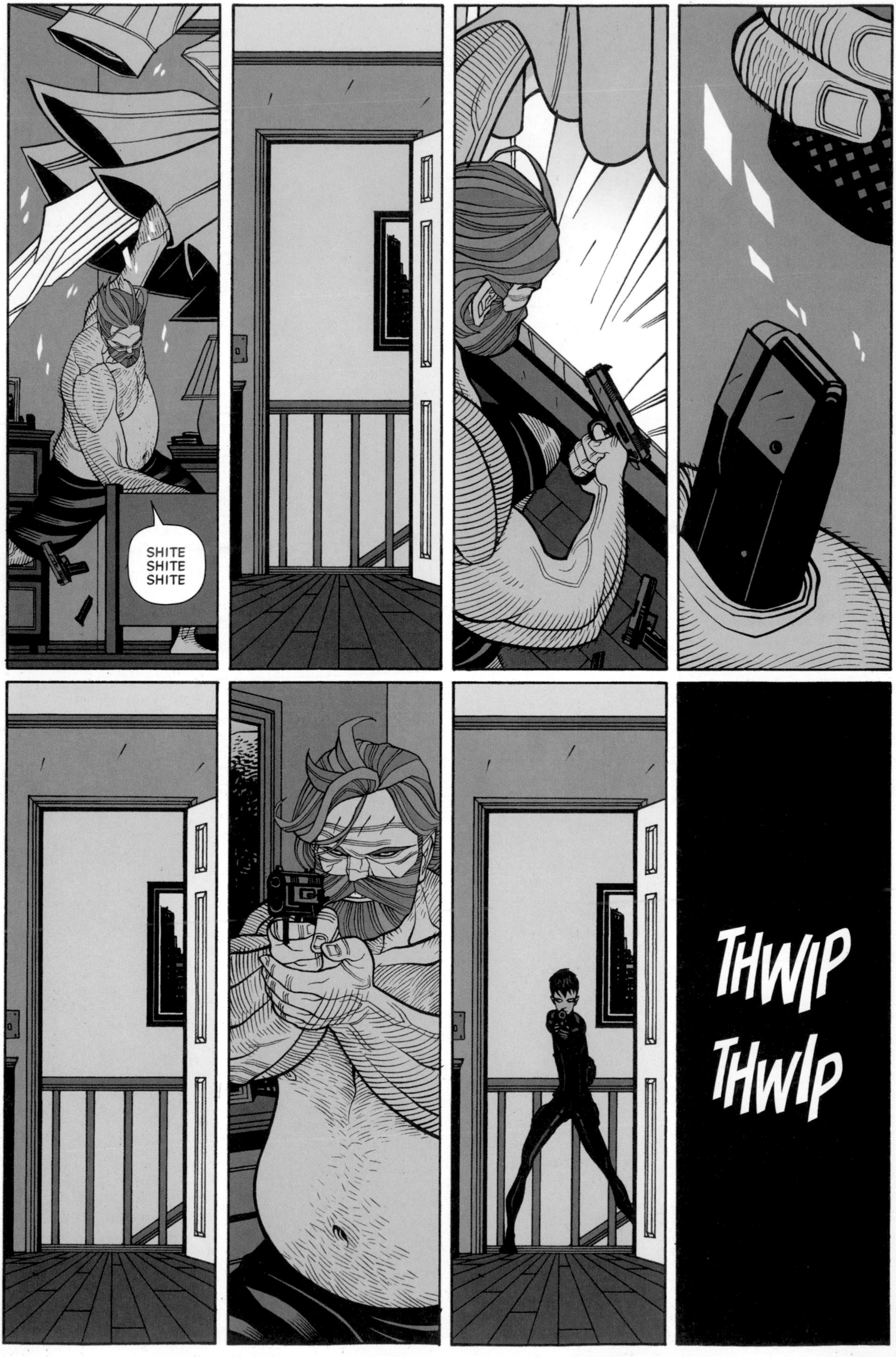
SHITE SHITE SHITE
THWIP
THWIP

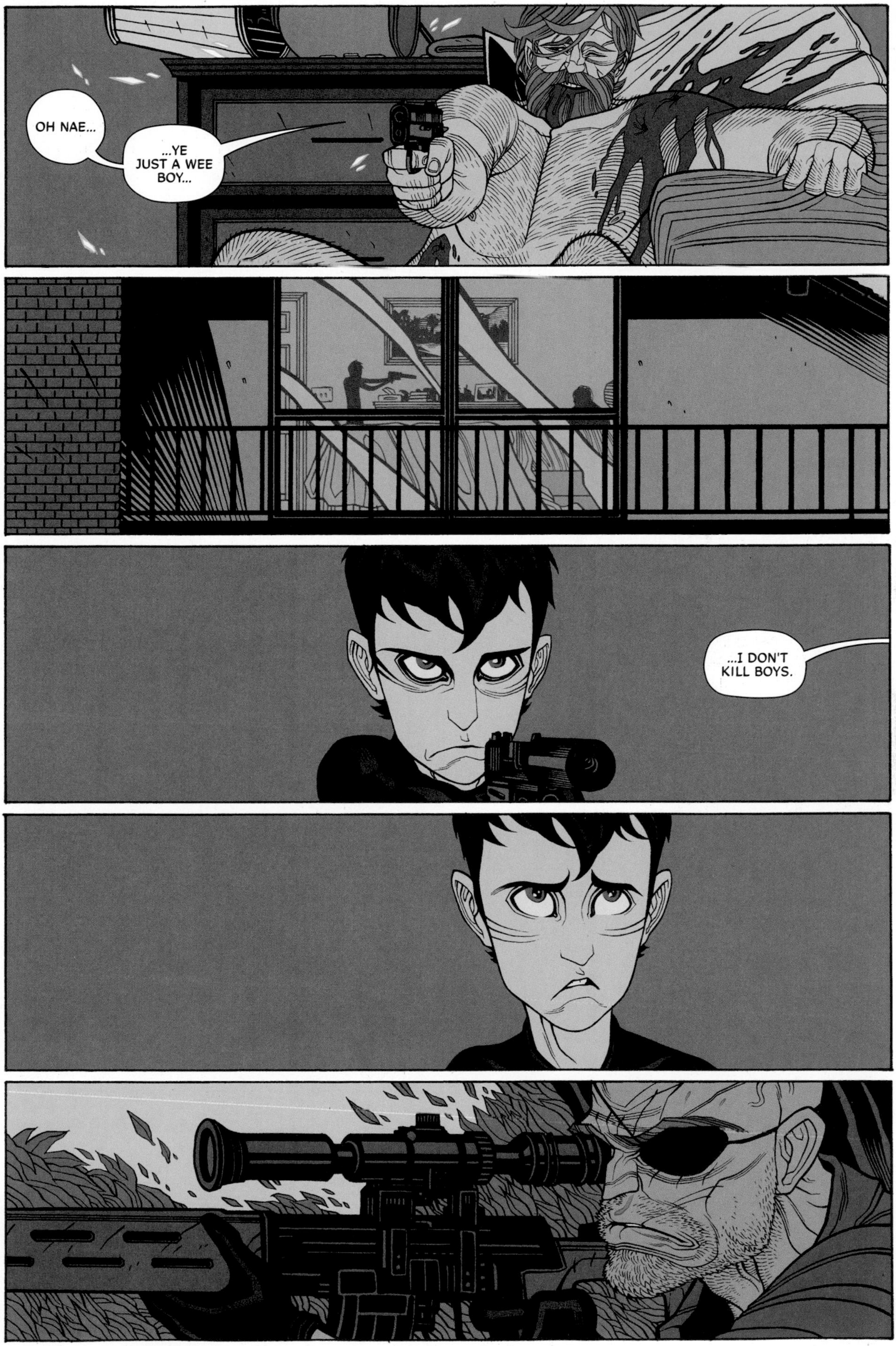
OH NAE...
...YE JUST A WEE BOY...
...I DON'T KILL BOYS.

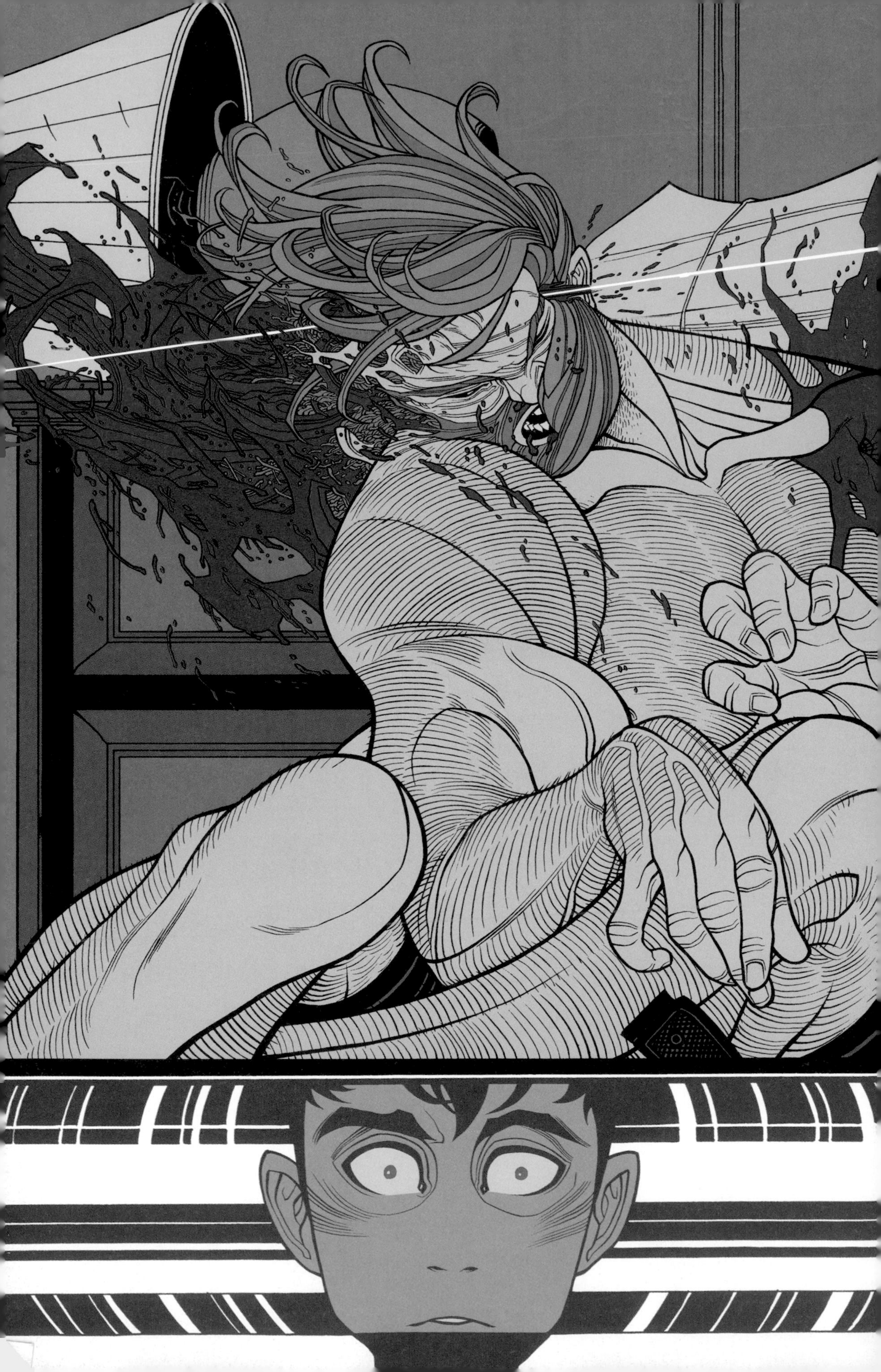

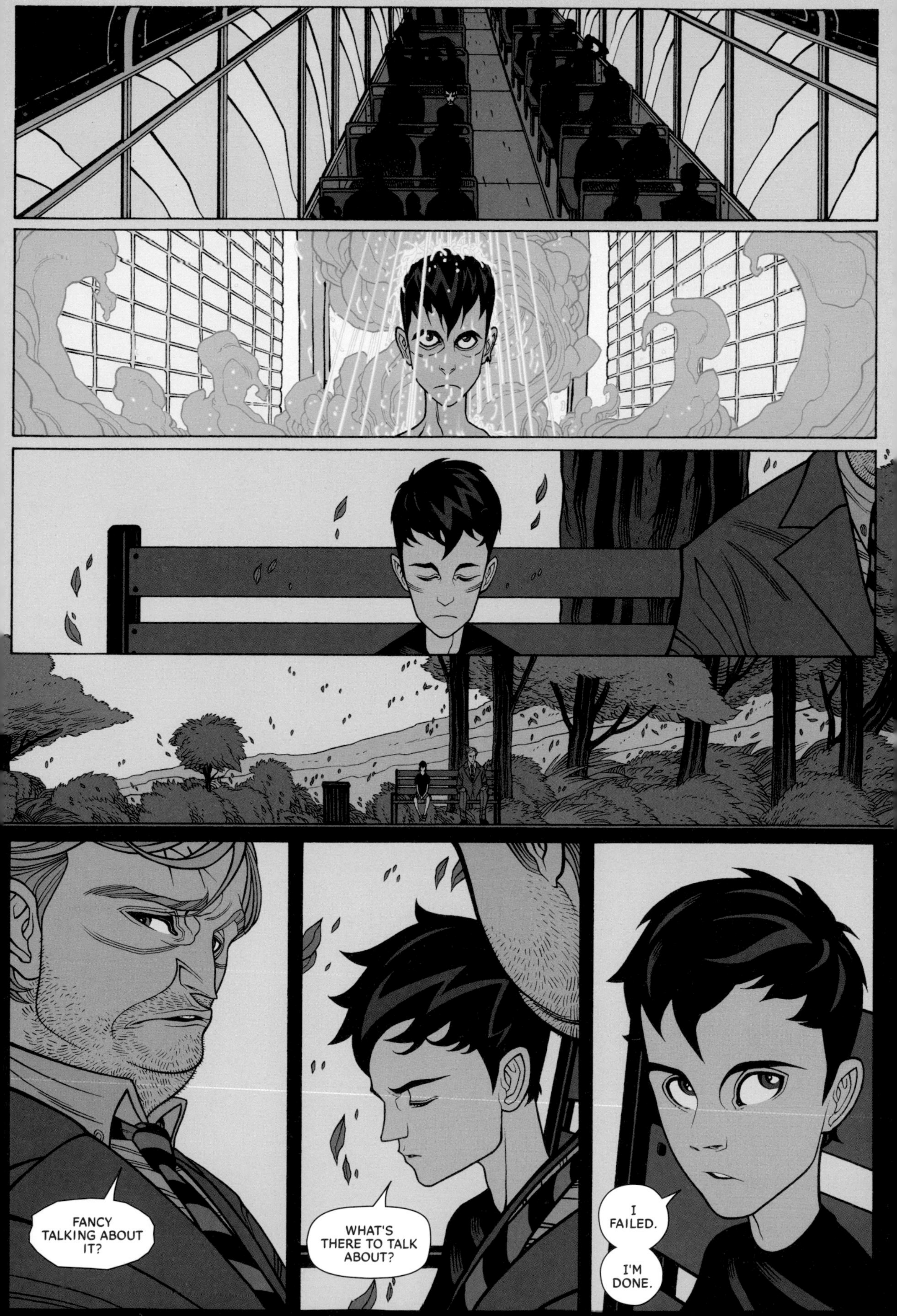
FANCY TALKING ABOUT IT?
WHAT'S THERE TO TALK ABOUT?
I FAILED.
I'M DONE.

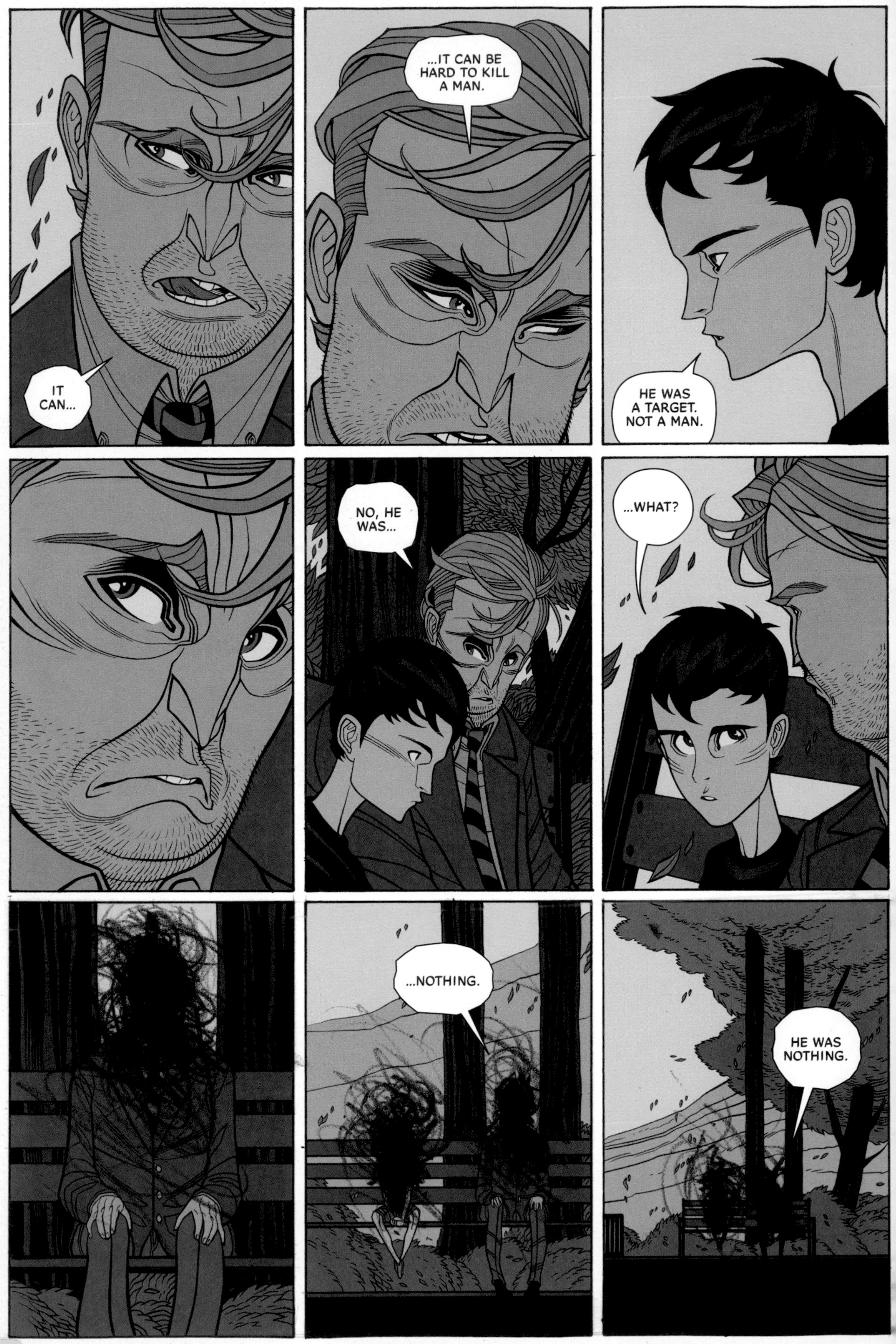
IT CAN...
...IT CAN BE HARD TO KILL A MAN.
HE WAS A TARGET. NOT A MAN.
NO, HE WAS...
...WHAT?
...NOTHING.
HE WAS NOTHING.

CHAPTER 2: I REMEMBER WHO YOU ARE.

DEDICATED TO GARTH ENNIS

ALMOST NO TRAINEE KILLS THE TARGET DURING THEIR FIRST MISSION. THEREIN LIES THE IMPORTANCE OF A HIGH-RANKING OFFICER PRESENT IN THE FIELD, OVERSEEING THE OPERATION FOR THE ENTIRETY OF ITS COURSE.

INTERROGATION OF ZIZEK, POST-MISSION.

1 ZIZEK: THE MISSION IS A SUCCESS.

2 (ERASED NAME): WHY DO YOU BELIEVE THAT?

3 ZIZEK: I KNOW THAT. WE CONTAINED THE TARGET.

4 (ERASED NAME): INCLUDING HIS FAMILY.

5 ZIZEK: DO YOU WANT THEM TO START BOMBING PLACES IN TEN YEARS?

6 ZIZEK: ME NEITHER.

7 ZIZEK: LOOK, YOU WANTED TO FUCKING PUT ME BEHIND THE DESK, SO HERE I AM. BUT IF YOU WANT TO TELL ME HOW TO DO MY JOB--

8 (ERASED NAME): CALM THE FUCK DOWN.

9 ZIZEK: ...OKAY.

10 (ERASED NAME): HE'S TESTING HIGH. ARE YOU TAKING APPROPRIATE MEASURES TO ENSURE THAT HE WON'T OVERLOAD?

11 ZIZEK: YES.

12 (ERASED NAME): ALL PROCEDURES ARE IN PLACE?

13 ZIZEK: YES. UPPED THE PILLS, TOO.

14 (ERASED NAME): GOOD.

15 ZIZEK: I DON'T BELIEVE THE PILLS DO ANY GOOD LONG-TERM.

16 (ERASED NAME): IT'S NOT ABOUT WHAT YOU BELIEVE IN. IT'S ABOUT SCIENCE.

17 ZIZEK: BECAUSE SCIENCE HAS NEVER BEEN WRONG, EH?

18 (ERASED NAME): DOES HE STILL HAVE NIGHT TERRORS?

19 ZIZEK: NO. HE STOPPED HAVING THOSE.

[redacted] [redacted] [redacted]

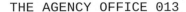

THE AGENCY OFFICE 013

URPDI

SPS FOR FRONT OFFICE, ART-1, AND UMP; FMI FOR
COOKE/ZIZEK/CRUMPTON

DT: 10/07/2018
TAGS: ISR, PLT, ZERO, MD-2, BTC, UR-15, BT-HN
SUBJECT: AGENT EVALUATION (POST-MISSION), ZERO, E.

REF: A. 68 BT-HN 03/2018
                        B. 389 JERUSALEM 04/2018
                        C. SEE ATTACHED B-5, C98

Classified By: ALTMAN, R.
for reasons: **CLASSIFIED**

  1.(A) Summary. The agent successfully returned from the
mission. The SAP-V enhancer remains fully functional and now
again in the Agency's care.

  During the mission, the agent had to dispose of five
Israeli combatants. These neutralizations were described as
necessary. Despite the agent testing highly on the H-scale,
the answers provided are satisfactory.

  The modified Palestinian combatant was neutralized by
a tank shell. The modified Israeli was neutralized by the
Israelis shortly after he failed to neutralize the Palestinian
combatant. The agent observed all this before leaving the
territory.

  The agent's wounds are minimal: dislodged jaw, a broken
index finger, multiple bruising. Psych evaluation successful.

Note: The loss of the SAP-V enhancer from the Agency
           laboratory is a clear proof that we have a mole
           within the Agency.

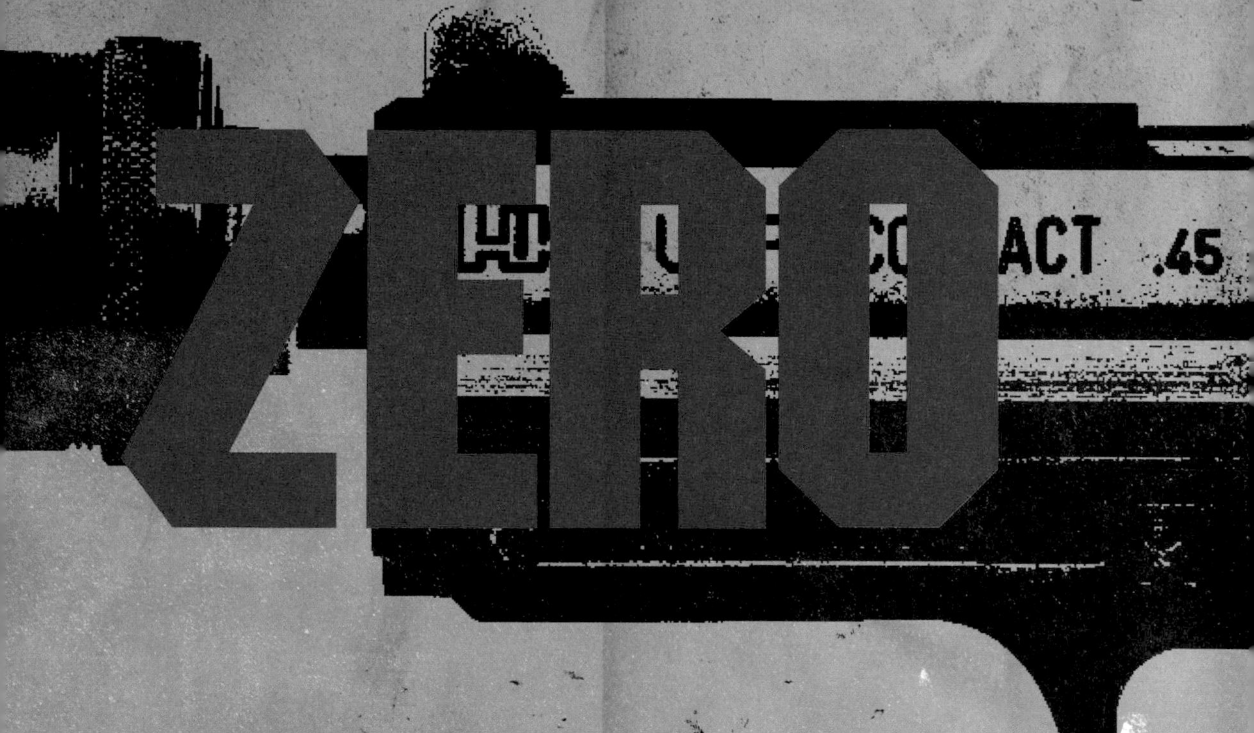
ZERO
ACT .45

CHAPTER 3

A NEEDLE IN YOUR EYE
Illustrated by Mateus Santolouco

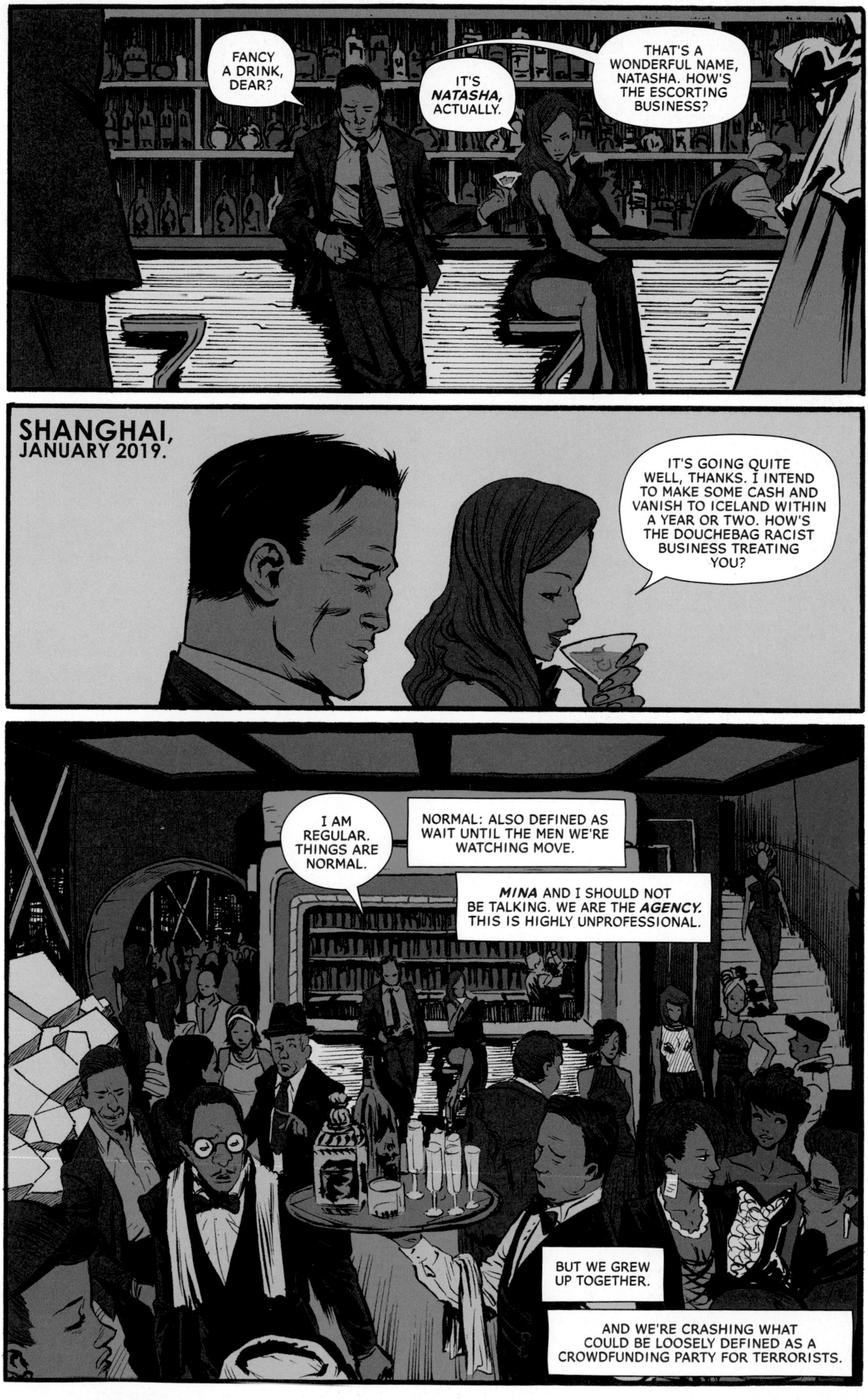
FANCY A DRINK, DEAR?
IT'S NATASHA, ACTUALLY.
THAT'S A WONDERFUL NAME, NATASHA. HOW'S THE ESCORTING BUSINESS?
SHANGHAI, JANUARY 2019.
IT'S GOING QUITE WELL, THANKS. I INTEND TO MAKE SOME CASH AND VANISH TO ICELAND WITHIN A YEAR OR TWO. HOW'S THE DOUCHEBAG RACIST BUSINESS TREATING YOU?
I AM REGULAR. THINGS ARE NORMAL.
NORMAL: ALSO DEFINED AS WAIT UNTIL THE MEN WE'RE WATCHING MOVE.
MINA AND I SHOULD NOT BE TALKING. WE ARE THE AGENCY. THIS IS HIGHLY UNPROFESSIONAL.
BUT WE GREW UP TOGETHER.
AND WE'RE CRASHING WHAT COULD BE LOOSELY DEFINED AS A CROWDFUNDING PARTY FOR TERRORISTS.

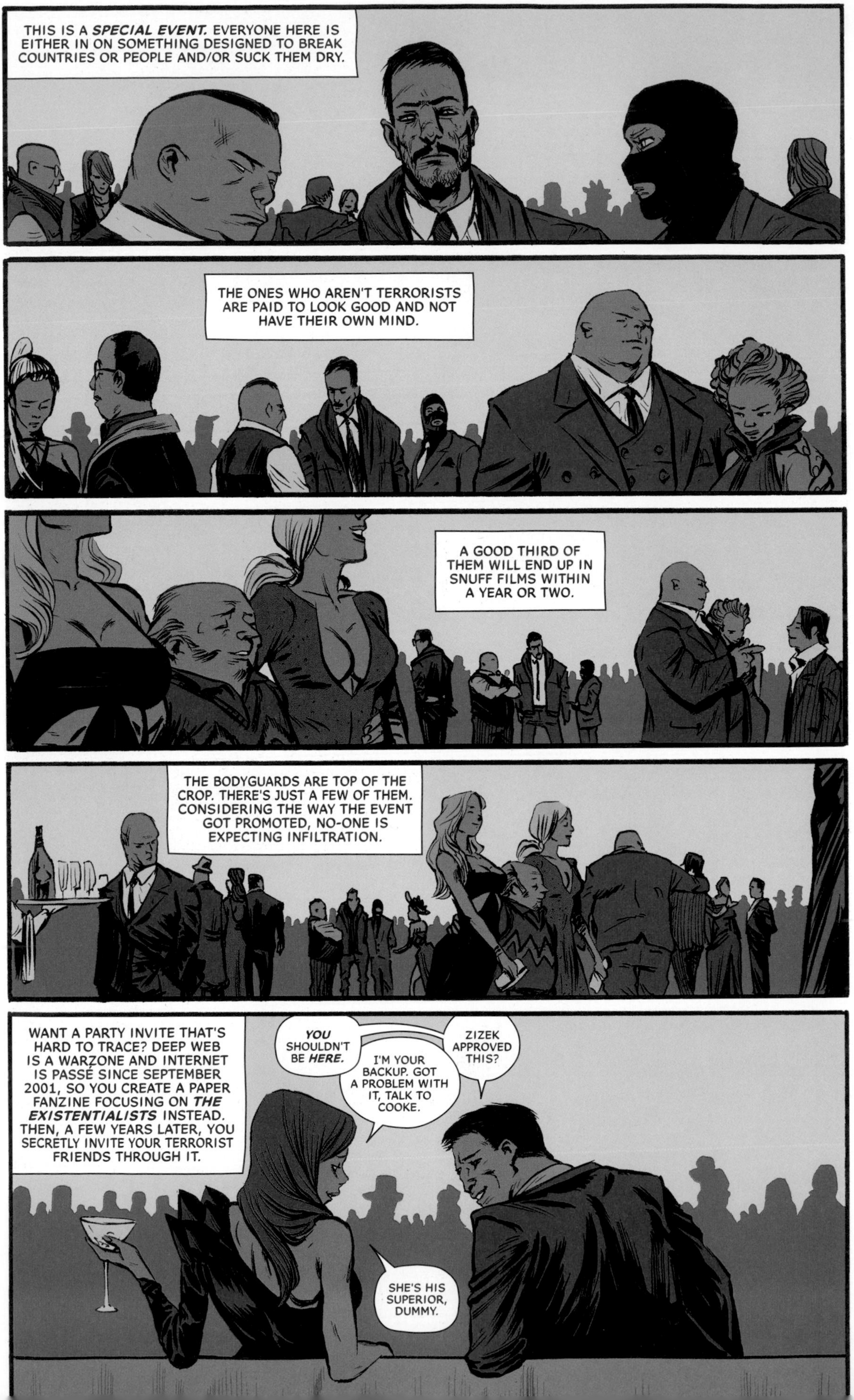
THIS IS A *SPECIAL EVENT.* EVERYONE HERE IS EITHER IN ON SOMETHING DESIGNED TO BREAK COUNTRIES OR PEOPLE AND/OR SUCK THEM DRY.
THE ONES WHO AREN'T TERRORISTS ARE PAID TO LOOK GOOD AND NOT HAVE THEIR OWN MIND.
A GOOD THIRD OF THEM WILL END UP IN SNUFF FILMS WITHIN A YEAR OR TWO.
THE BODYGUARDS ARE TOP OF THE CROP. THERE'S JUST A FEW OF THEM. CONSIDERING THE WAY THE EVENT GOT PROMOTED, NO-ONE IS EXPECTING INFILTRATION.
WANT A PARTY INVITE THAT'S HARD TO TRACE? DEEP WEB IS A WARZONE AND INTERNET IS PASSÉ SINCE SEPTEMBER 2001, SO YOU CREATE A PAPER FANZINE FOCUSING ON *THE EXISTENTIALISTS* INSTEAD. THEN, A FEW YEARS LATER, YOU SECRETLY INVITE YOUR TERRORIST FRIENDS THROUGH IT.
YOU SHOULDN'T BE *HERE.*
ZIZEK APPROVED THIS?
I'M YOUR BACKUP. GOT A PROBLEM WITH IT, TALK TO COOKE.
SHE'S HIS SUPERIOR, DUMMY.

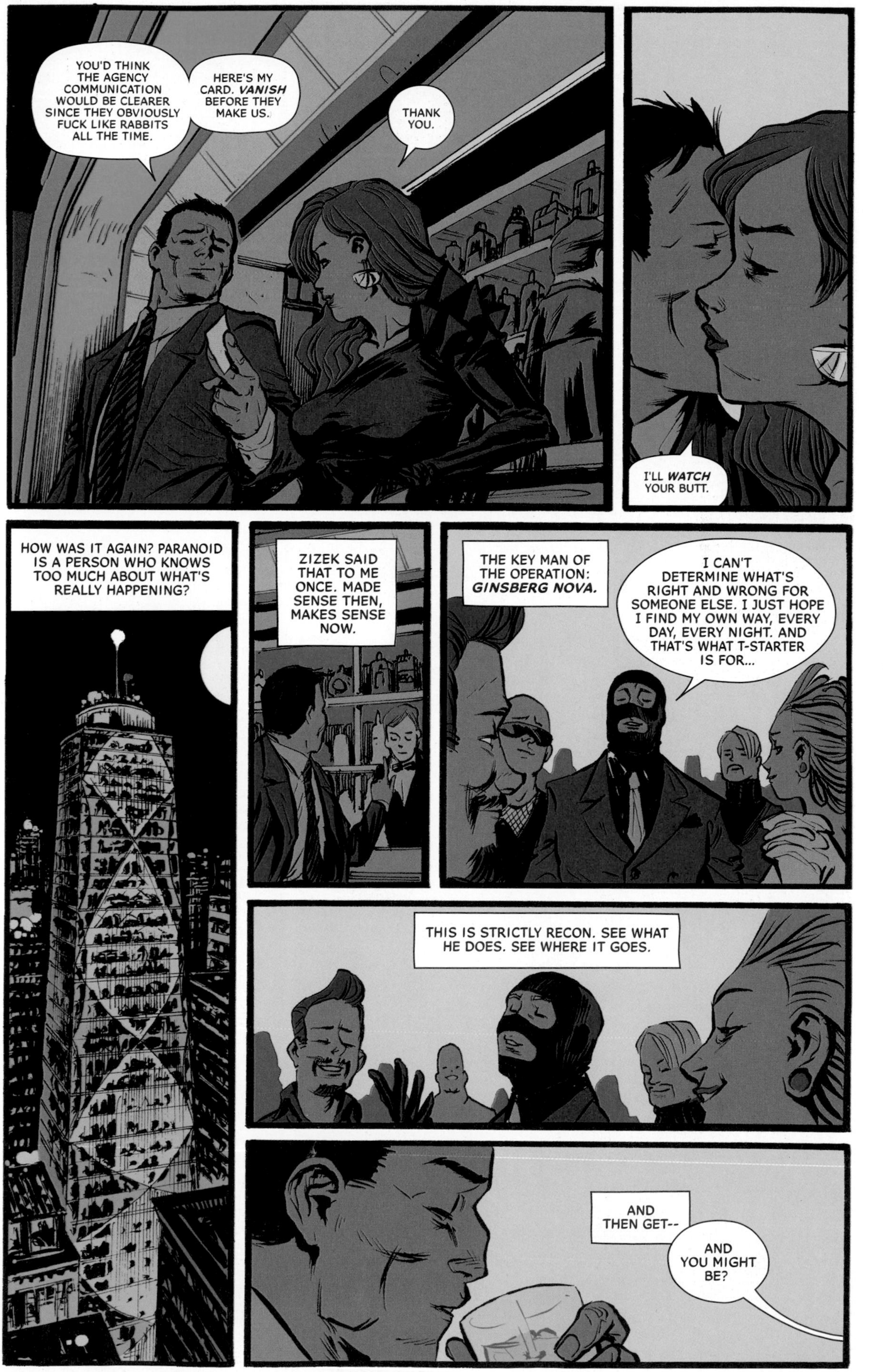
YOU'D THINK THE AGENCY COMMUNICATION WOULD BE CLEARER SINCE THEY OBVIOUSLY FUCK LIKE RABBITS ALL THE TIME.
HERE'S MY CARD. VANISH BEFORE THEY MAKE US.
THANK YOU.
I'LL WATCH YOUR BUTT.
HOW WAS IT AGAIN? PARANOID IS A PERSON WHO KNOWS TOO MUCH ABOUT WHAT'S REALLY HAPPENING?
ZIZEK SAID THAT TO ME ONCE. MADE SENSE THEN, MAKES SENSE NOW.
THE KEY MAN OF THE OPERATION: GINSBERG NOVA.
I CAN'T DETERMINE WHAT'S RIGHT AND WRONG FOR SOMEONE ELSE. I JUST HOPE I FIND MY OWN WAY, EVERY DAY, EVERY NIGHT. AND THAT'S WHAT T-STARTER IS FOR...
THIS IS STRICTLY RECON. SEE WHAT HE DOES. SEE WHERE IT GOES.
AND THEN GET--
AND YOU MIGHT BE?

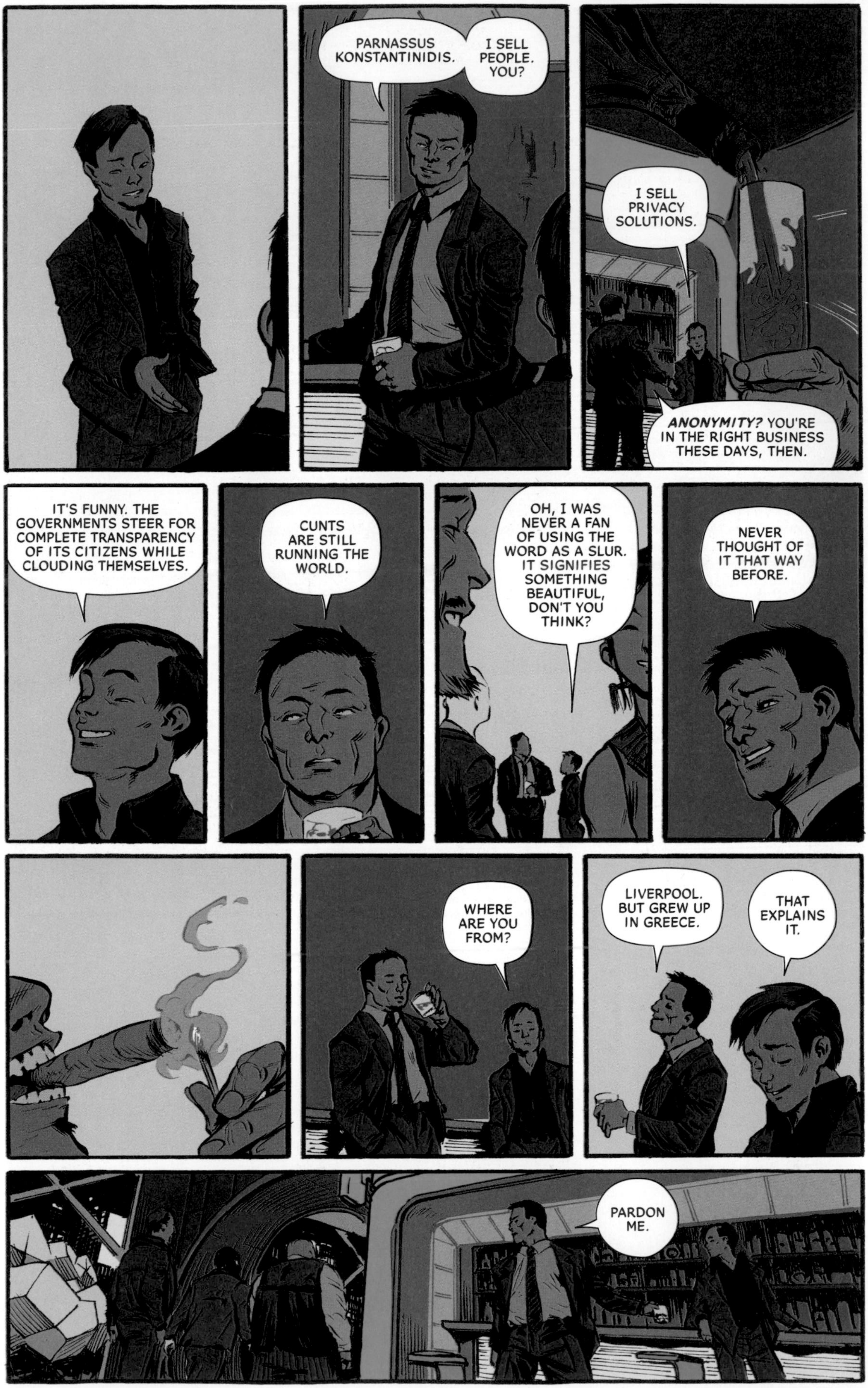

PARNASSUS KONSTANTINIDIS.
I SELL PEOPLE. YOU?
I SELL PRIVACY SOLUTIONS.
ANONYMITY? YOU'RE IN THE RIGHT BUSINESS THESE DAYS, THEN.
IT'S FUNNY. THE GOVERNMENTS STEER FOR COMPLETE TRANSPARENCY OF ITS CITIZENS WHILE CLOUDING THEMSELVES.
CUNTS ARE STILL RUNNING THE WORLD.
OH, I WAS NEVER A FAN OF USING THE WORD AS A SLUR. IT SIGNIFIES SOMETHING BEAUTIFUL, DON'T YOU THINK?
NEVER THOUGHT OF IT THAT WAY BEFORE.
WHERE ARE YOU FROM?
LIVERPOOL. BUT GREW UP IN GREECE.
THAT EXPLAINS IT.
PARDON ME.

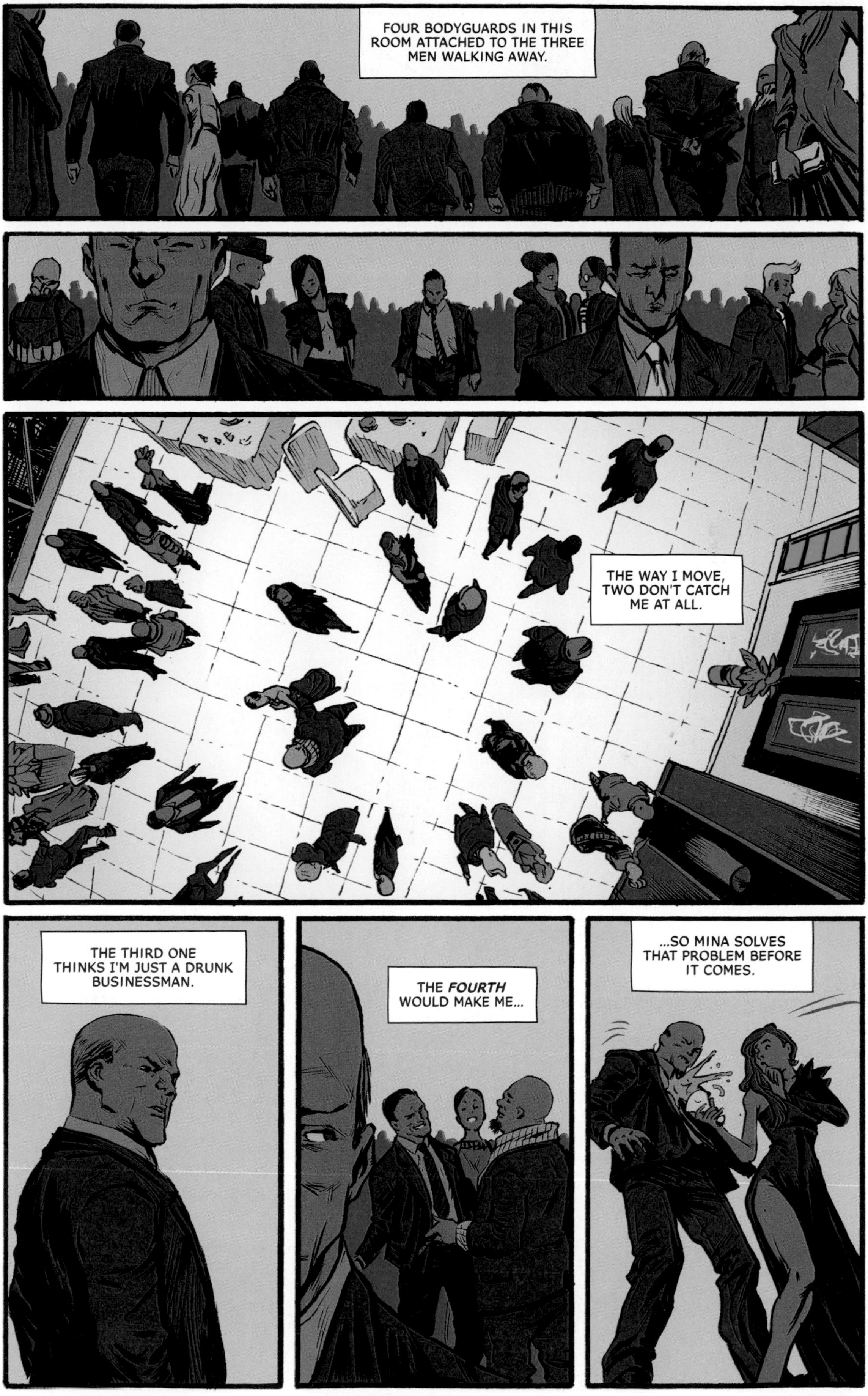
FOUR BODYGUARDS IN THIS ROOM ATTACHED TO THE THREE MEN WALKING AWAY.
THE WAY I MOVE, TWO DON'T CATCH ME AT ALL.
THE THIRD ONE THINKS I'M JUST A DRUNK BUSINESSMAN.
THE *FOURTH* WOULD MAKE ME...
...SO MINA SOLVES THAT PROBLEM BEFORE IT COMES.

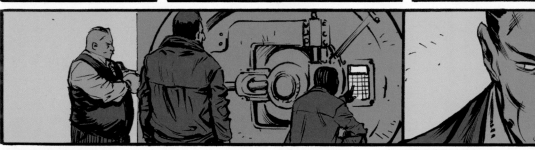

I AM *SO SORRY.* IS THERE *ANYTHING* I CAN *DO* TO MAKE THIS UP TO *YOU?*

THAT'S ALL RIGHT, *MISS...?*

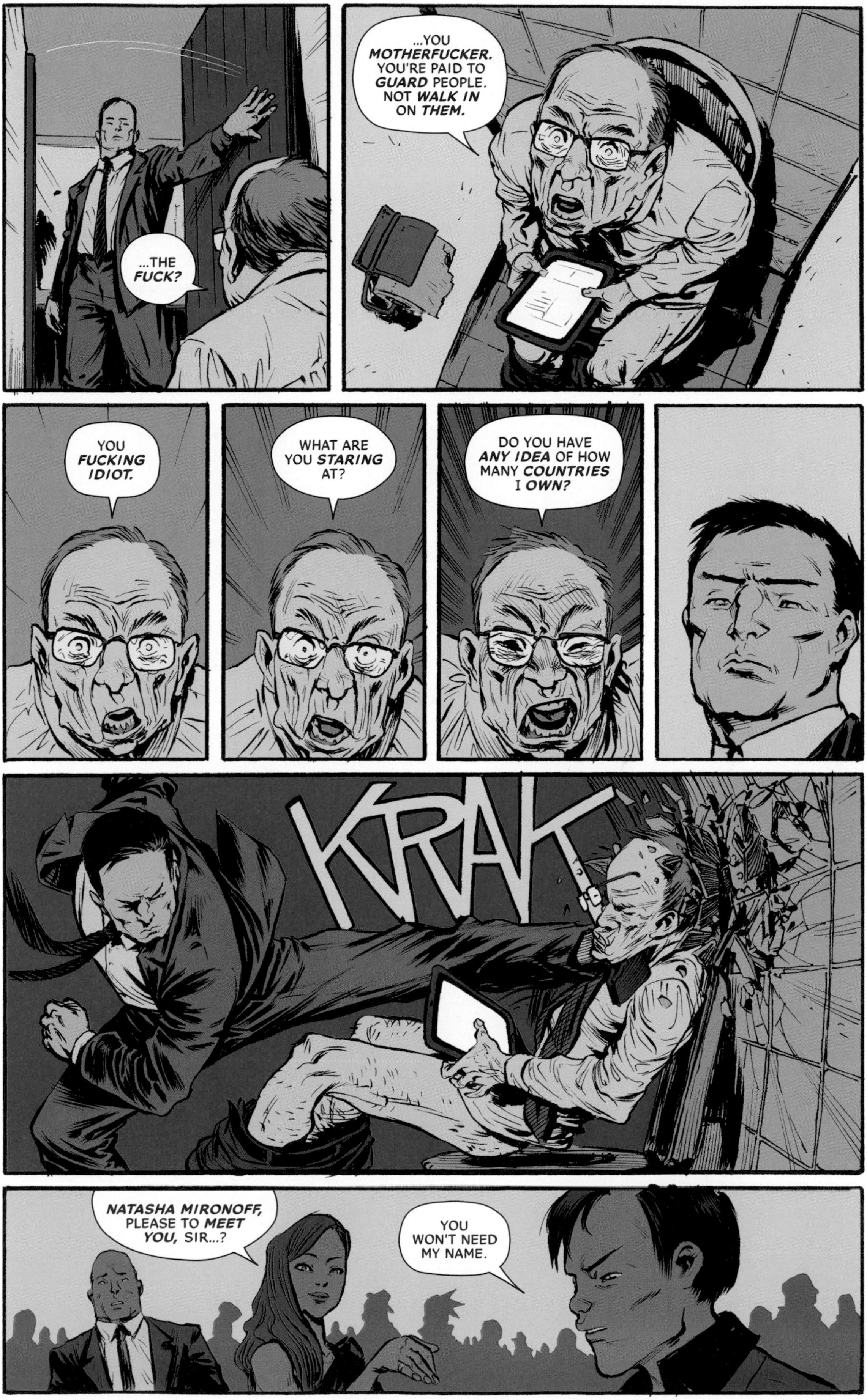
...THE FUCK?
...YOU MOTHERFUCKER. YOU'RE PAID TO GUARD PEOPLE. NOT WALK IN ON THEM.
YOU FUCKING IDIOT.
WHAT ARE YOU STARING AT?
DO YOU HAVE ANY IDEA OF HOW MANY COUNTRIES I OWN?
KRAK
NATASHA MIRONOFF, PLEASE TO MEET YOU, SIR...?
YOU WON'T NEED MY NAME.

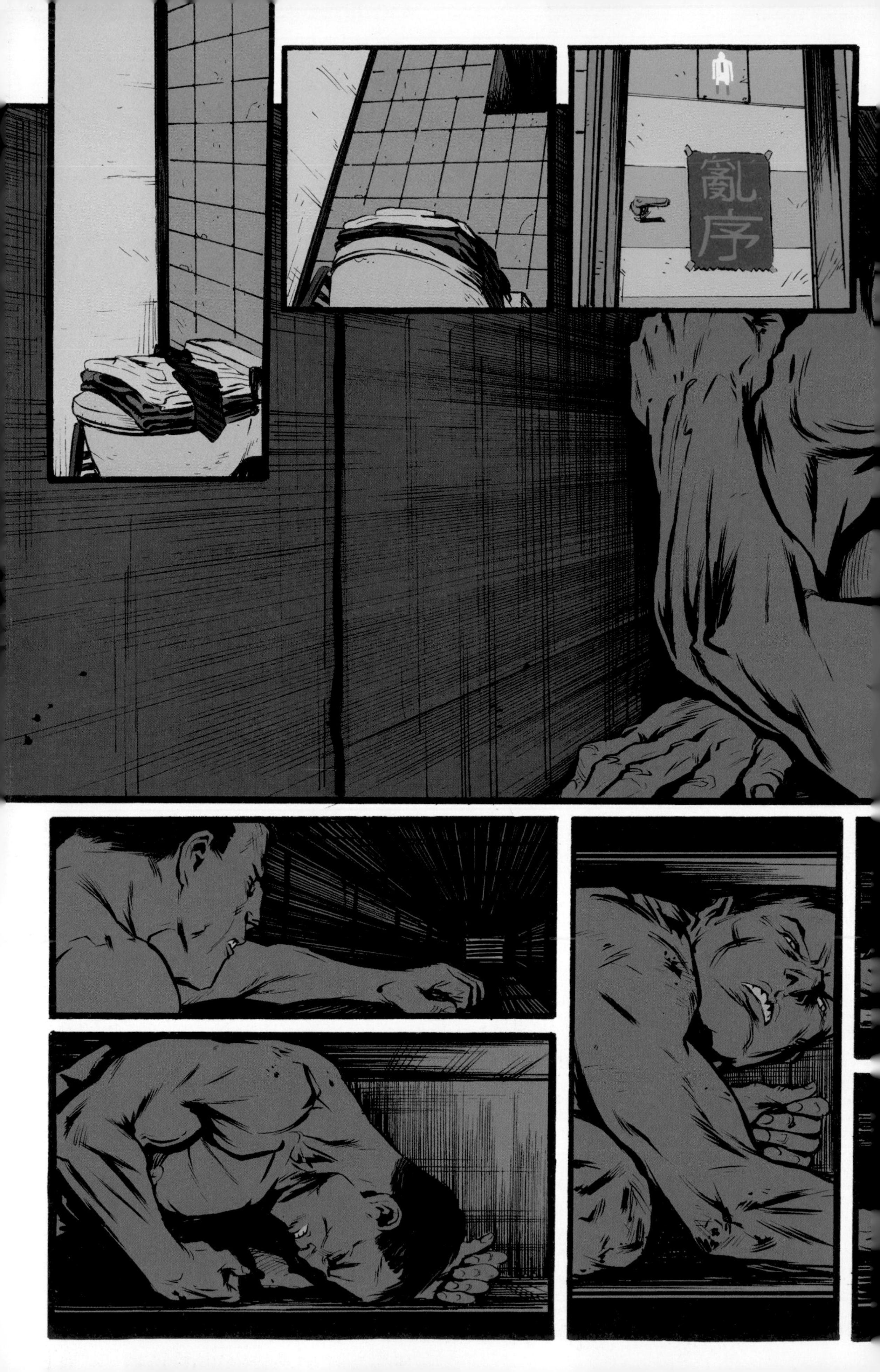
亂序

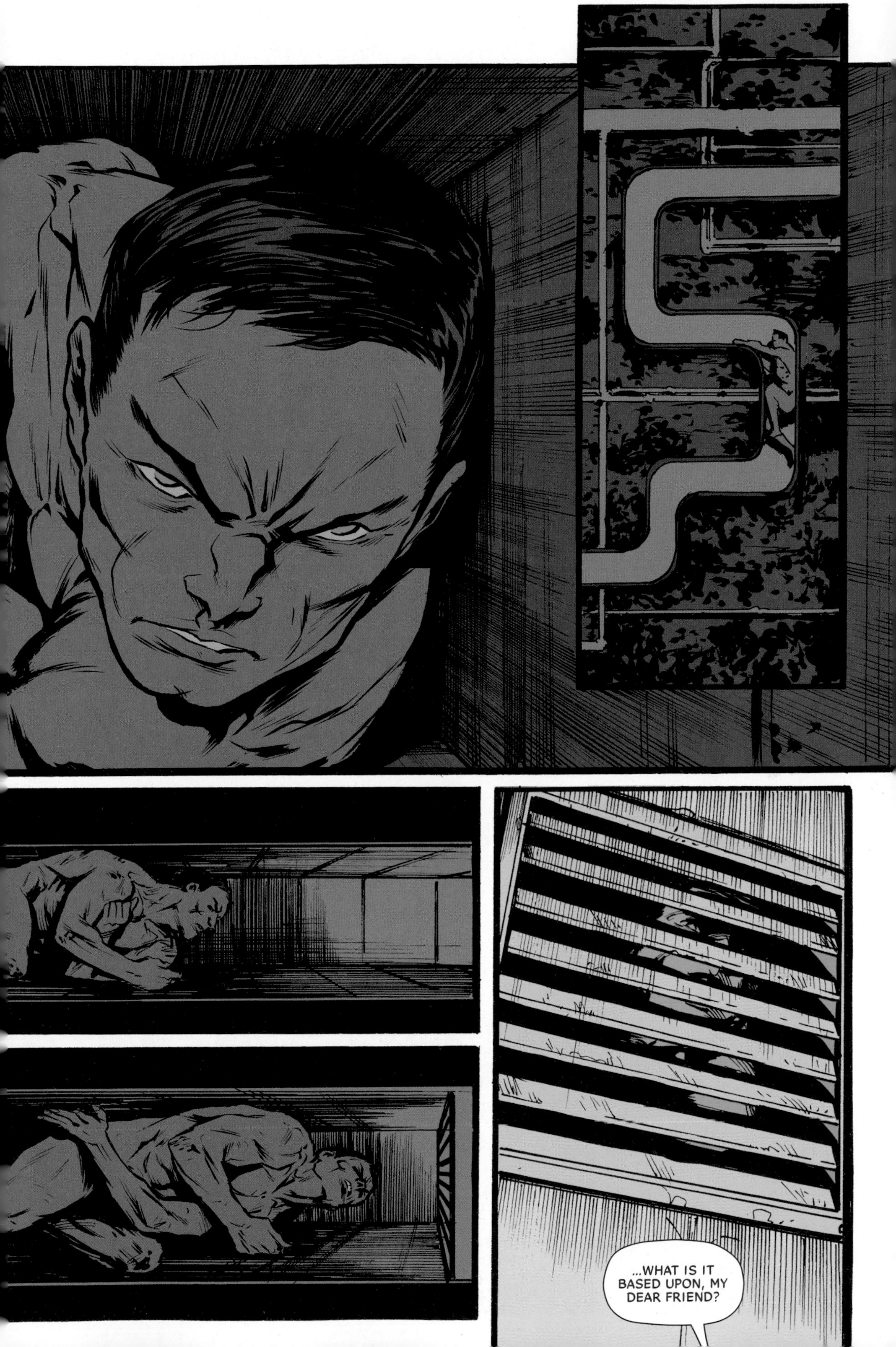
...WHAT IS IT BASED UPON, MY DEAR FRIEND?

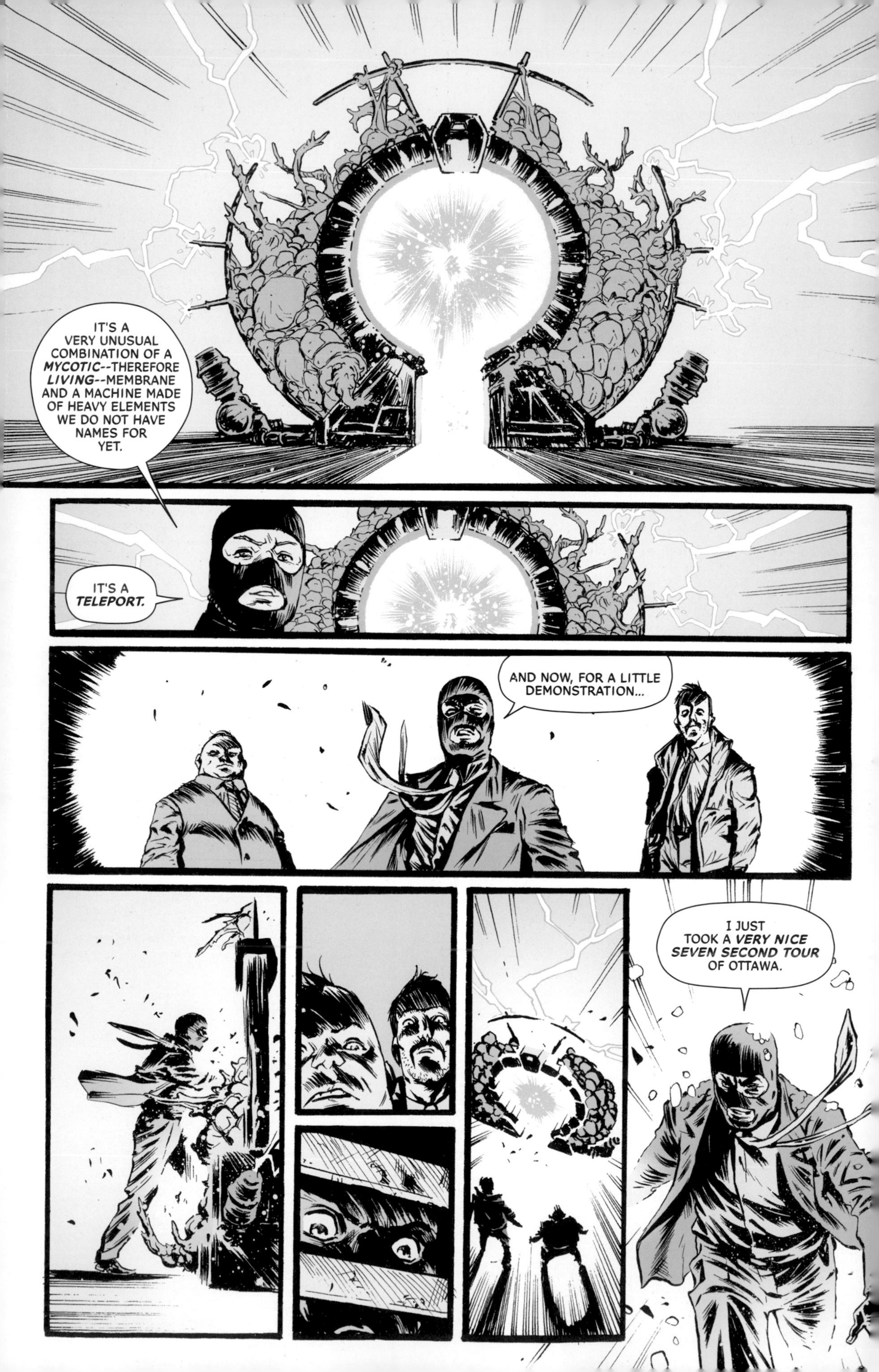

IT'S A VERY UNUSUAL COMBINATION OF A *MYCOTIC*--THEREFORE *LIVING*--MEMBRANE AND A MACHINE MADE OF HEAVY ELEMENTS WE DO NOT HAVE NAMES FOR YET.
IT'S A ***TELEPORT.***
AND NOW, FOR A LITTLE DEMONSTRATION...
I JUST TOOK A ***VERY NICE SEVEN SECOND TOUR*** OF OTTAWA.

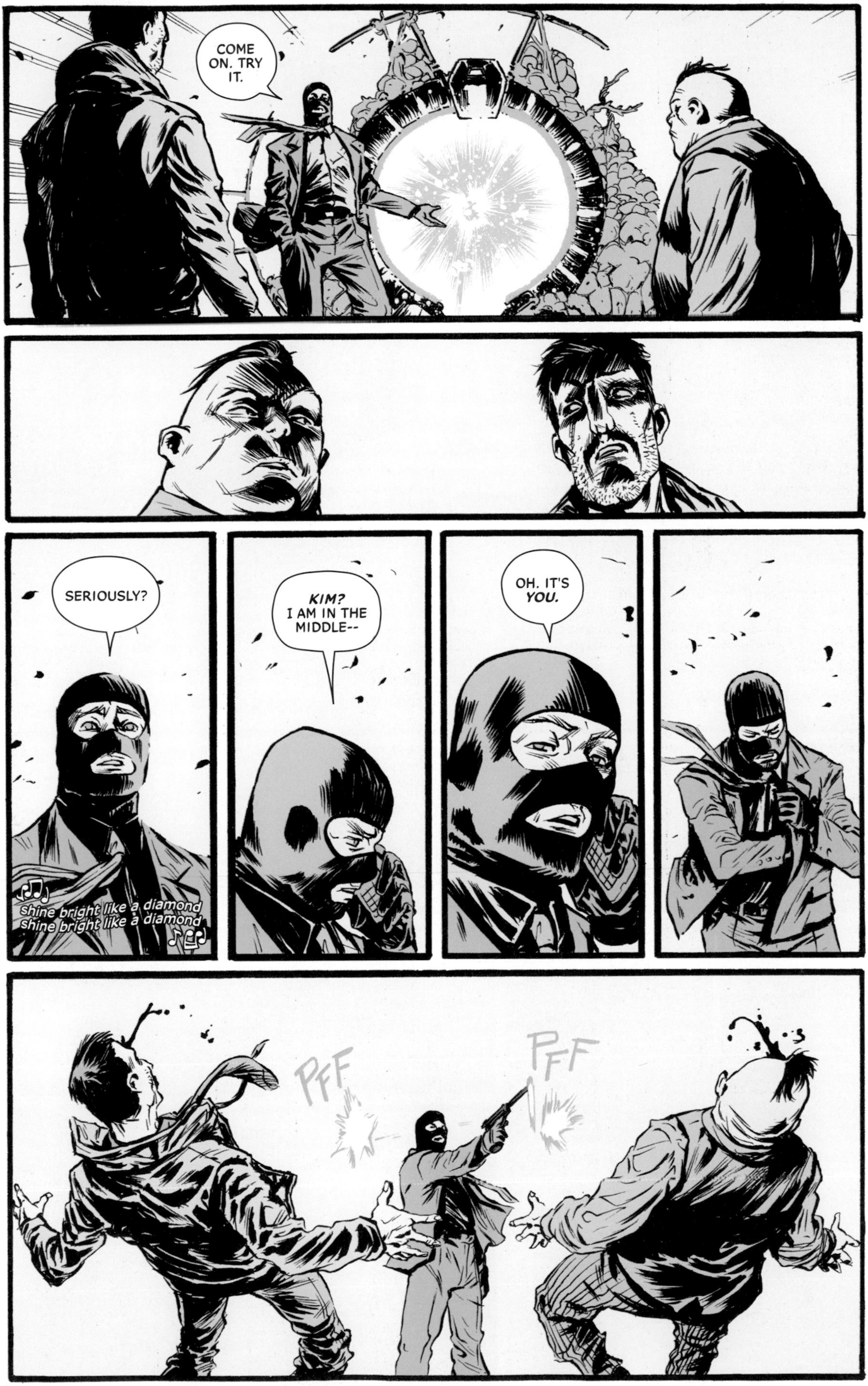
COME ON. TRY IT.
SERIOUSLY?
shine bright like a diamond
shine bright like a diamond
KIM? I AM IN THE MIDDLE--
OH. IT'S YOU.
PFF
PFF

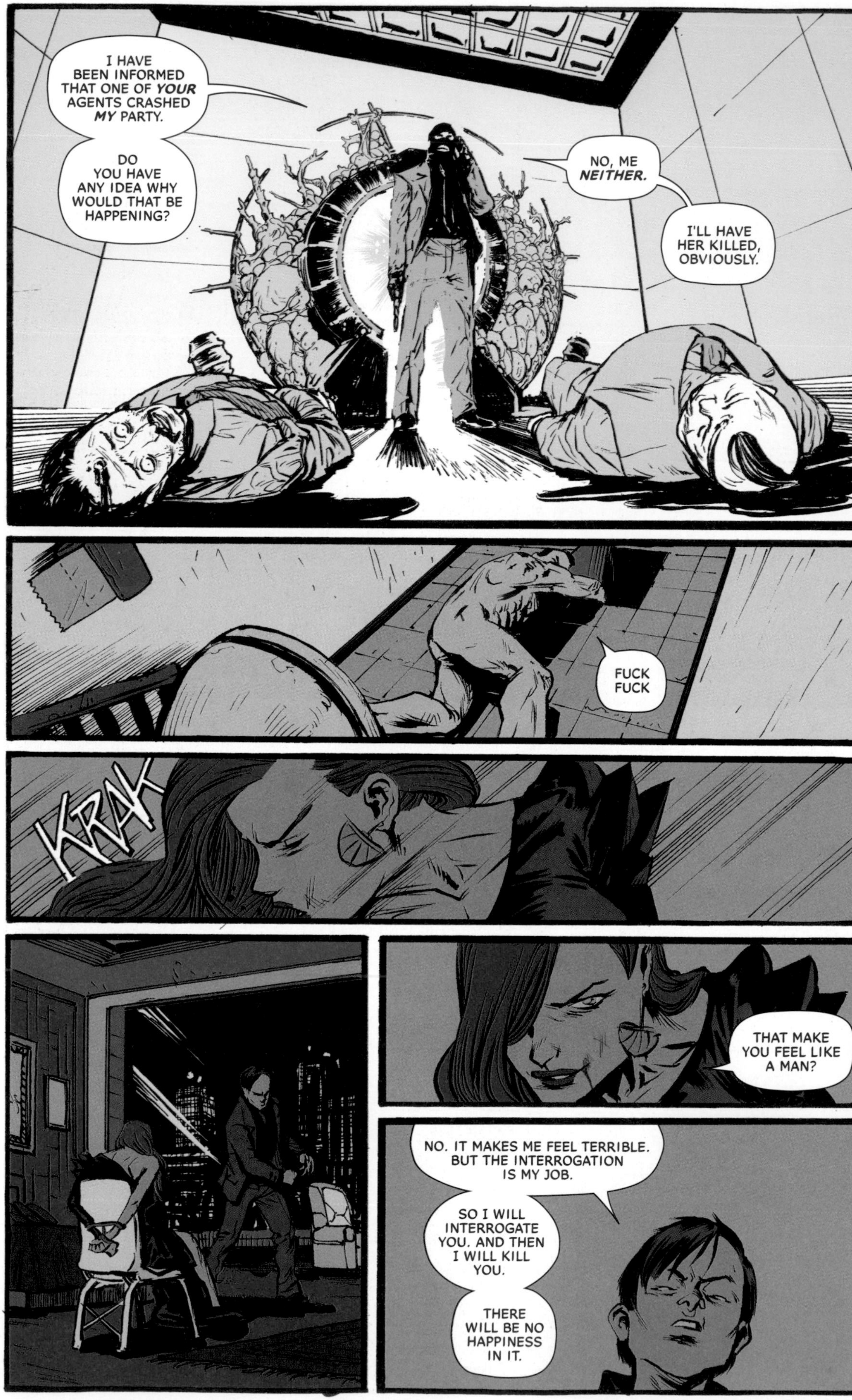
I HAVE BEEN INFORMED THAT ONE OF *YOUR* AGENTS CRASHED *MY* PARTY.
DO YOU HAVE ANY IDEA WHY WOULD THAT BE HAPPENING?
NO, ME ***NEITHER.***
I'LL HAVE HER KILLED, OBVIOUSLY.
FUCK FUCK
KRAK
THAT MAKE YOU FEEL LIKE A MAN?
NO. IT MAKES ME FEEL TERRIBLE. BUT THE INTERROGATION IS MY JOB.
SO I WILL INTERROGATE YOU. AND THEN I WILL KILL YOU.
THERE WILL BE NO HAPPINESS IN IT.

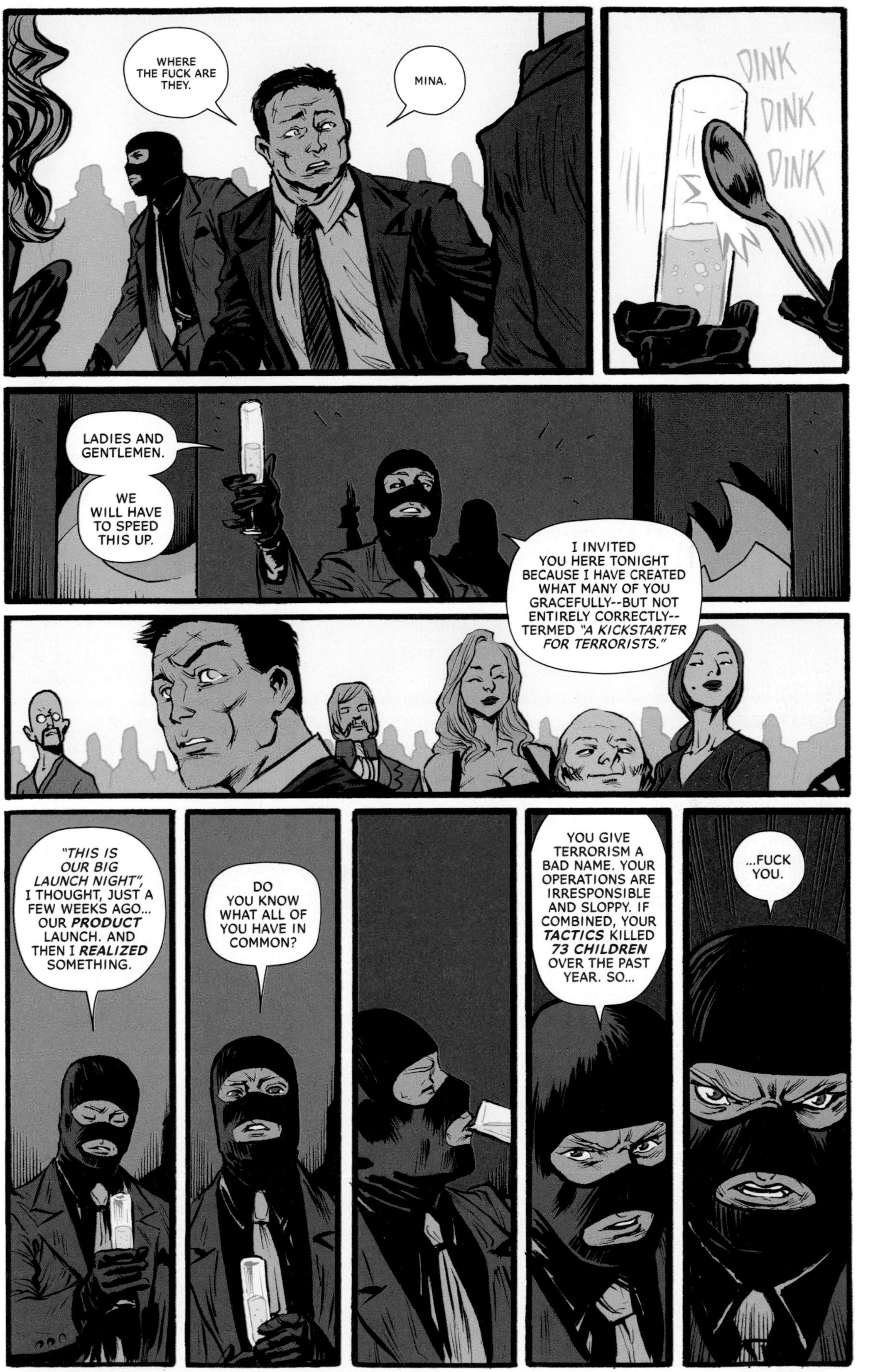

WHERE THE FUCK ARE THEY.
MINA.
DINK DINK DINK
LADIES AND GENTLEMEN.
WE WILL HAVE TO SPEED THIS UP.
I INVITED YOU HERE TONIGHT BECAUSE I HAVE CREATED WHAT MANY OF YOU GRACEFULLY--BUT NOT ENTIRELY CORRECTLY--TERMED "A KICKSTARTER FOR TERRORISTS."
"THIS IS OUR BIG LAUNCH NIGHT", I THOUGHT, JUST A FEW WEEKS AGO... OUR PRODUCT LAUNCH. AND THEN I REALIZED SOMETHING.
DO YOU KNOW WHAT ALL OF YOU HAVE IN COMMON?
YOU GIVE TERRORISM A BAD NAME. YOUR OPERATIONS ARE IRRESPONSIBLE AND SLOPPY. IF COMBINED, YOUR TACTICS KILLED 73 CHILDREN OVER THE PAST YEAR. SO...
...FUCK YOU.

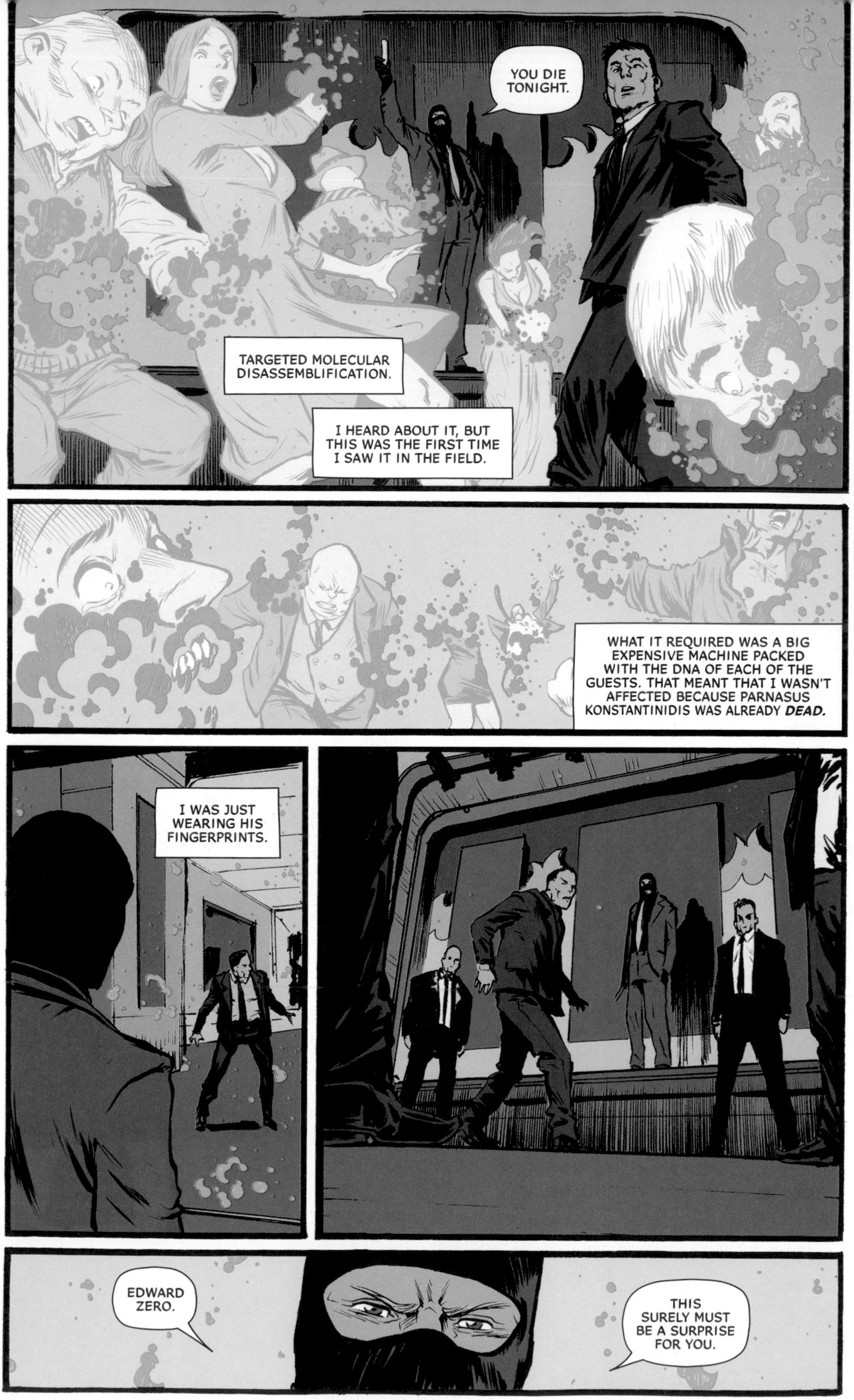
YOU DIE TONIGHT.
TARGETED MOLECULAR DISASSEMBLIFICATION.
I HEARD ABOUT IT, BUT THIS WAS THE FIRST TIME I SAW IT IN THE FIELD.
WHAT IT REQUIRED WAS A BIG EXPENSIVE MACHINE PACKED WITH THE DNA OF EACH OF THE GUESTS. THAT MEANT THAT I WASN'T AFFECTED BECAUSE PARNASUS KONSTANTINIDIS WAS ALREADY *DEAD.*
I WAS JUST WEARING HIS FINGERPRINTS.
EDWARD ZERO.
THIS SURELY MUST BE A SURPRISE FOR YOU.

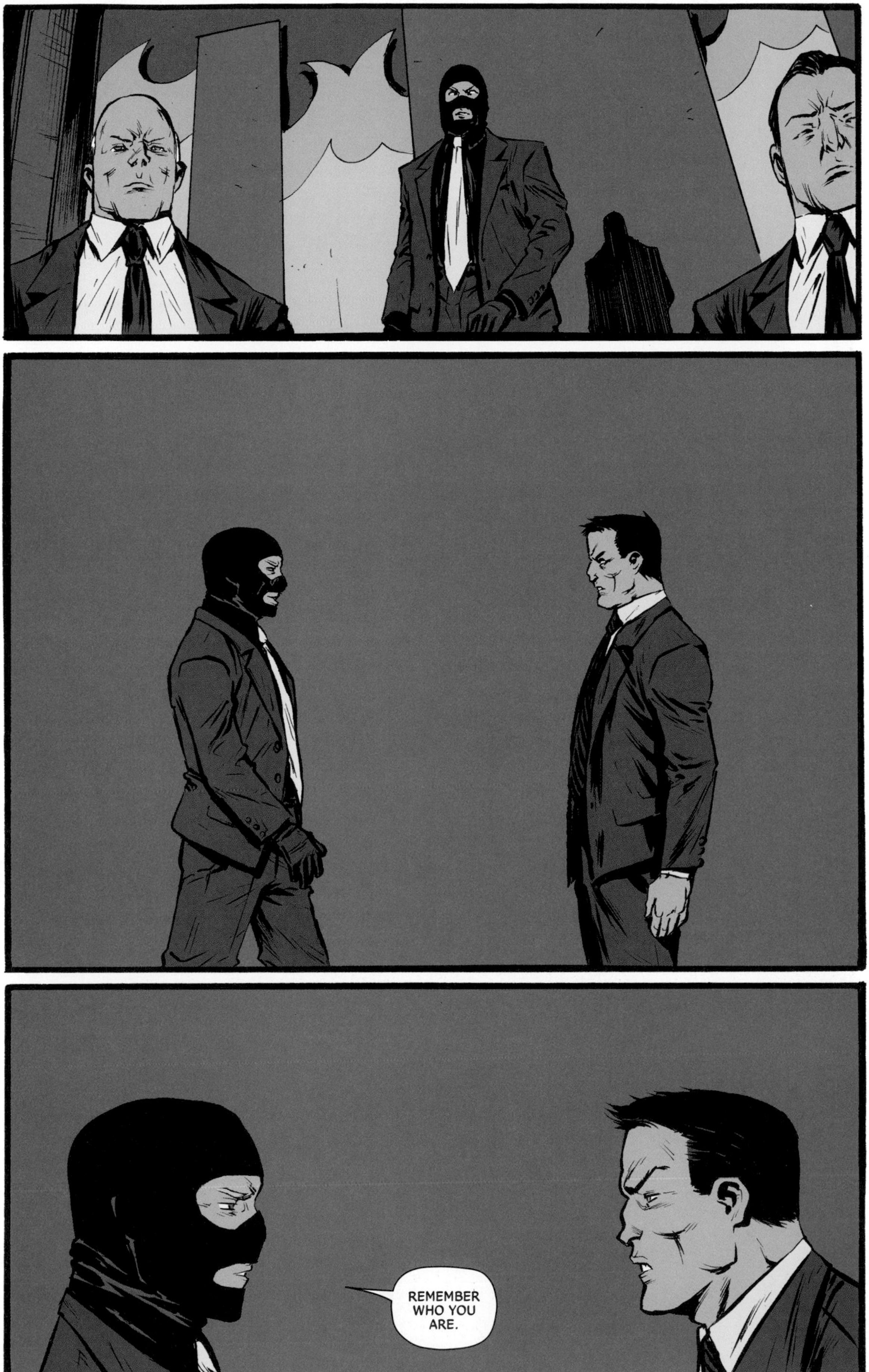
REMEMBER WHO YOU ARE.

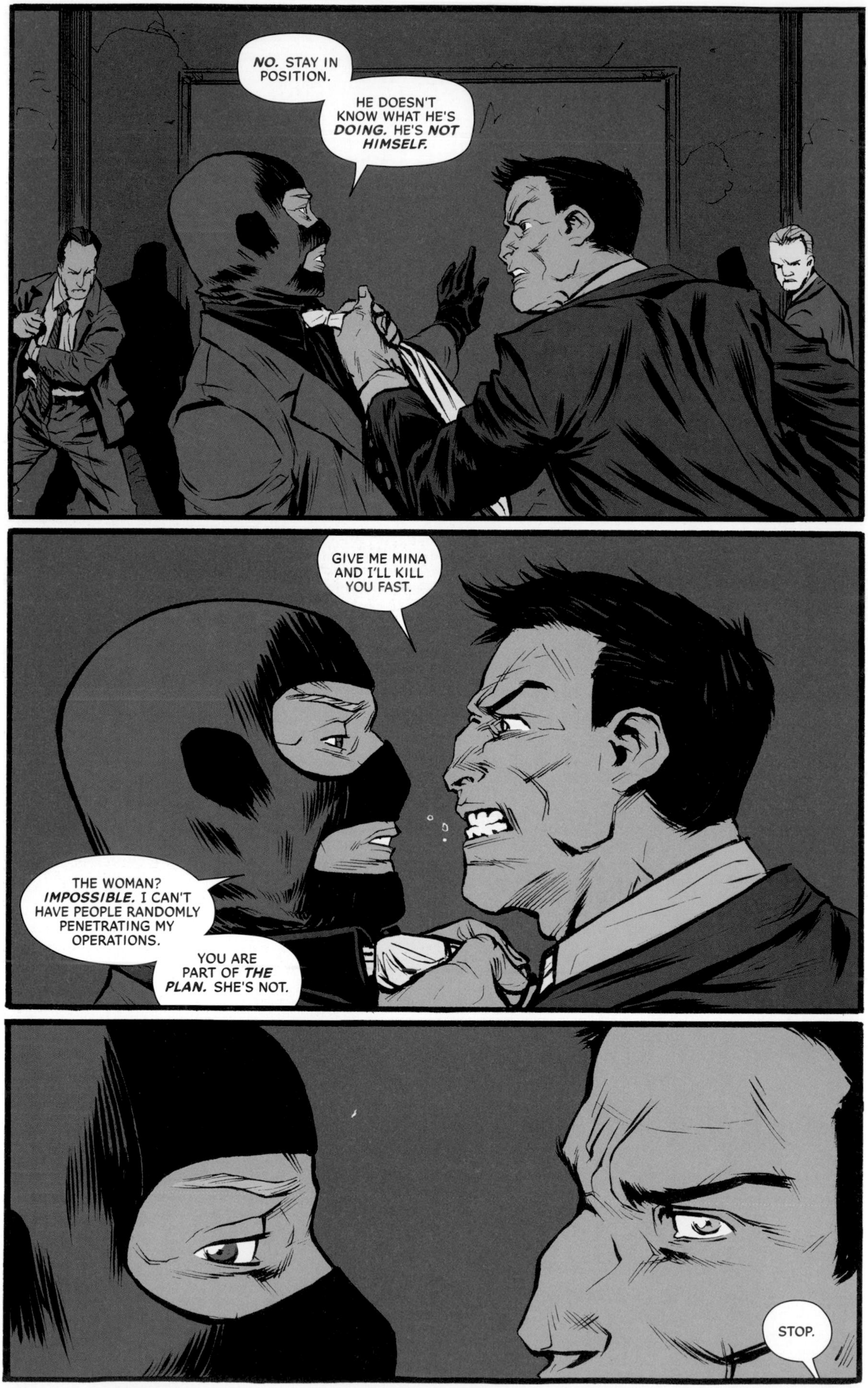
NO. STAY IN POSITION.
HE DOESN'T KNOW WHAT HE'S DOING. HE'S NOT HIMSELF.
GIVE ME MINA AND I'LL KILL YOU FAST.
THE WOMAN? IMPOSSIBLE. I CAN'T HAVE PEOPLE RANDOMLY PENETRATING MY OPERATIONS.
YOU ARE PART OF THE PLAN. SHE'S NOT.
STOP.

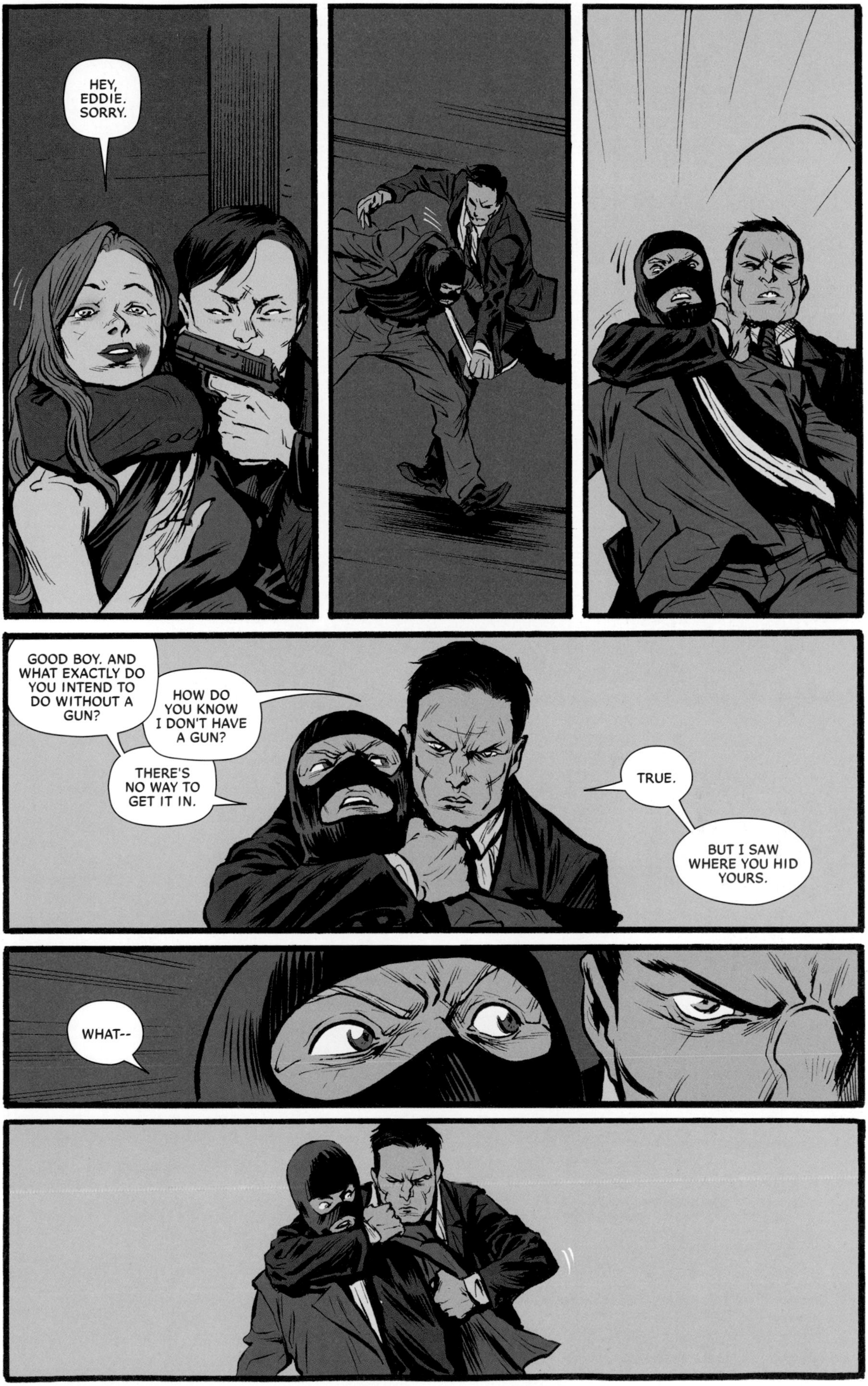
HEY, EDDIE. SORRY.
GOOD BOY. AND WHAT EXACTLY DO YOU INTEND TO DO WITHOUT A GUN?
HOW DO YOU KNOW I DON'T HAVE A GUN?
THERE'S NO WAY TO GET IT IN.
TRUE.
BUT I SAW WHERE YOU HID YOURS.
WHAT--

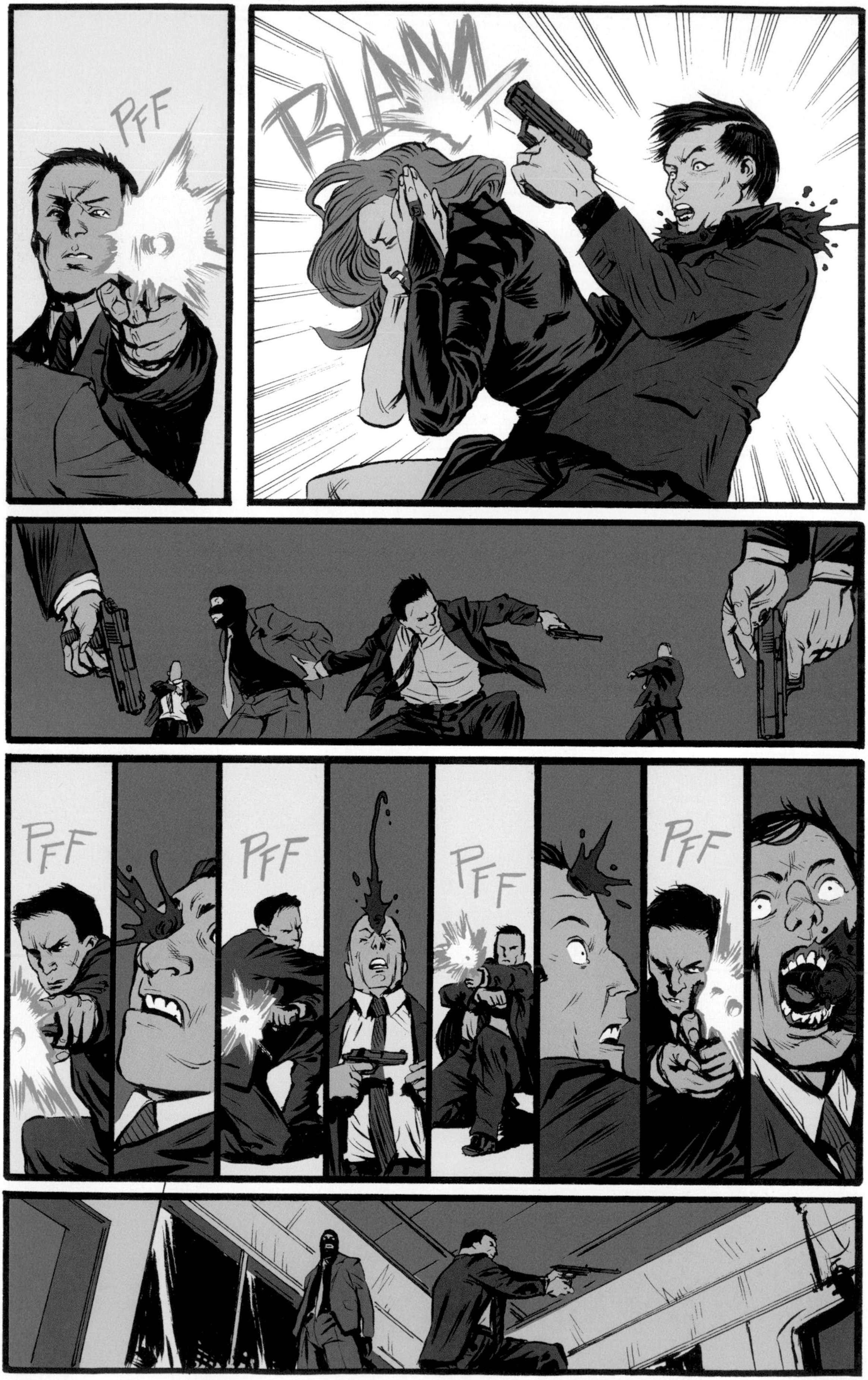
PFF
BLAM
PFF
PFF
PFF
PFF

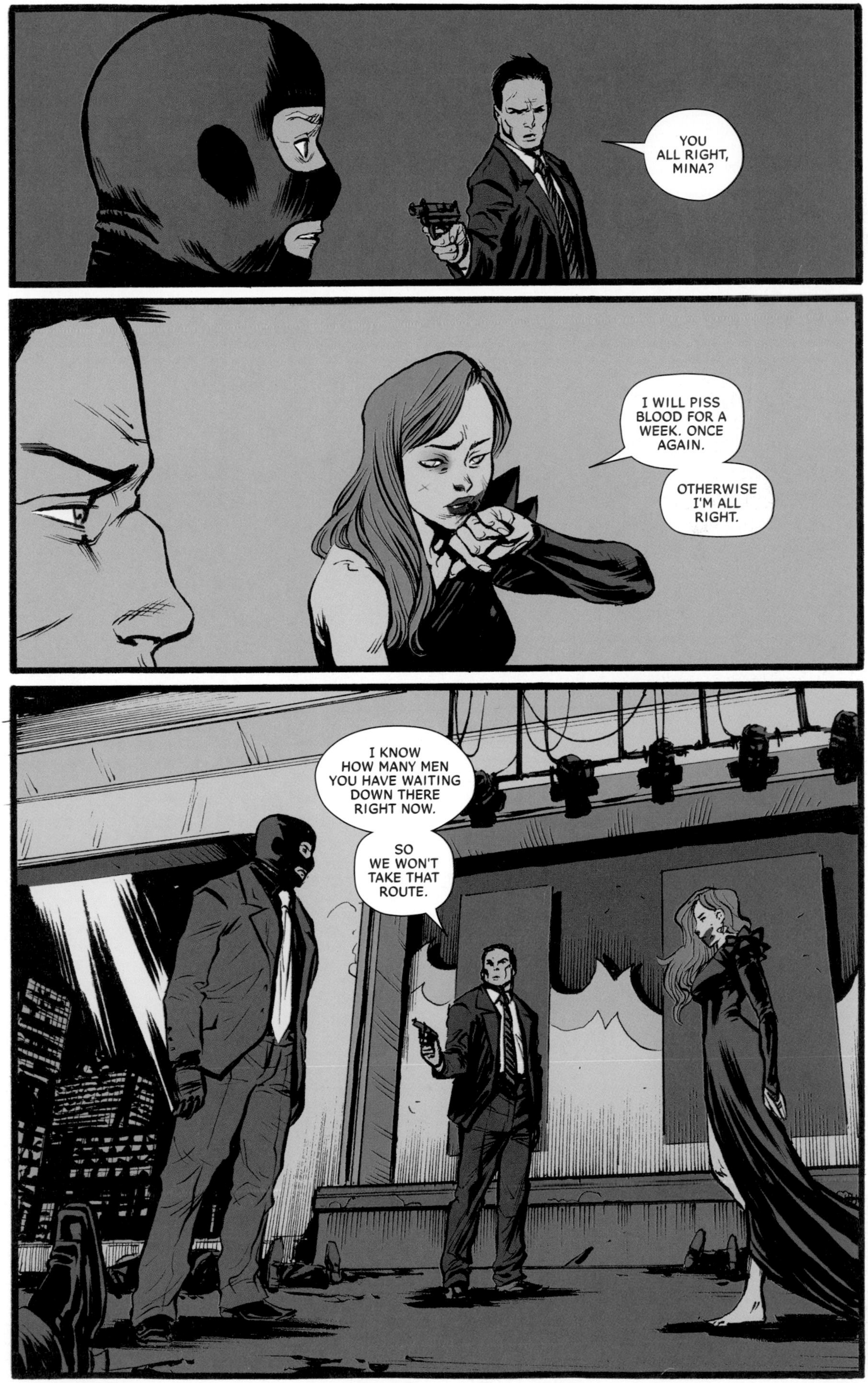
YOU ALL RIGHT, MINA?
I WILL PISS BLOOD FOR A WEEK. ONCE AGAIN.
OTHERWISE I'M ALL RIGHT.
I KNOW HOW MANY MEN YOU HAVE WAITING DOWN THERE RIGHT NOW.
SO WE WON'T TAKE THAT ROUTE.

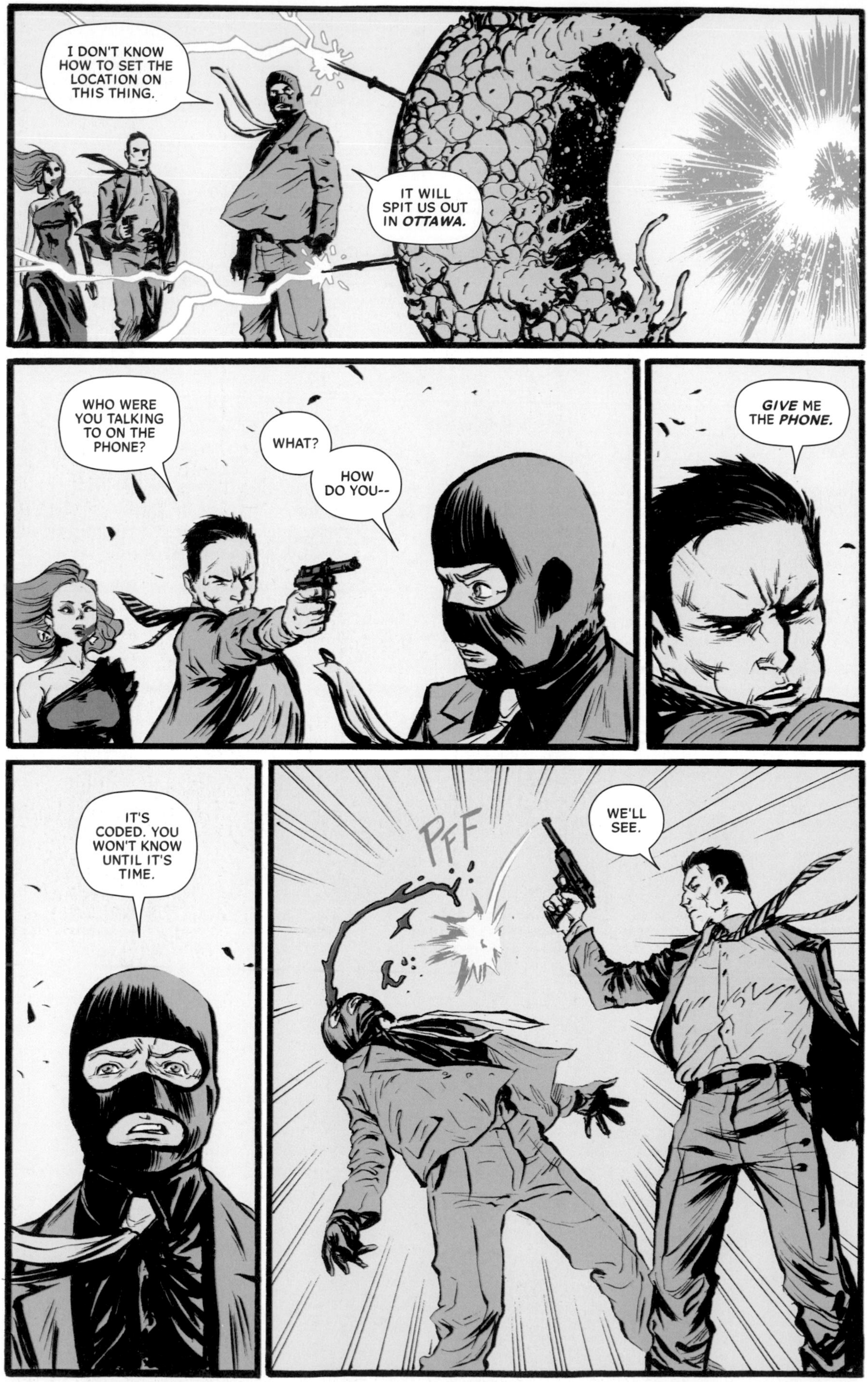
I DON'T KNOW HOW TO SET THE LOCATION ON THIS THING.
IT WILL SPIT US OUT IN *OTTAWA.*
WHO WERE YOU TALKING TO ON THE PHONE?
WHAT?
HOW DO YOU--
GIVE ME THE *PHONE.*
IT'S CODED. YOU WON'T KNOW UNTIL IT'S TIME.
PFF
WE'LL SEE.

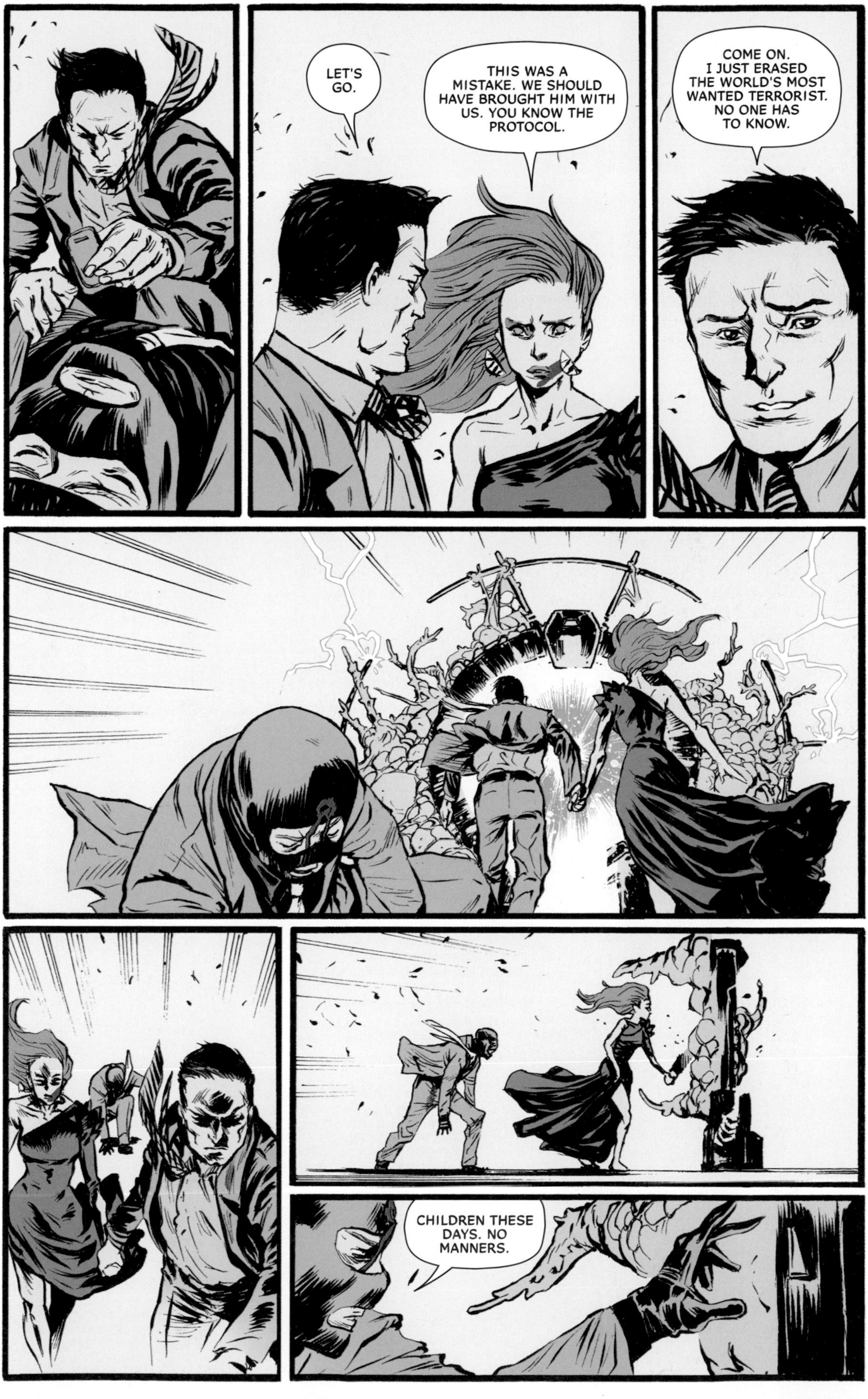
LET'S GO.
THIS WAS A MISTAKE. WE SHOULD HAVE BROUGHT HIM WITH US. YOU KNOW THE PROTOCOL.
COME ON. I JUST ERASED THE WORLD'S MOST WANTED TERRORIST. NO ONE HAS TO KNOW.
CHILDREN THESE DAYS. NO MANNERS.

A LOT CHANGED
THAT NIGHT.

WHEN WE WALKED
THROUGH THE GATE,
THERE WAS NO COLOR.
NOT BLACK, NOT WHITE.

IT WAS...LIKE ALL COLORS,
BUT WITHOUT COLOR.
I COULDN'T DESCRIBE IT
BACK THEN, AND I DON'T
THINK I'M DOING A MUCH
BETTER JOB OF IT NOW.

THERE WAS A SOUND,
A THOUSAND WINGS
CLAPPING, SMALL BIRDS
EVERYWHERE. BUT YOU
COULDN'T SEE EVEN
ONE OF THEM.

ANOTHER SOUND,
LIKE PAPER BEING
RIPPED APART.

AN ECHO THAT SOUNDED THE WAY I IMAGINED
A TORNADO WOULD SOUND IF YOU SHUT ALL THE
DOORS AND WINDOWS AND HID UNDERNEATH
THE HOUSE AND YOU COULD STILL FEEL IT
CIRCLING...BUT IT WOULD BE UNDERNEATH
YOU, SOMEHOW, NOT JUST ABOVE YOU,
IT WOULD BE BELOW AND ABOVE AND
EVERYWHERE AT ONCE.

I REMEMBER MINA'S HAND
IN MINE. I REMEMBER THINKING,
WE SHOULD HAVE RAN AWAY
WHEN WE WERE CHILDREN.

I REMEMBER THINKING,
I CAN FEEL THE ROUGH SPOTS
ON YOUR HAND BECAUSE OF
THE WAY YOU PLACE IT ON THE
CEMENT FLOOR WHEN YOU DO
PUSH-UPS EVERY MORNING.

I REMEMBER THINKING,
NO, NOT THINKING,
I REMEMBER FEELING...

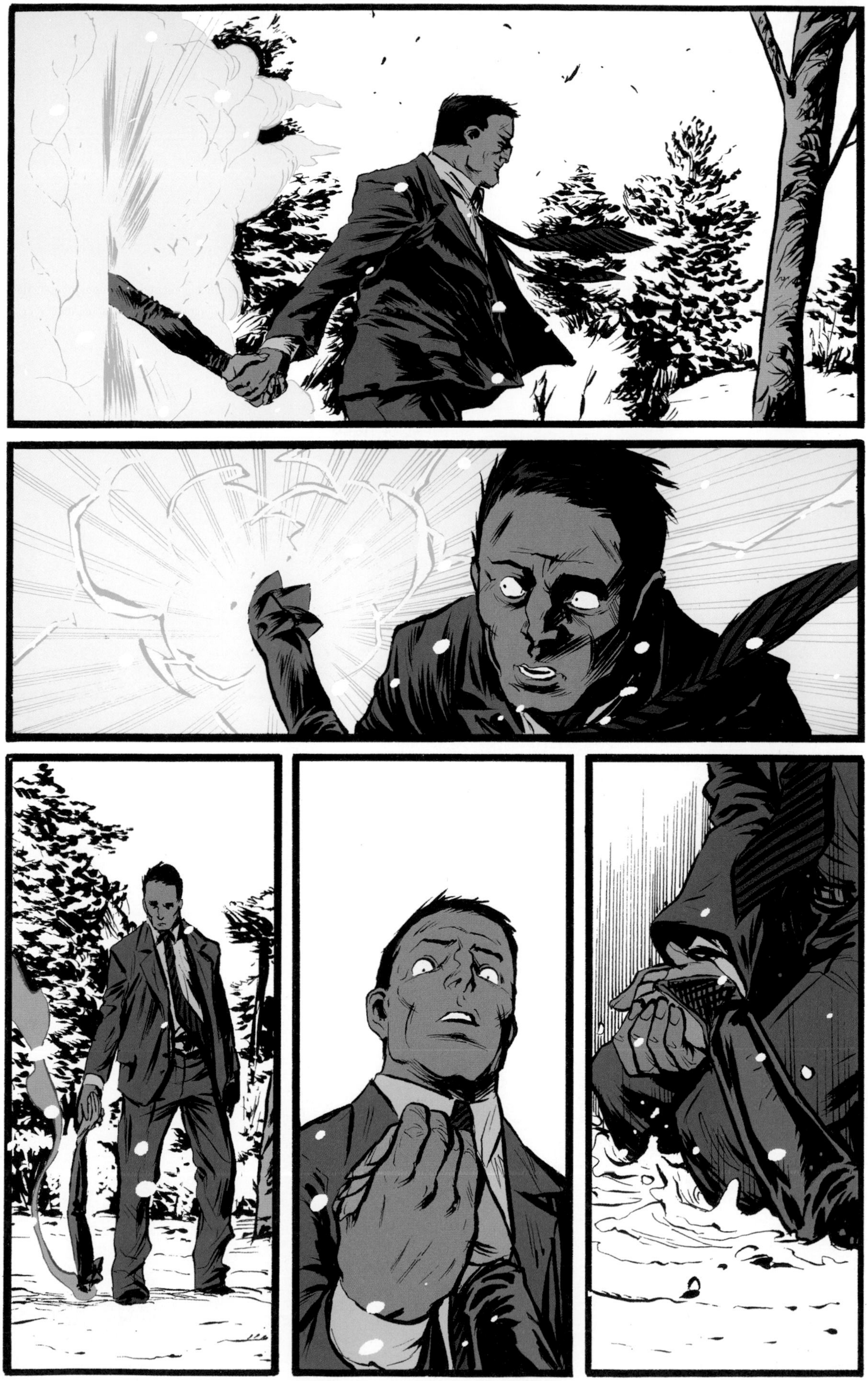

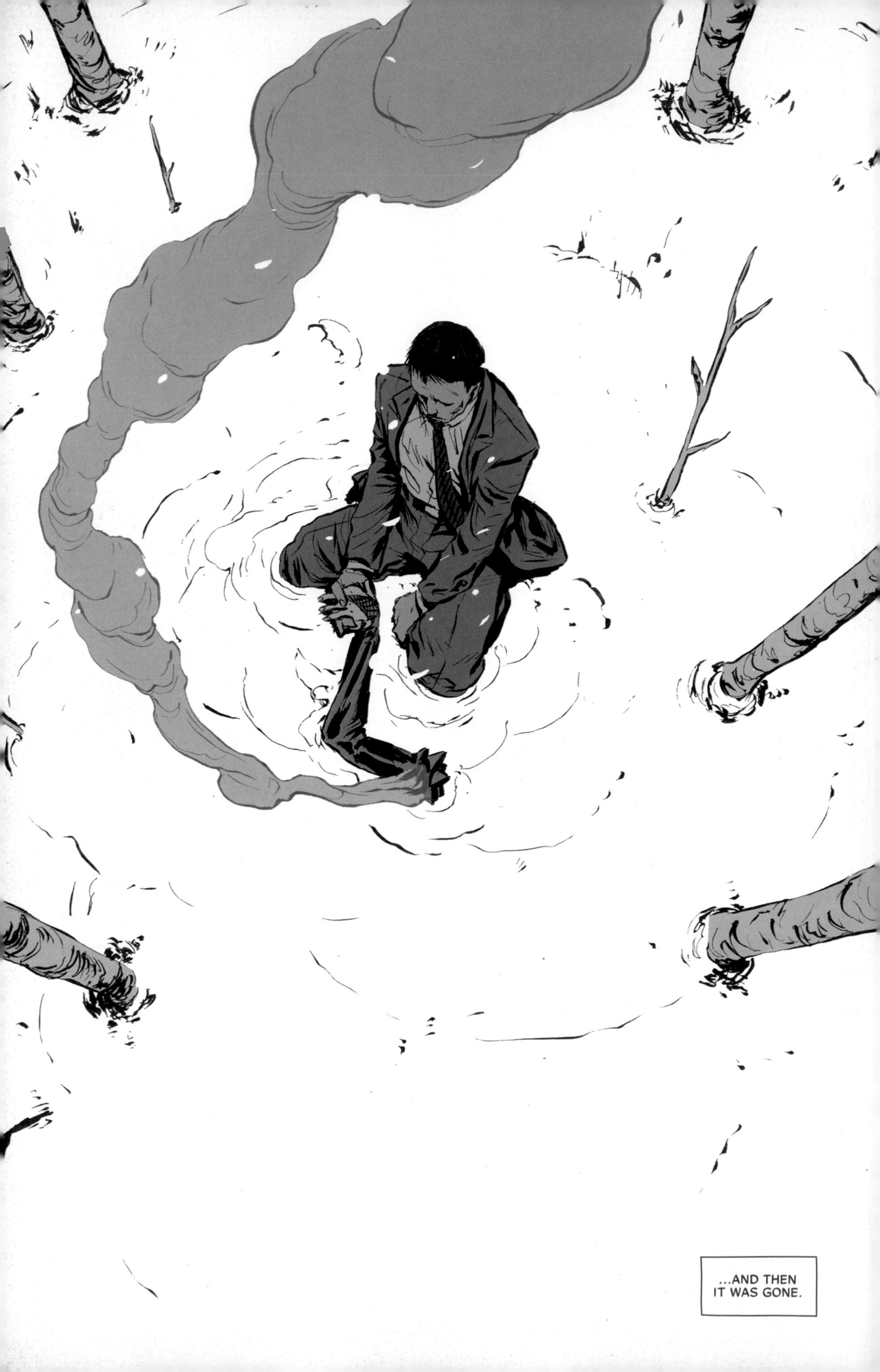
...AND THEN IT WAS GONE.

零

CHAPTER 3: A NEEDLE IN YOUR EYE.

THE MENNONITE WATCHES THE ENSHADOWED DARK BEFORE THEM AS IT IS REFLECTED TO HIM IN THE MIRROR OVER THE BAR. HE TURNS TO THEM. HIS EYES ARE WET, HE SPEAKS SLOWLY. THE WRATH OF GOD LIES SLEEPING. IT WAS HID A MILLION YEARS BEFORE MEN WERE AND ONLY MEN HAVE POWER TO WAKE IT. HELL AINT HALF FULL. HEAR ME. YE CARRY WAR OF A MADMAN'S MAKING ONTO A FOREIGN LAND. YE'LL WAKE MORE THAN THE DOGS. CORMAC MCCARTHY

Blood Meridian: Or the Evening Redness in the West

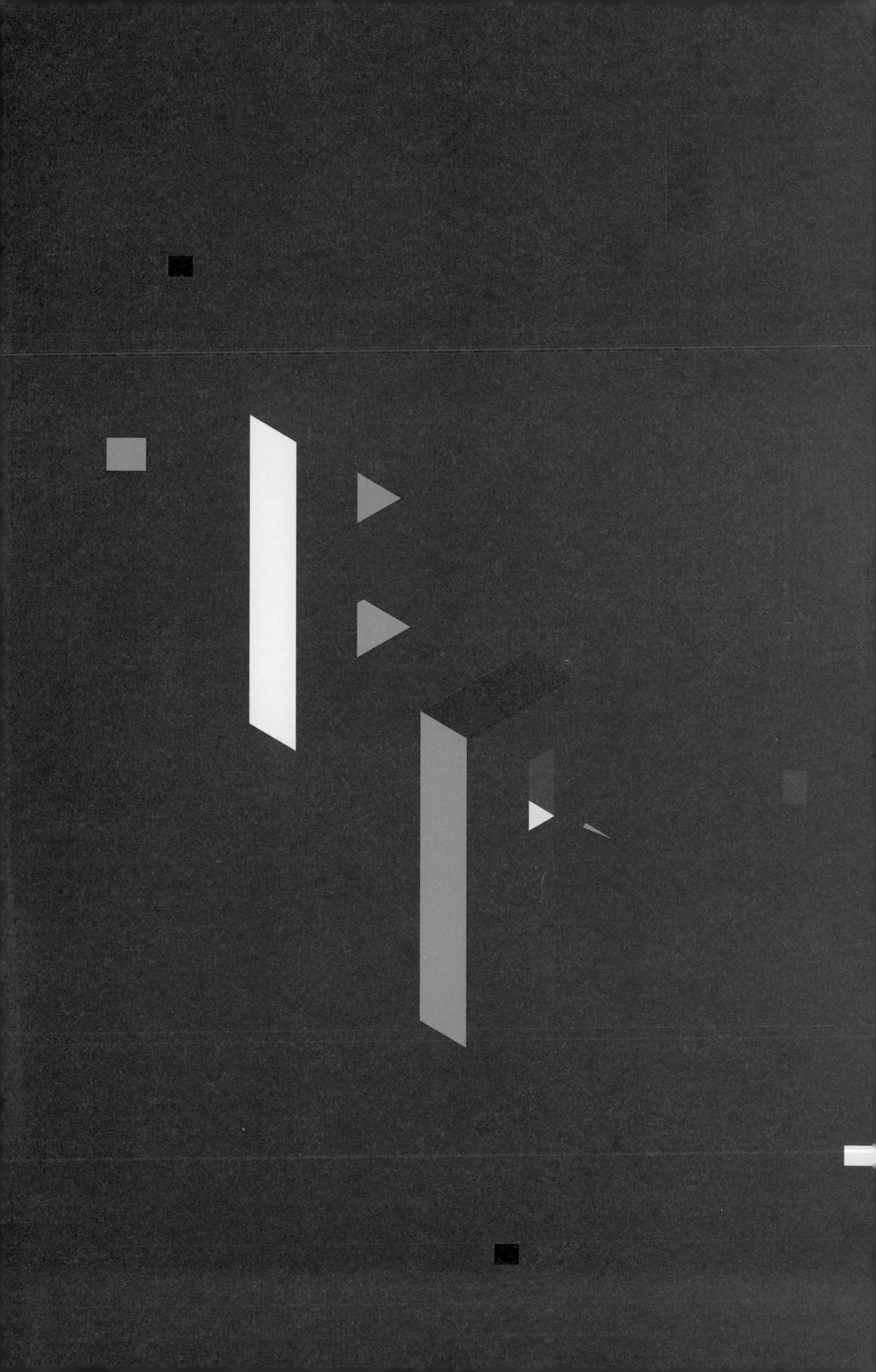

CHAPTER 4

VISION IMPAIRMENT
Illustrated by Morgan Jeske

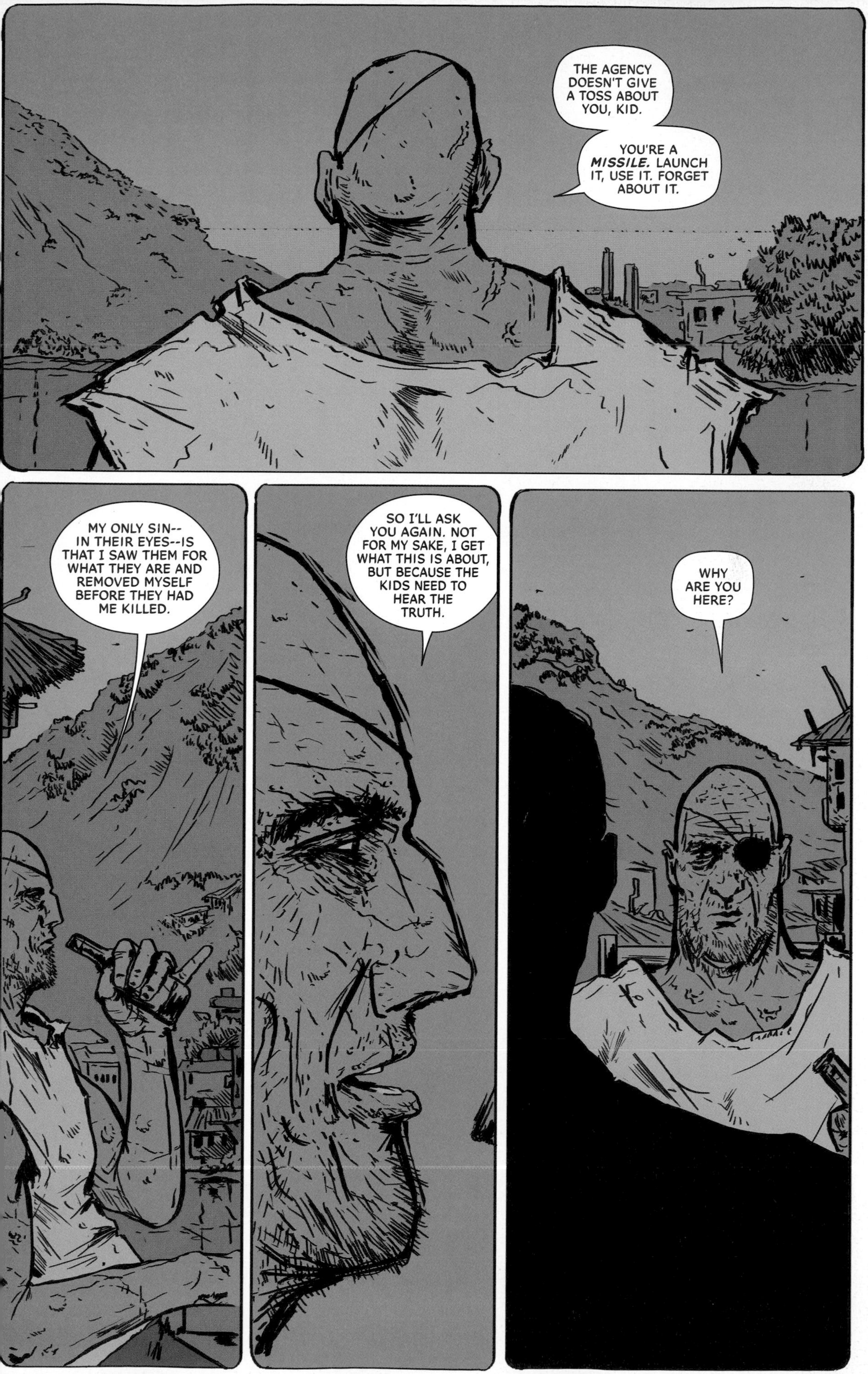
THE AGENCY DOESN'T GIVE A TOSS ABOUT YOU, KID.
YOU'RE A *MISSILE.* LAUNCH IT, USE IT. FORGET ABOUT IT.
MY ONLY SIN-- IN THEIR EYES--IS THAT I SAW THEM FOR WHAT THEY ARE AND REMOVED MYSELF BEFORE THEY HAD ME KILLED.
SO I'LL ASK YOU AGAIN. NOT FOR MY SAKE, I GET WHAT THIS IS ABOUT, BUT BECAUSE THE KIDS NEED TO HEAR THE TRUTH.
WHY ARE YOU HERE?

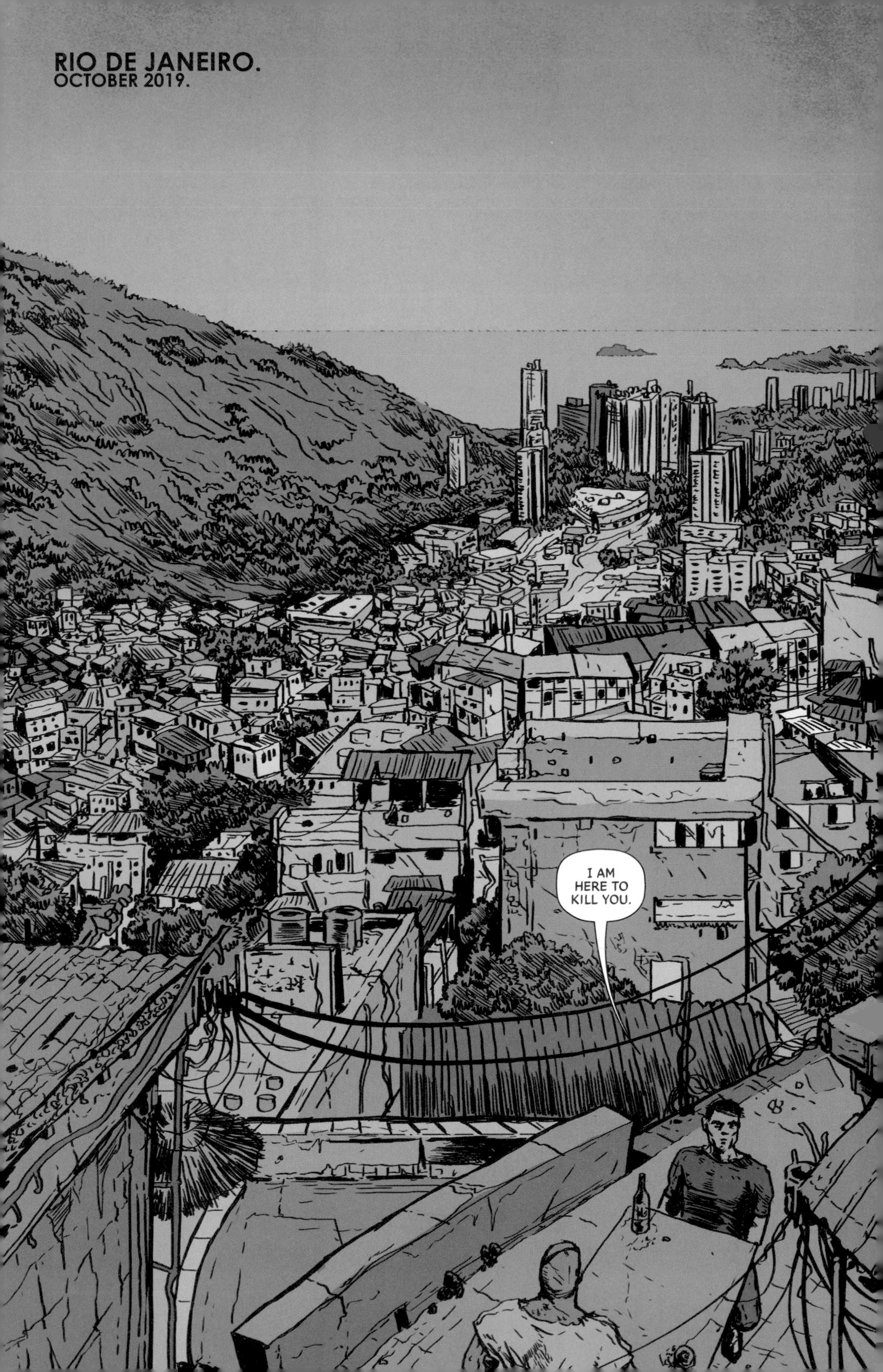
RIO DE JANEIRO.
OCTOBER 2019.
I AM HERE TO KILL YOU.

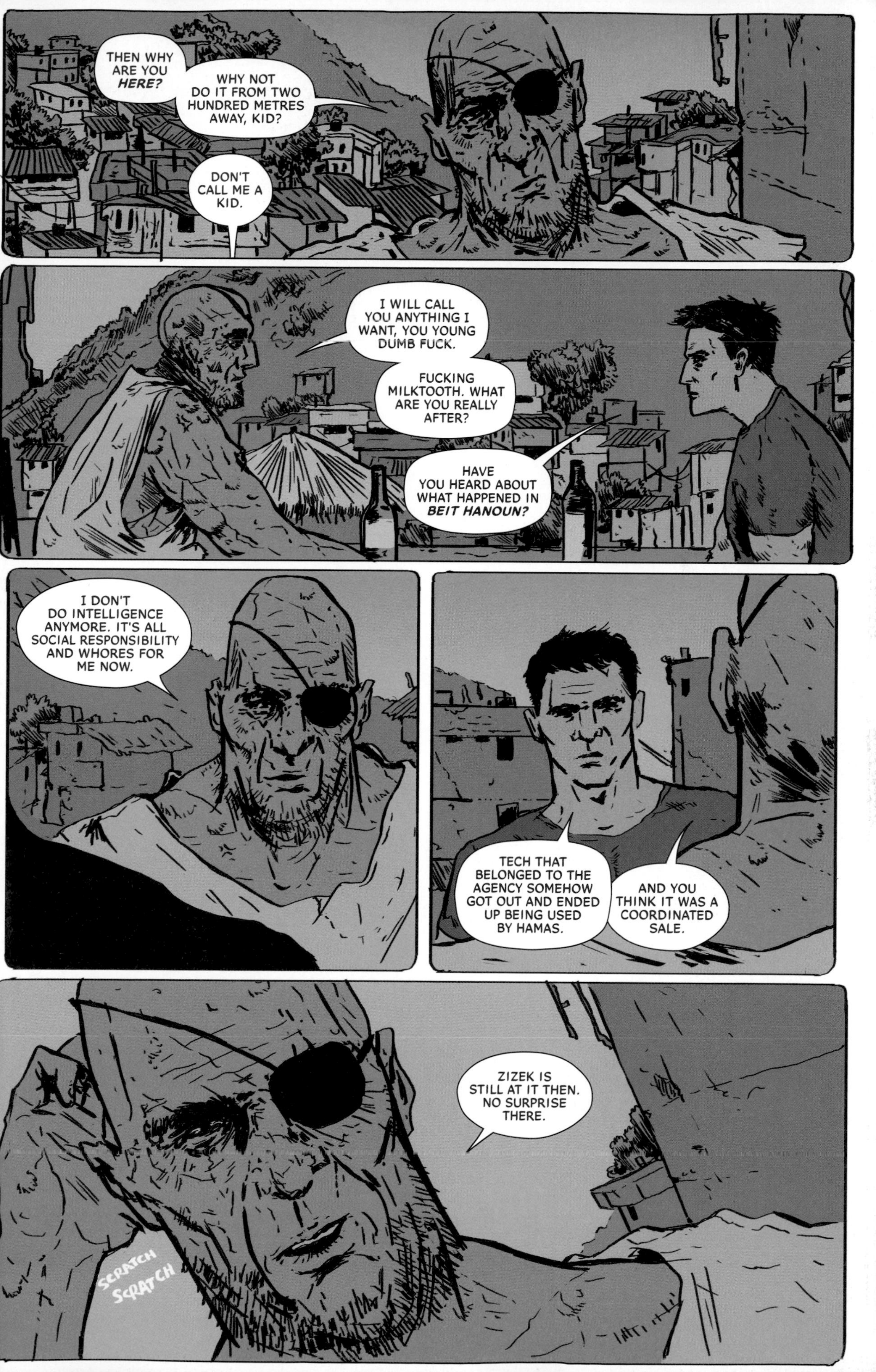
THEN WHY ARE YOU *HERE?*
WHY NOT DO IT FROM TWO HUNDRED METRES AWAY, KID?
DON'T CALL ME A KID.
I WILL CALL YOU ANYTHING I WANT, YOU YOUNG DUMB FUCK.
FUCKING MILKTOOTH. WHAT ARE YOU REALLY AFTER?
HAVE YOU HEARD ABOUT WHAT HAPPENED IN *BEIT HANOUN?*
I DON'T DO INTELLIGENCE ANYMORE. IT'S ALL SOCIAL RESPONSIBILITY AND WHORES FOR ME NOW.
TECH THAT BELONGED TO THE AGENCY SOMEHOW GOT OUT AND ENDED UP BEING USED BY HAMAS.
AND YOU THINK IT WAS A COORDINATED SALE.
ZIZEK IS STILL AT IT THEN. NO SURPRISE THERE.
SCRATCH SCRATCH

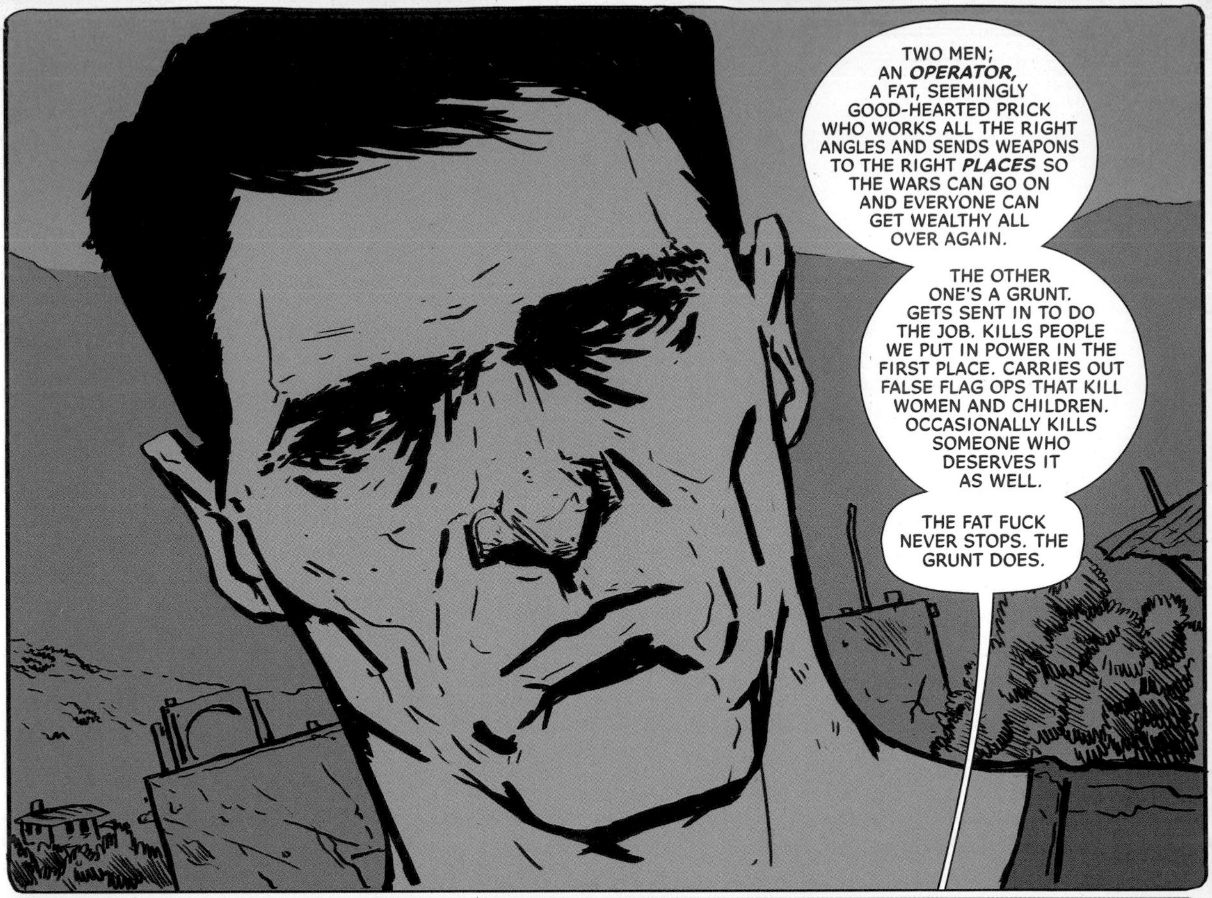
TWO MEN; AN *OPERATOR,* A FAT, SEEMINGLY GOOD-HEARTED PRICK WHO WORKS ALL THE RIGHT ANGLES AND SENDS WEAPONS TO THE RIGHT *PLACES* SO THE WARS CAN GO ON AND EVERYONE CAN GET WEALTHY ALL OVER AGAIN.
THE OTHER ONE'S A GRUNT. GETS SENT IN TO DO THE JOB. KILLS PEOPLE WE PUT IN POWER IN THE FIRST PLACE. CARRIES OUT FALSE FLAG OPS THAT KILL WOMEN AND CHILDREN. OCCASIONALLY KILLS SOMEONE WHO DESERVES IT AS *WELL.*
THE FAT FUCK NEVER STOPS. THE GRUNT DOES.

VISION IMPAIRMENT

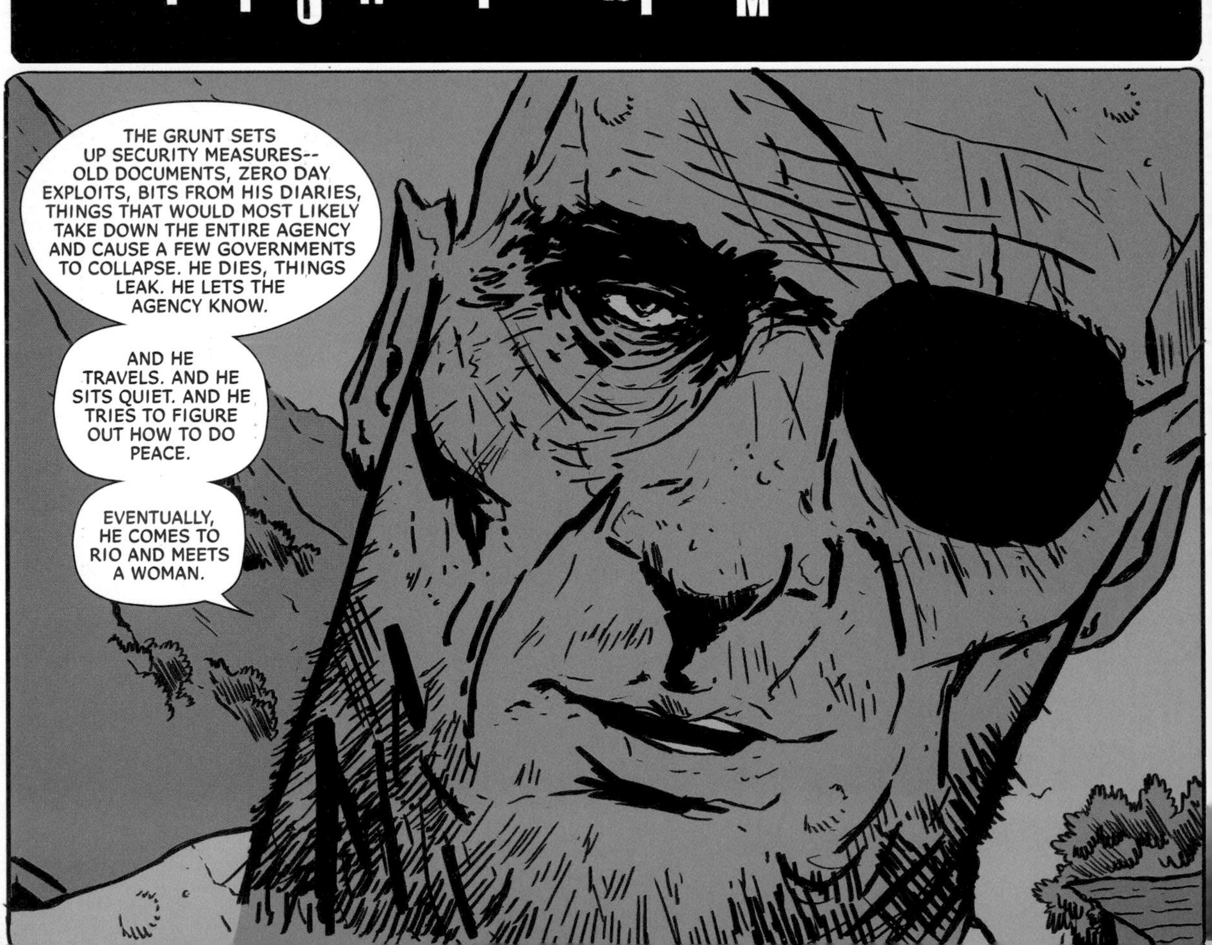
THE GRUNT SETS UP SECURITY MEASURES-- OLD DOCUMENTS, ZERO DAY EXPLOITS, BITS FROM HIS DIARIES, THINGS THAT WOULD MOST LIKELY TAKE DOWN THE ENTIRE AGENCY AND CAUSE A FEW GOVERNMENTS TO COLLAPSE. HE DIES, THINGS LEAK. HE LETS THE AGENCY *KNOW.*
AND HE TRAVELS. AND HE SITS QUIET. AND HE TRIES TO FIGURE OUT HOW TO DO PEACE.
EVENTUALLY, HE COMES TO RIO AND MEETS A WOMAN.

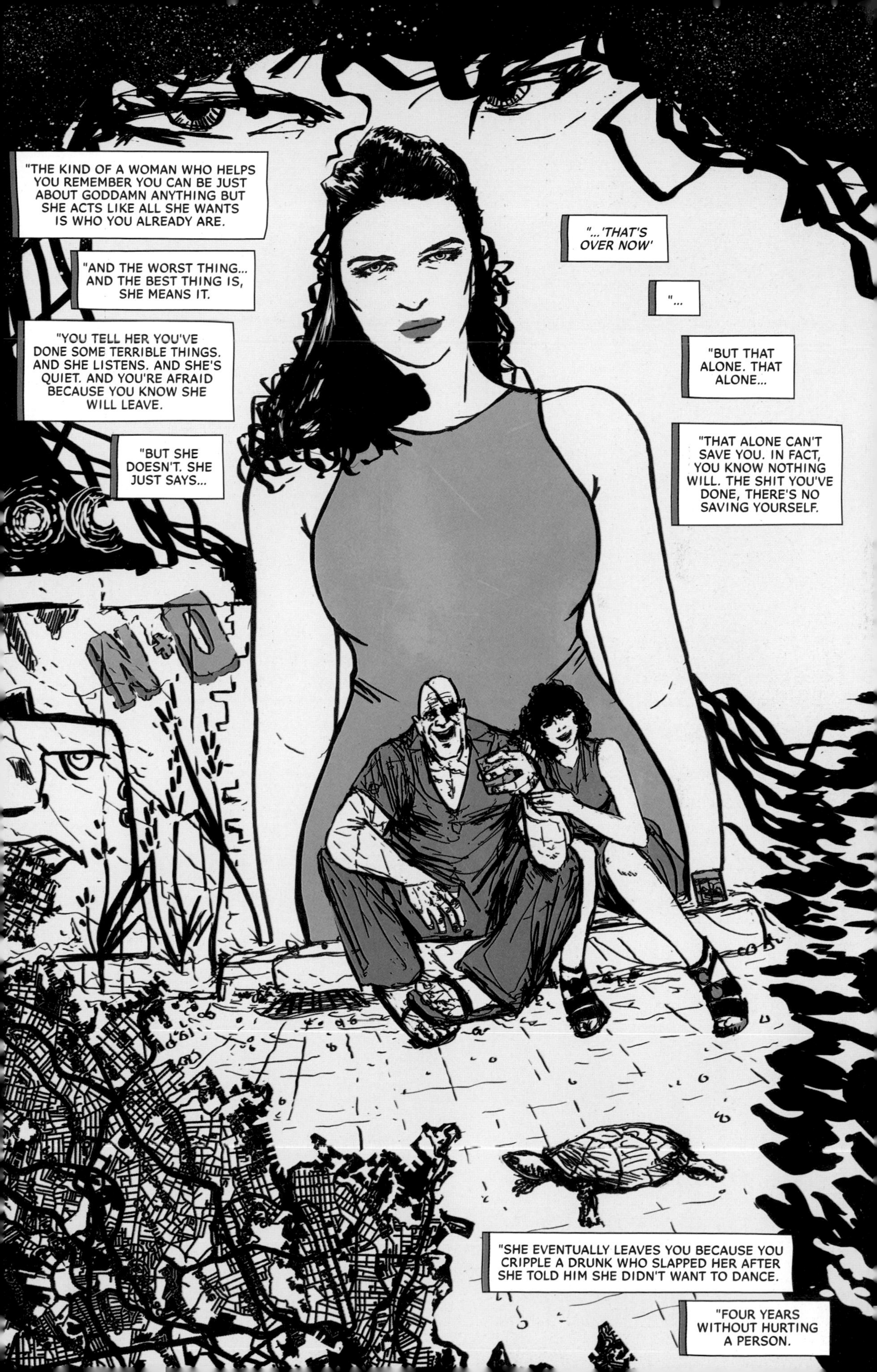
"THE KIND OF A WOMAN WHO HELPS YOU REMEMBER YOU CAN BE JUST ABOUT GODDAMN ANYTHING BUT SHE ACTS LIKE ALL SHE WANTS IS WHO YOU ALREADY ARE.
"AND THE WORST THING... AND THE BEST THING IS, SHE MEANS IT.
"YOU TELL HER YOU'VE DONE SOME TERRIBLE THINGS. AND SHE LISTENS. AND SHE'S QUIET. AND YOU'RE AFRAID BECAUSE YOU KNOW SHE WILL LEAVE.
"BUT SHE DOESN'T. SHE JUST SAYS...
"...'THAT'S OVER NOW'
"...
"BUT THAT ALONE. THAT ALONE...
"THAT ALONE CAN'T SAVE YOU. IN FACT, YOU KNOW NOTHING WILL. THE SHIT YOU'VE DONE, THERE'S NO SAVING YOURSELF.
"SHE EVENTUALLY LEAVES YOU BECAUSE YOU CRIPPLE A DRUNK WHO SLAPPED HER AFTER SHE TOLD HIM SHE DIDN'T WANT TO DANCE.
"FOUR YEARS WITHOUT HURTING A PERSON.

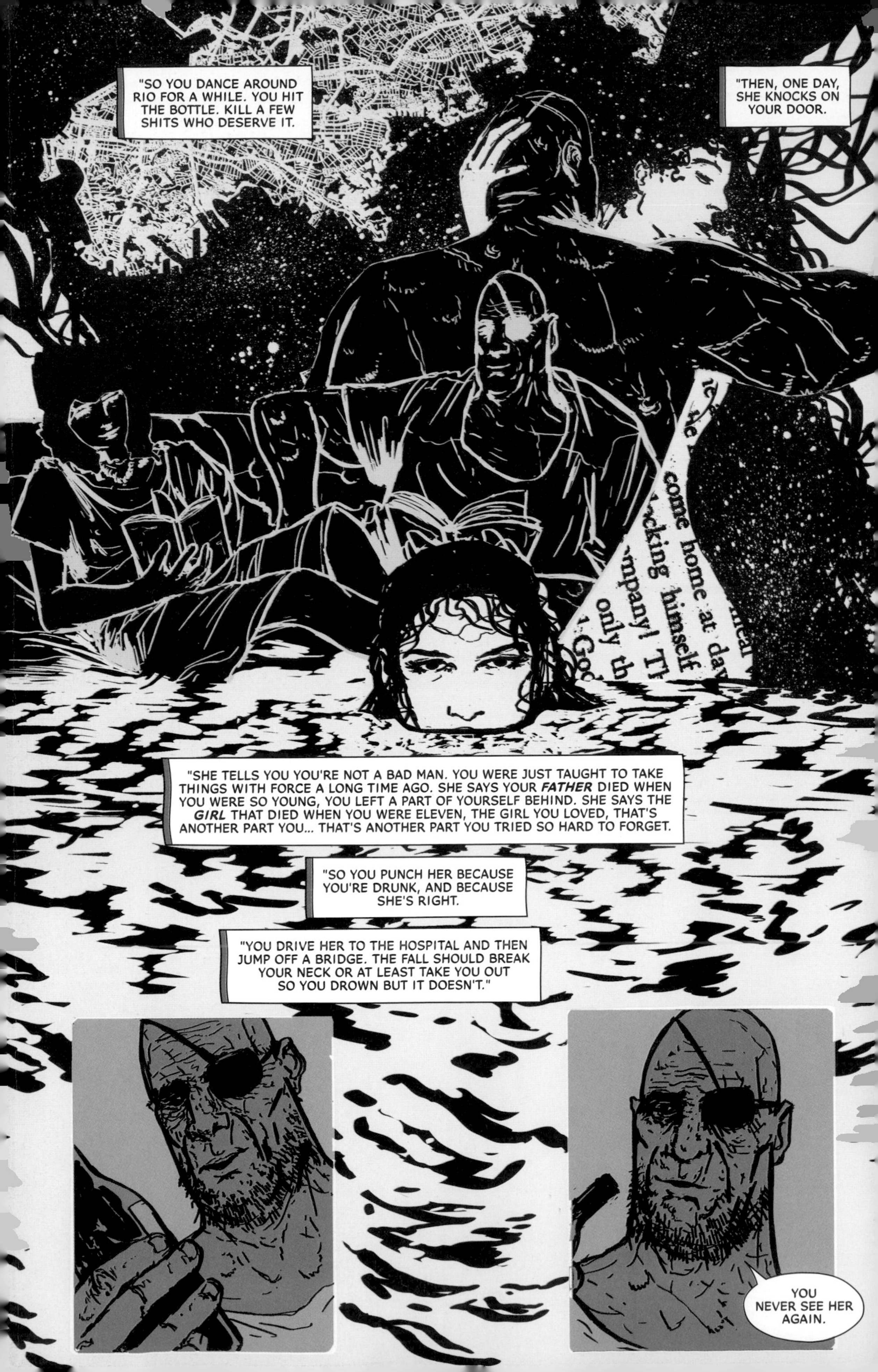
"SO YOU DANCE AROUND RIO FOR A WHILE. YOU HIT THE BOTTLE. KILL A FEW SHITS WHO DESERVE IT.
"THEN, ONE DAY, SHE KNOCKS ON YOUR DOOR.
come home at day
king himself
mpany! Th
only th
"SHE TELLS YOU YOU'RE NOT A BAD MAN. YOU WERE JUST TAUGHT TO TAKE THINGS WITH FORCE A LONG TIME AGO. SHE SAYS YOUR *FATHER* DIED WHEN YOU WERE SO YOUNG, YOU LEFT A PART OF YOURSELF BEHIND. SHE SAYS THE *GIRL* THAT DIED WHEN YOU WERE ELEVEN, THE GIRL YOU LOVED, THAT'S ANOTHER PART YOU... THAT'S ANOTHER PART YOU TRIED SO HARD TO FORGET.
"SO YOU PUNCH HER BECAUSE YOU'RE DRUNK, AND BECAUSE SHE'S RIGHT.
"YOU DRIVE HER TO THE HOSPITAL AND THEN JUMP OFF A BRIDGE. THE FALL SHOULD BREAK YOUR NECK OR AT LEAST TAKE YOU OUT SO YOU DROWN BUT IT DOESN'T."
YOU NEVER SEE HER AGAIN.

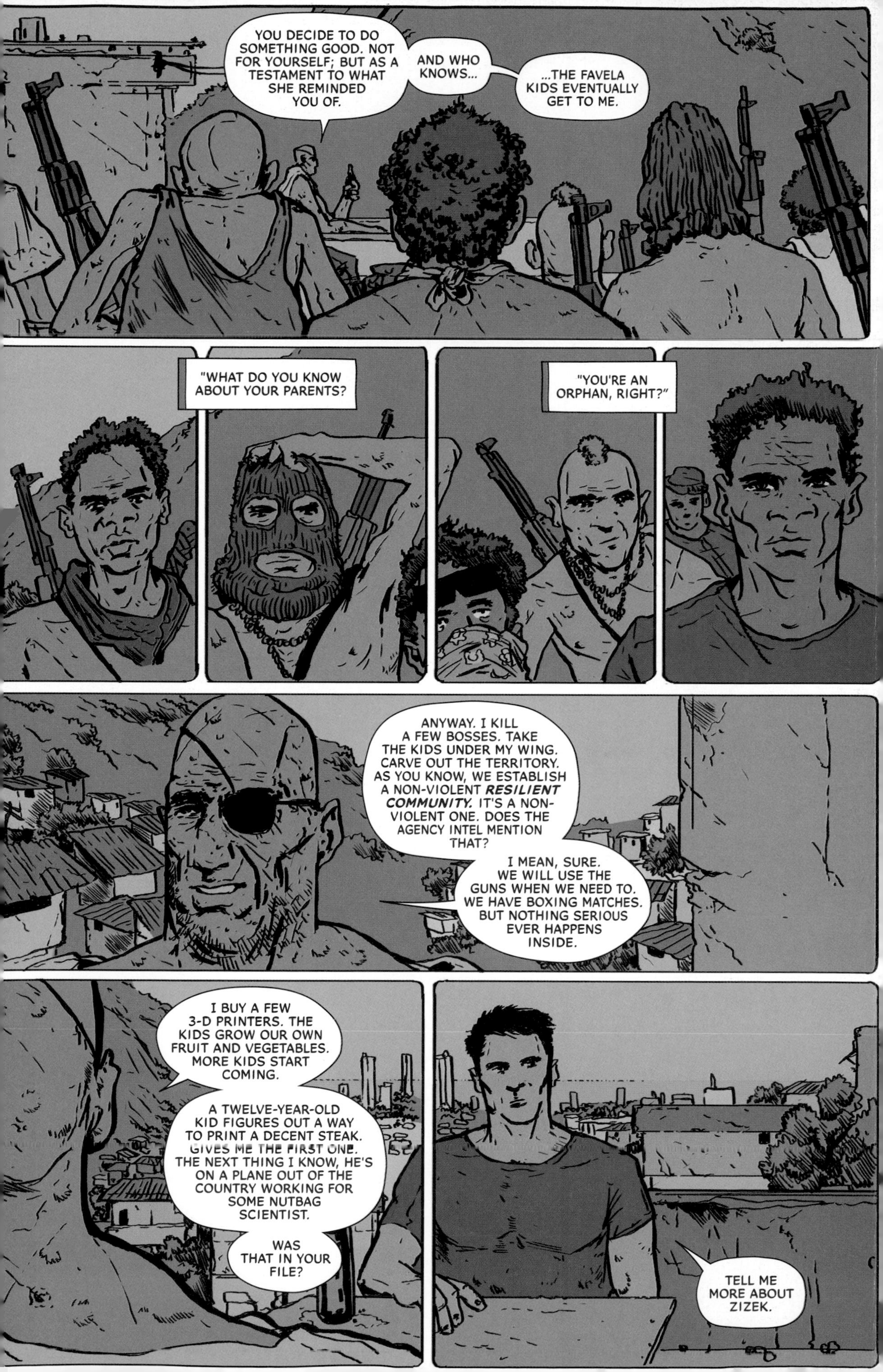
YOU DECIDE TO DO SOMETHING GOOD. NOT FOR YOURSELF; BUT AS A TESTAMENT TO WHAT SHE REMINDED YOU OF.
AND WHO KNOWS...
...THE FAVELA KIDS EVENTUALLY GET TO ME.
"WHAT DO YOU KNOW ABOUT YOUR PARENTS?
"YOU'RE AN ORPHAN, RIGHT?"
ANYWAY. I KILL A FEW BOSSES. TAKE THE KIDS UNDER MY WING. CARVE OUT THE TERRITORY. AS YOU KNOW, WE ESTABLISH A NON-VIOLENT ***RESILIENT COMMUNITY.*** IT'S A NON-VIOLENT ONE. DOES THE AGENCY INTEL MENTION THAT?
I MEAN, SURE. WE WILL USE THE GUNS WHEN WE NEED TO. WE HAVE BOXING MATCHES. BUT NOTHING SERIOUS EVER HAPPENS INSIDE.
I BUY A FEW 3-D PRINTERS. THE KIDS GROW OUR OWN FRUIT AND VEGETABLES. MORE KIDS START COMING.
A TWELVE-YEAR-OLD KID FIGURES OUT A WAY TO PRINT A DECENT STEAK. GIVES ME THE FIRST ONE. THE NEXT THING I KNOW, HE'S ON A PLANE OUT OF THE COUNTRY WORKING FOR SOME NUTBAG SCIENTIST.
WAS THAT IN YOUR FILE?
TELL ME MORE ABOUT ZIZEK.

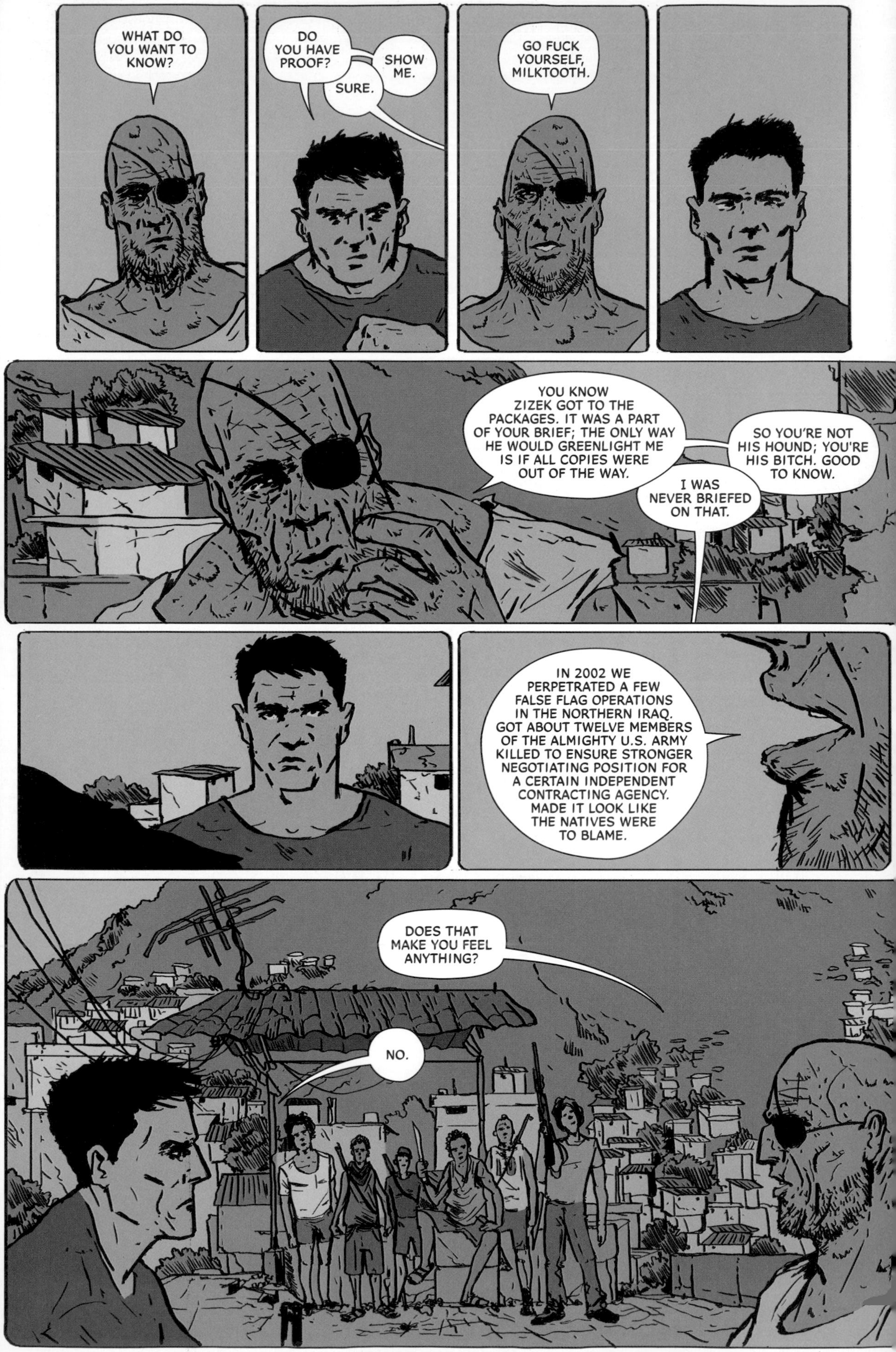
WHAT DO YOU WANT TO KNOW?
DO YOU HAVE PROOF?
SURE.
SHOW ME.
GO FUCK YOURSELF, MILKTOOTH.
YOU KNOW ZIZEK GOT TO THE PACKAGES. IT WAS A PART OF YOUR BRIEF; THE ONLY WAY HE WOULD GREENLIGHT ME IS IF ALL COPIES WERE OUT OF THE WAY.
I WAS NEVER BRIEFED ON THAT.
SO YOU'RE NOT HIS HOUND; YOU'RE HIS BITCH. GOOD TO KNOW.
IN 2002 WE PERPETRATED A FEW FALSE FLAG OPERATIONS IN THE NORTHERN IRAQ. GOT ABOUT TWELVE MEMBERS OF THE ALMIGHTY U.S. ARMY KILLED TO ENSURE STRONGER NEGOTIATING POSITION FOR A CERTAIN INDEPENDENT CONTRACTING AGENCY. MADE IT LOOK LIKE THE NATIVES WERE TO BLAME.
DOES THAT MAKE YOU FEEL ANYTHING?
NO.

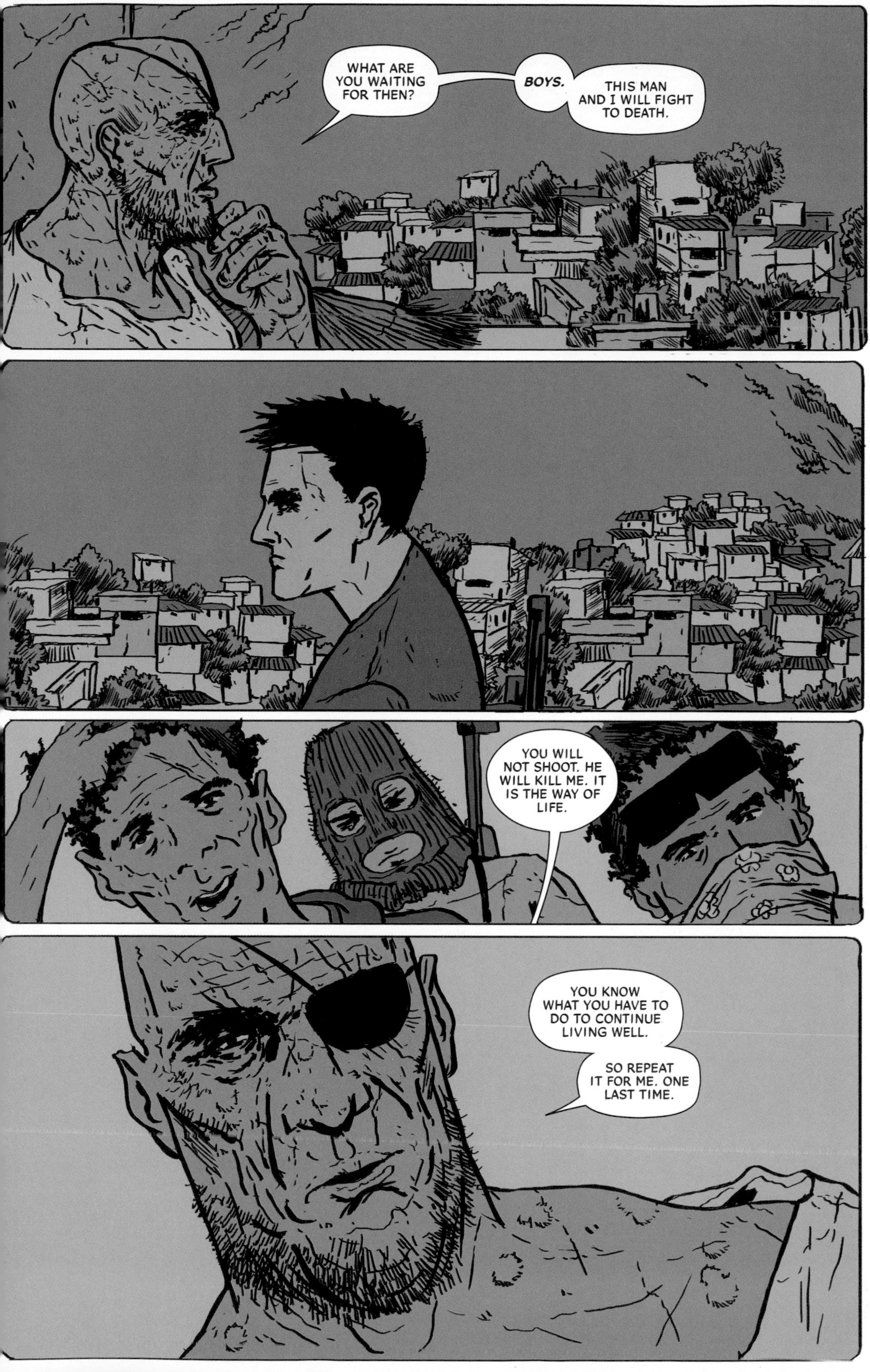
WHAT ARE YOU WAITING FOR THEN?
BOYS.
THIS MAN AND I WILL FIGHT TO DEATH.
YOU WILL NOT SHOOT. HE WILL KILL ME. IT IS THE WAY OF LIFE.
YOU KNOW WHAT YOU HAVE TO DO TO CONTINUE LIVING WELL.
SO REPEAT IT FOR ME. ONE LAST TIME.

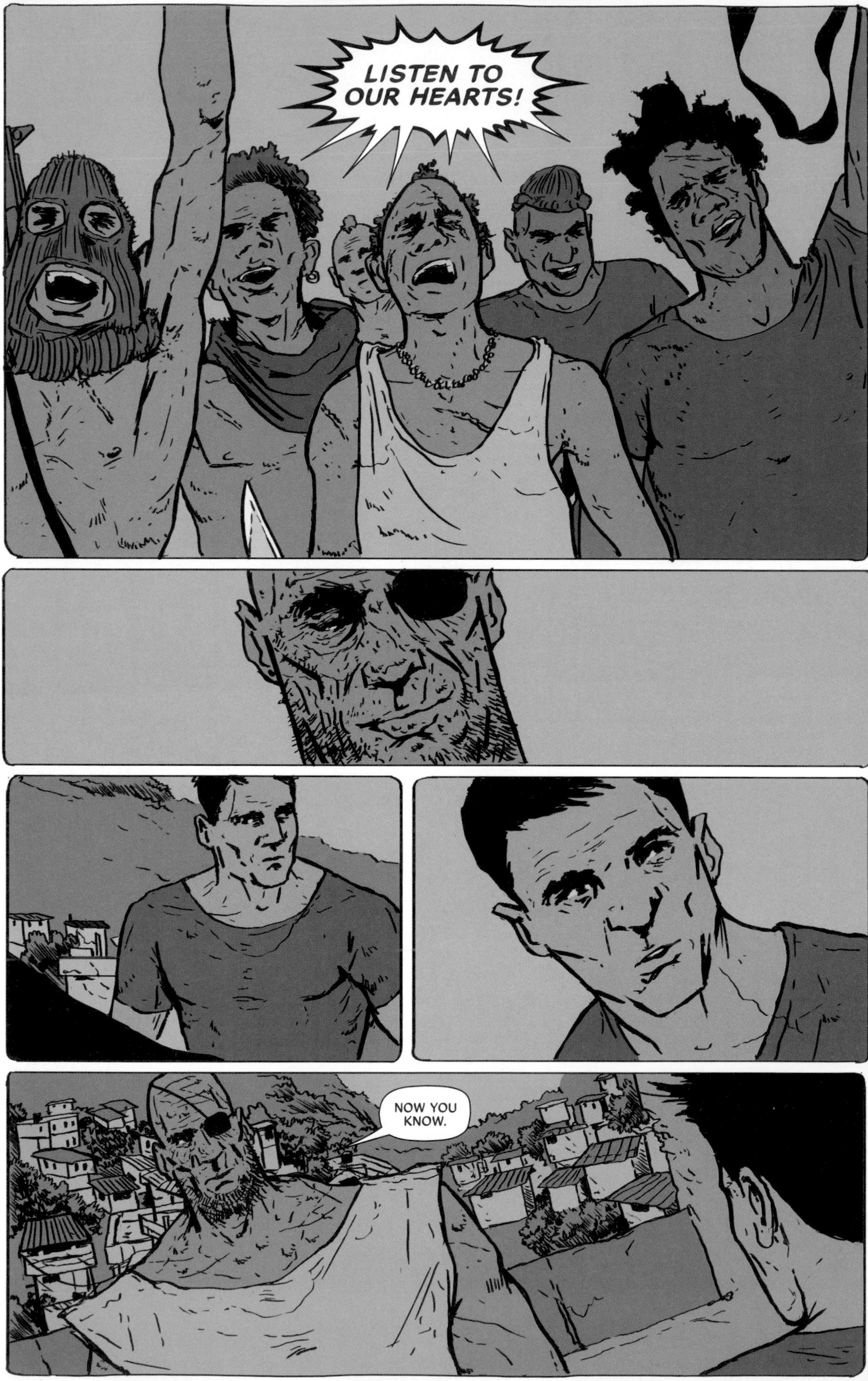
LISTEN TO OUR HEARTS!
NOW YOU KNOW.

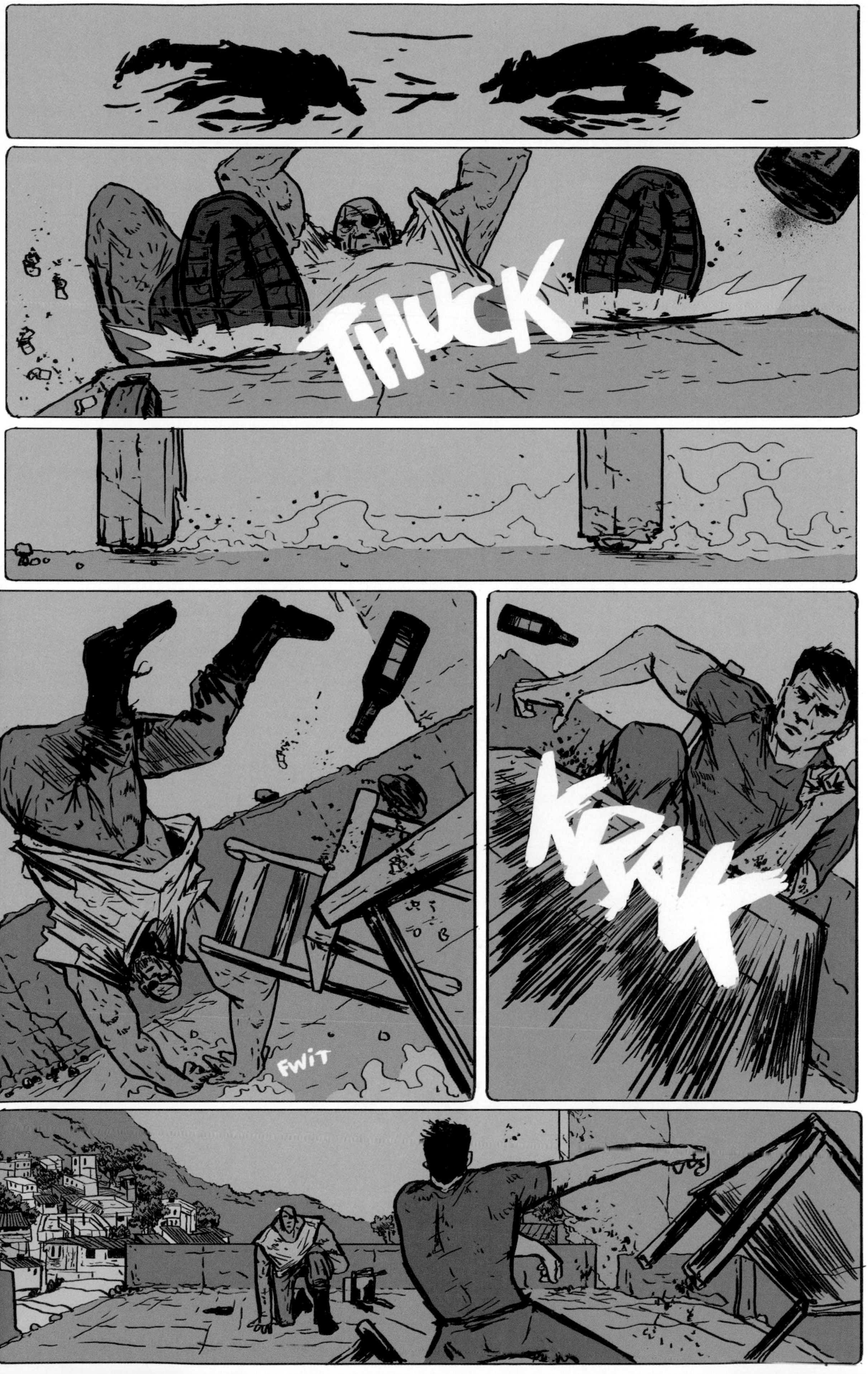
THUCK
KRAK
FWIT

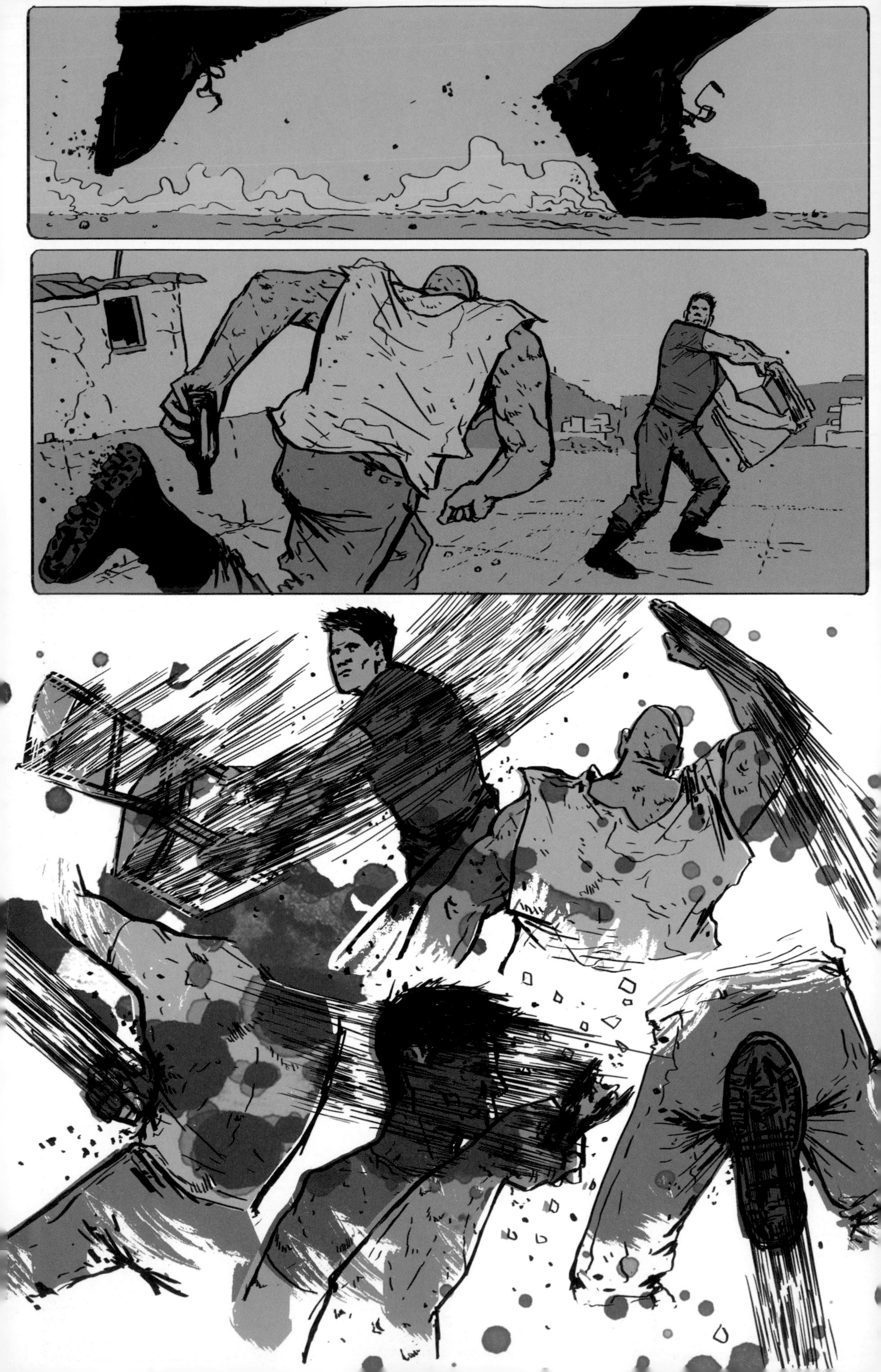

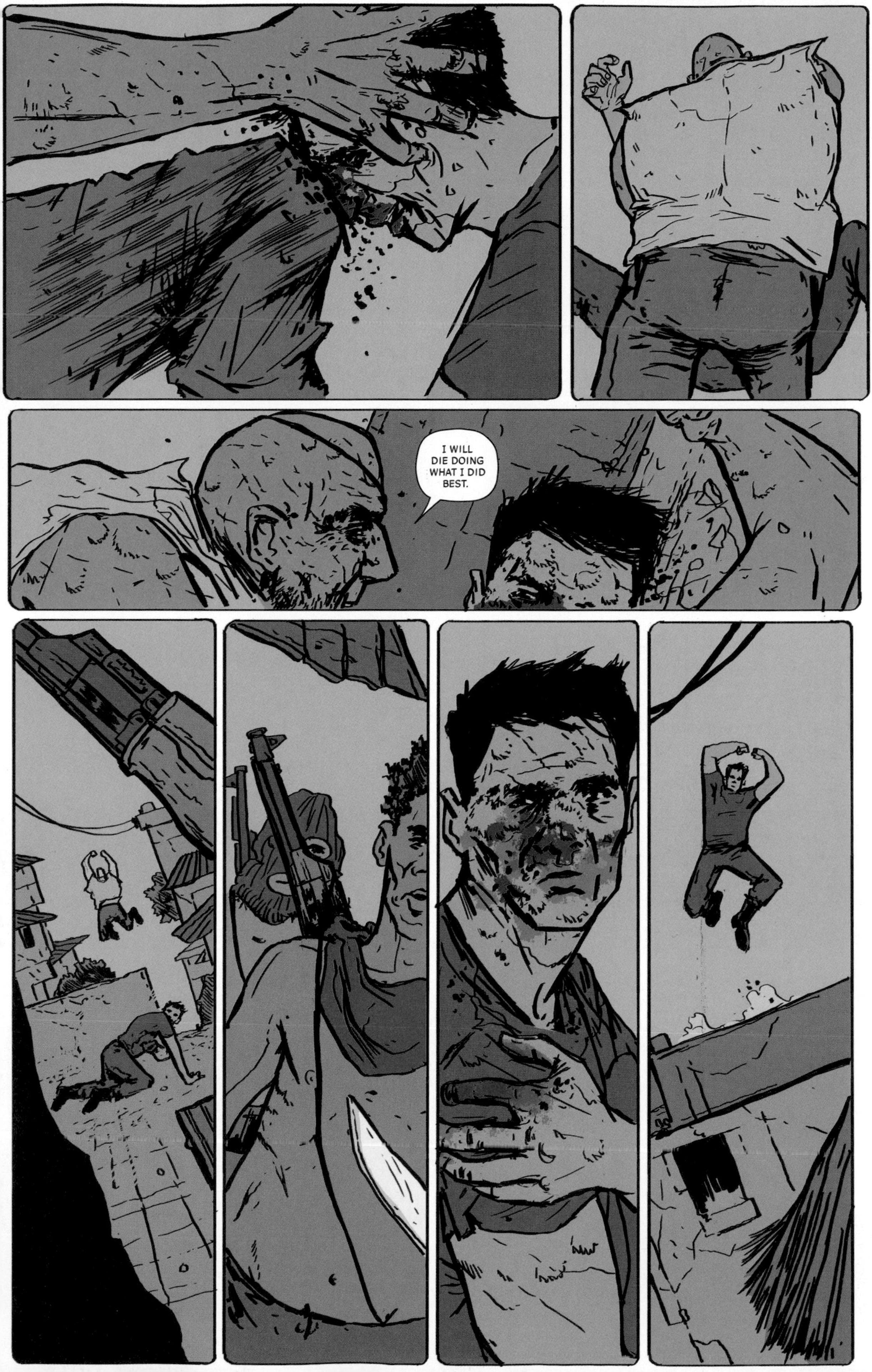
I WILL DIE DOING WHAT I DID BEST.

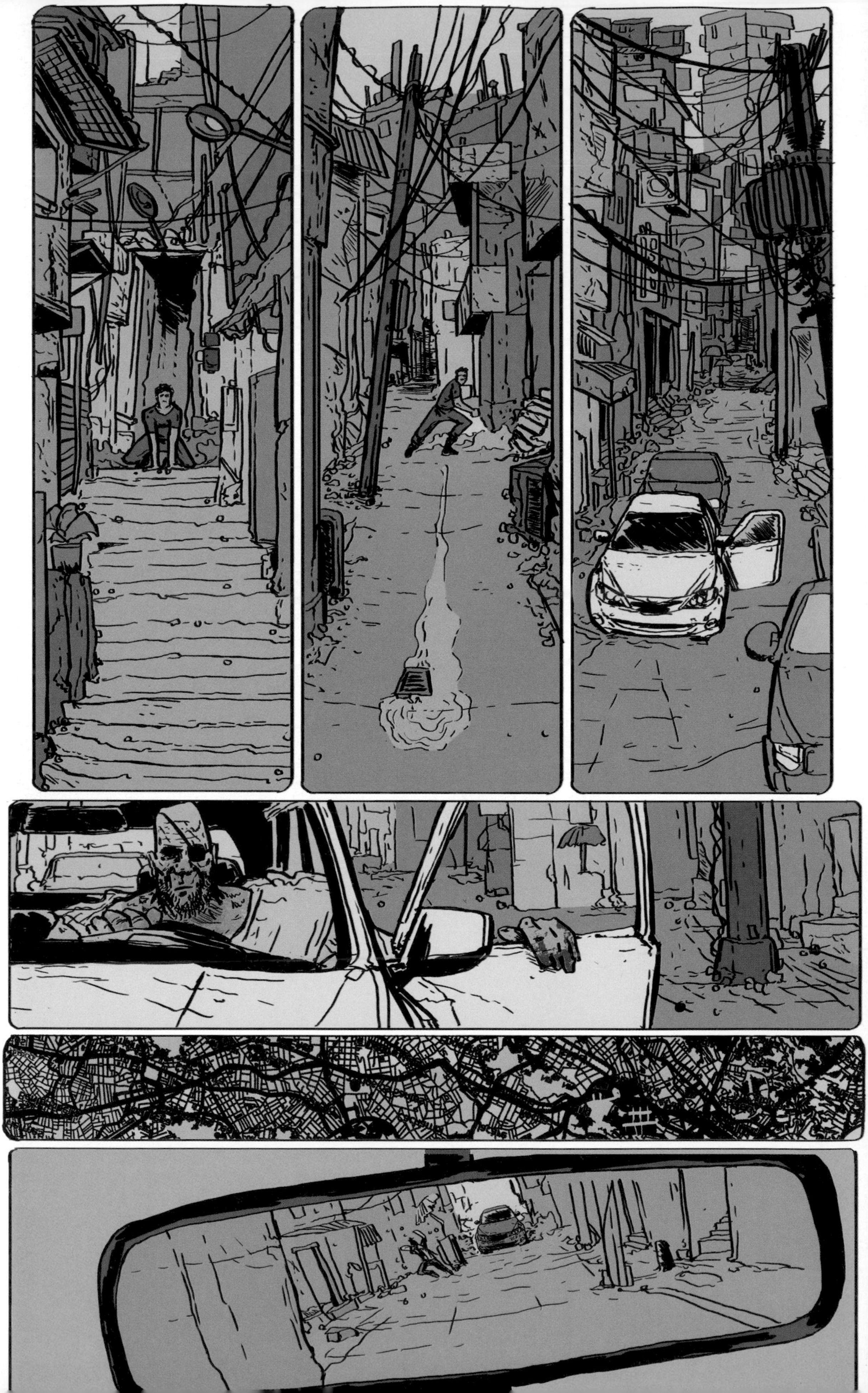

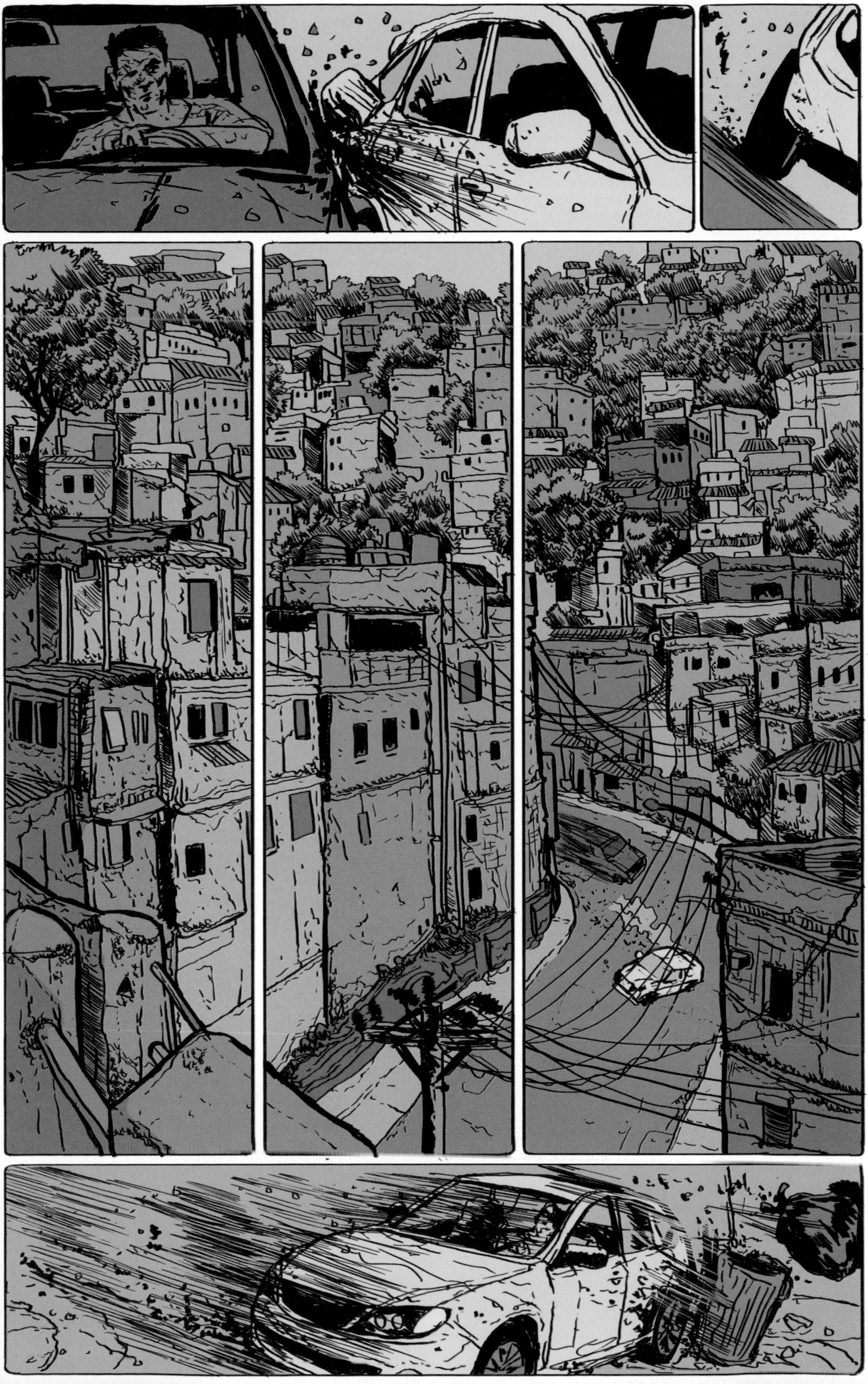

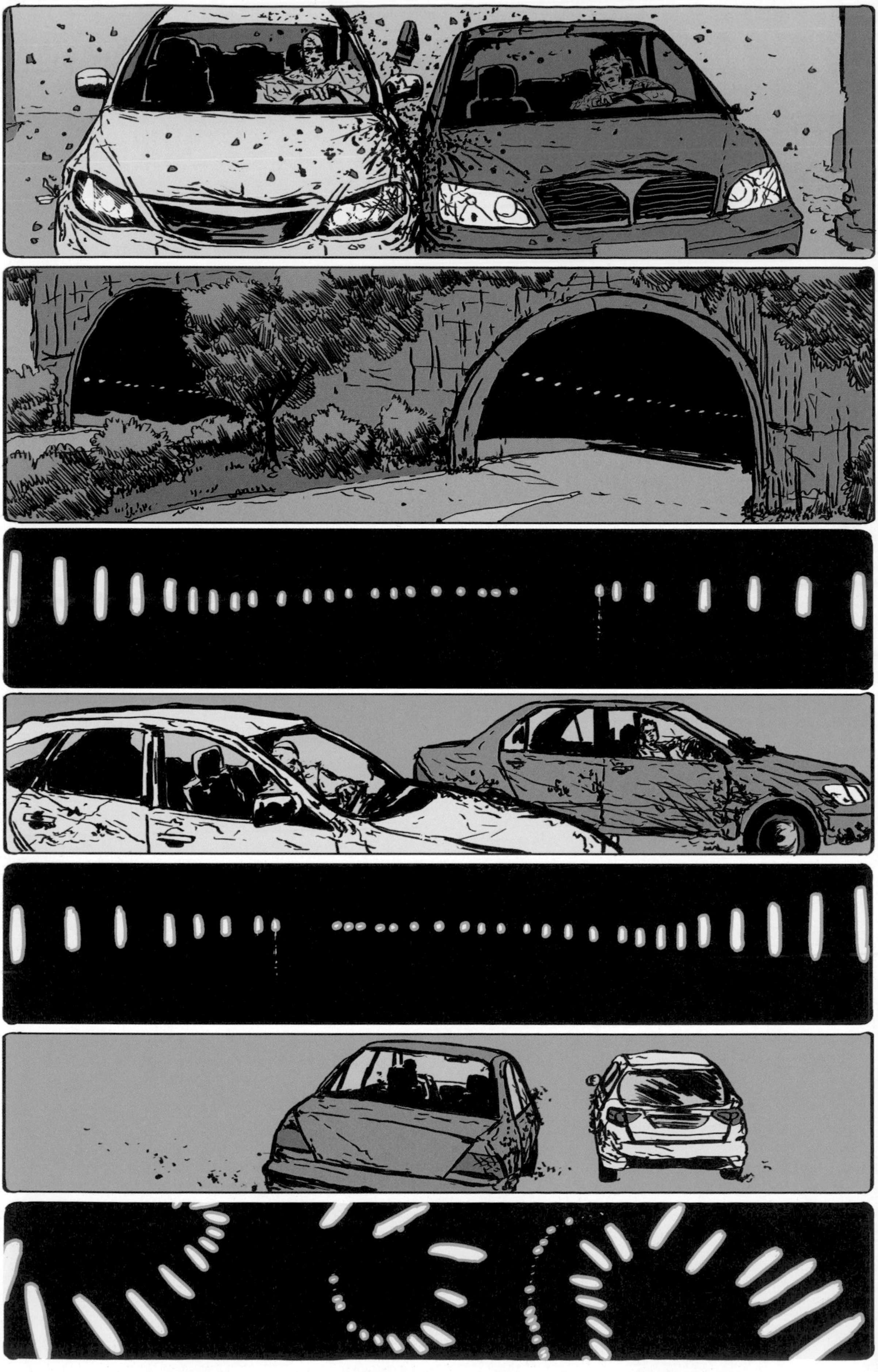

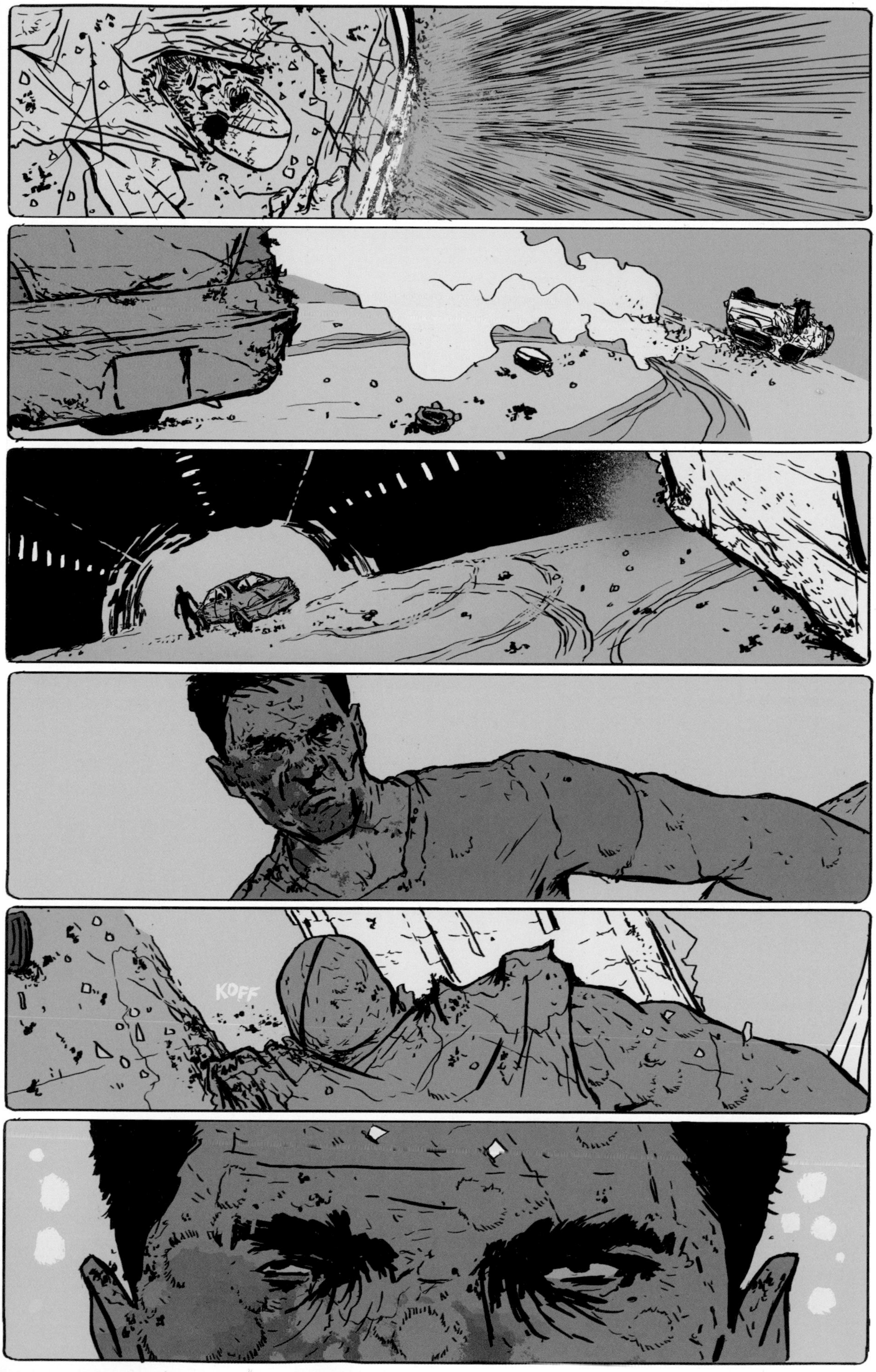
KOFF

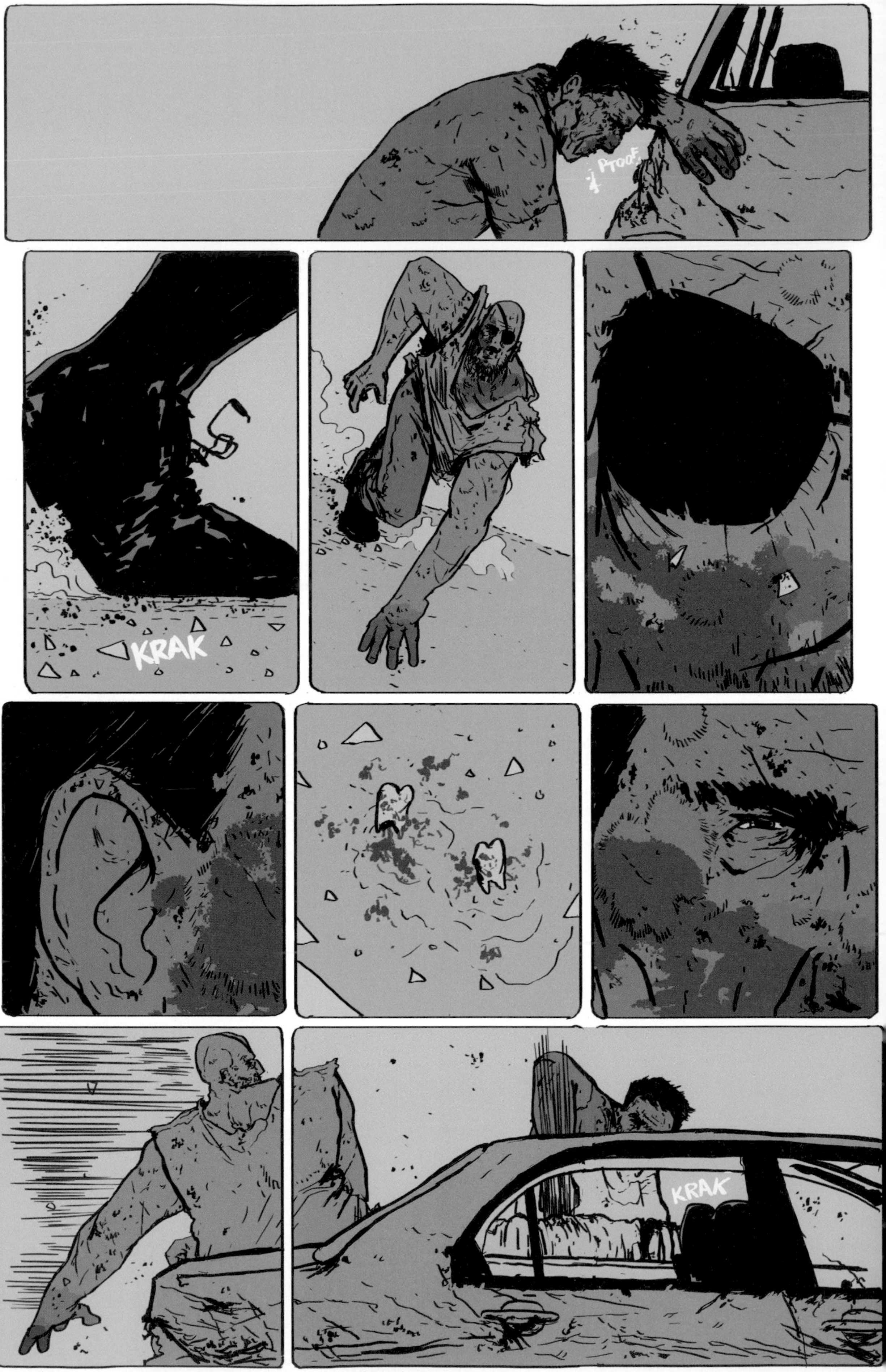
PTOOF
KRAK
KRAK

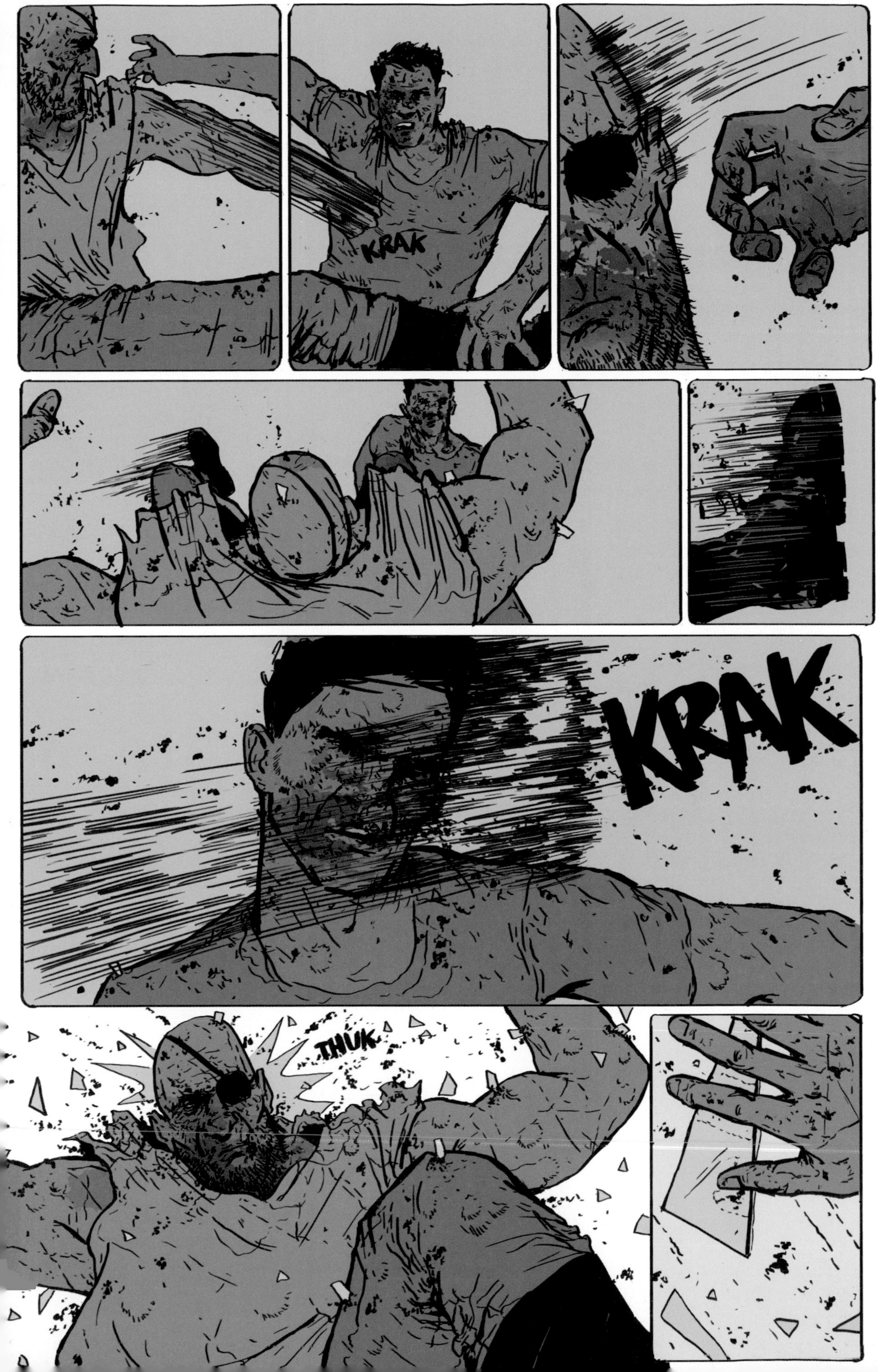
KRAK
KRAK
THUK

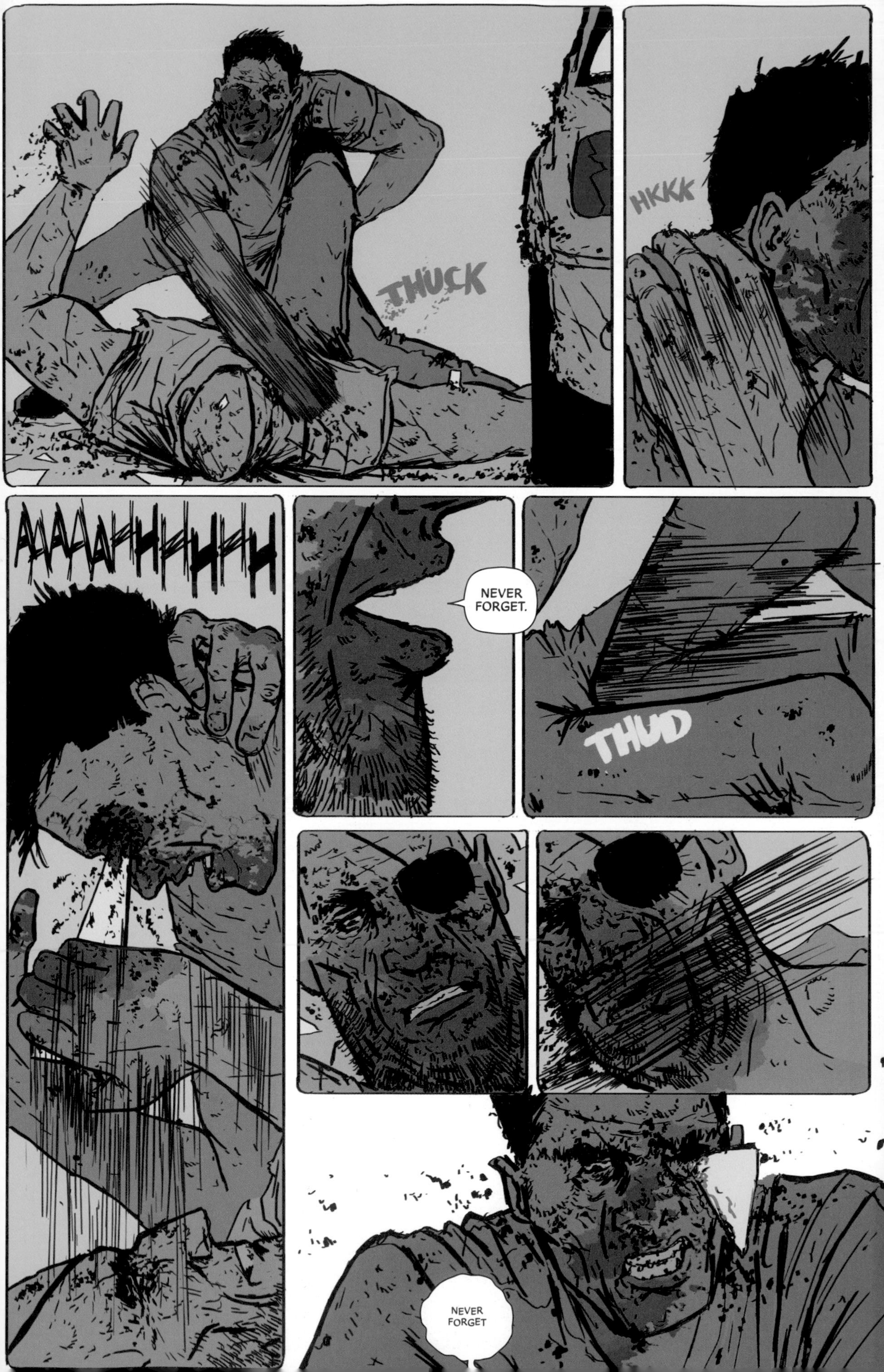
THUCK
HKKK
AAAAAHHHHHH
NEVER FORGET.
THUD
NEVER FORGET

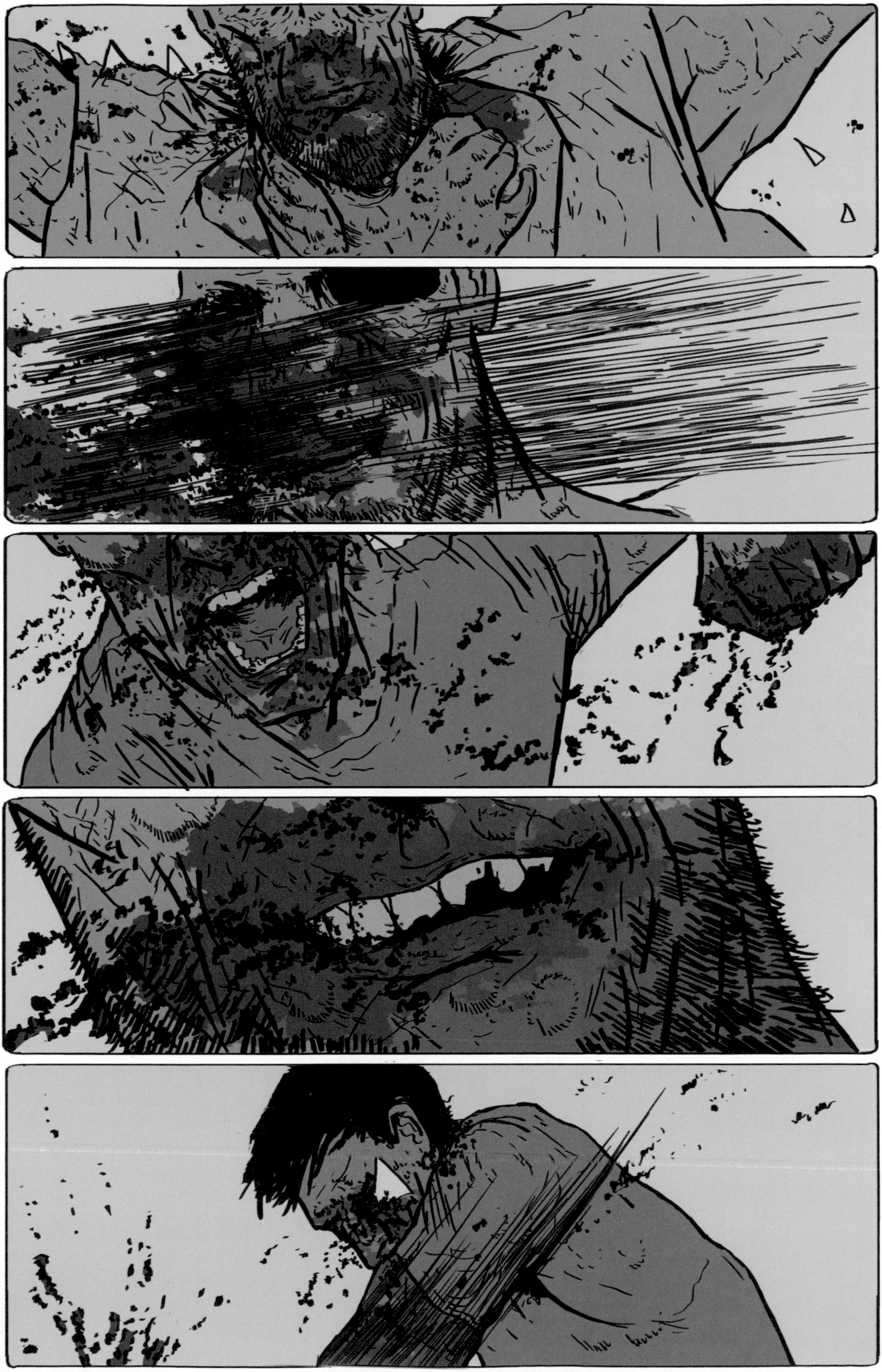

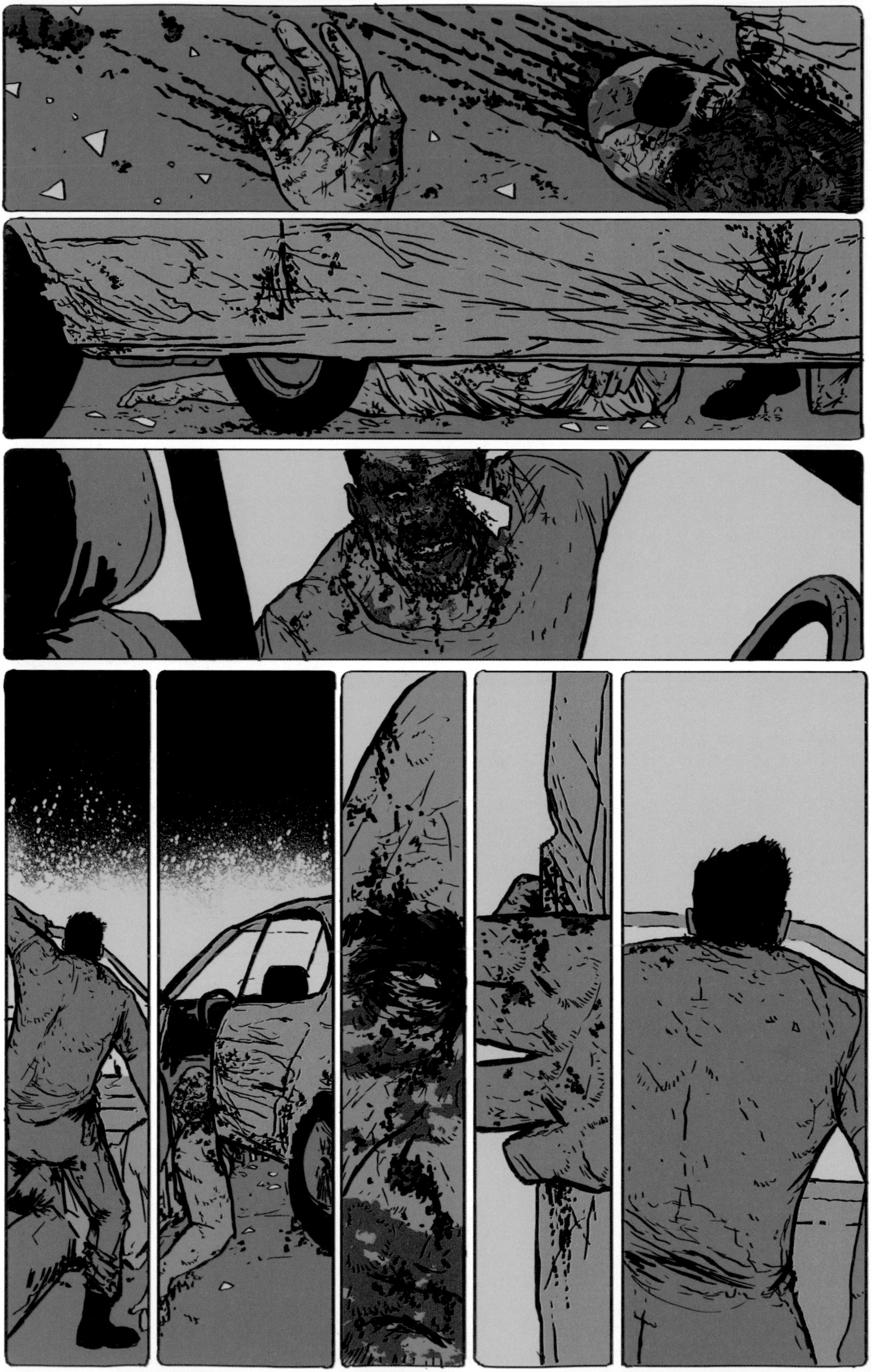

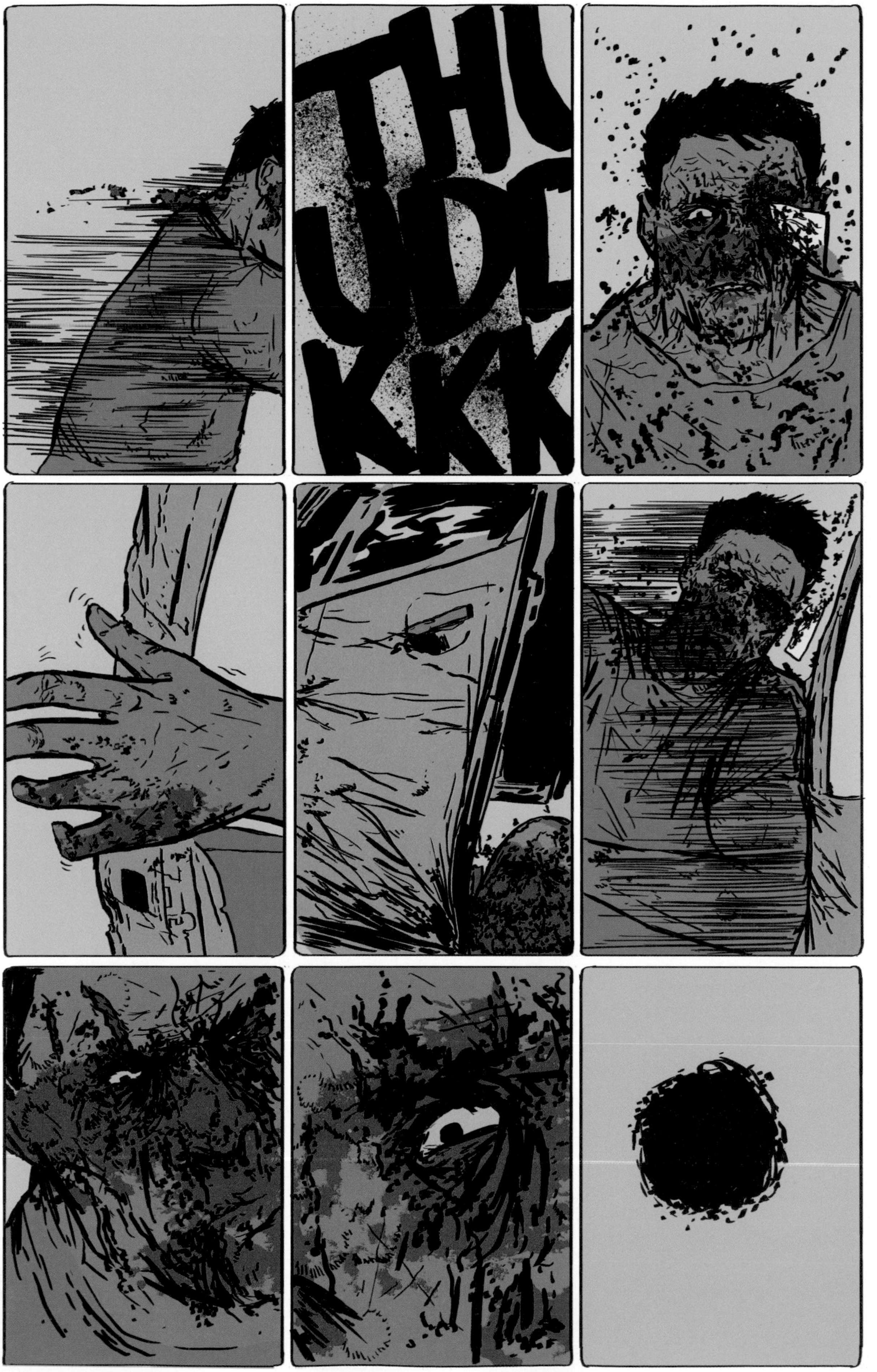
THU
UDD
KKK

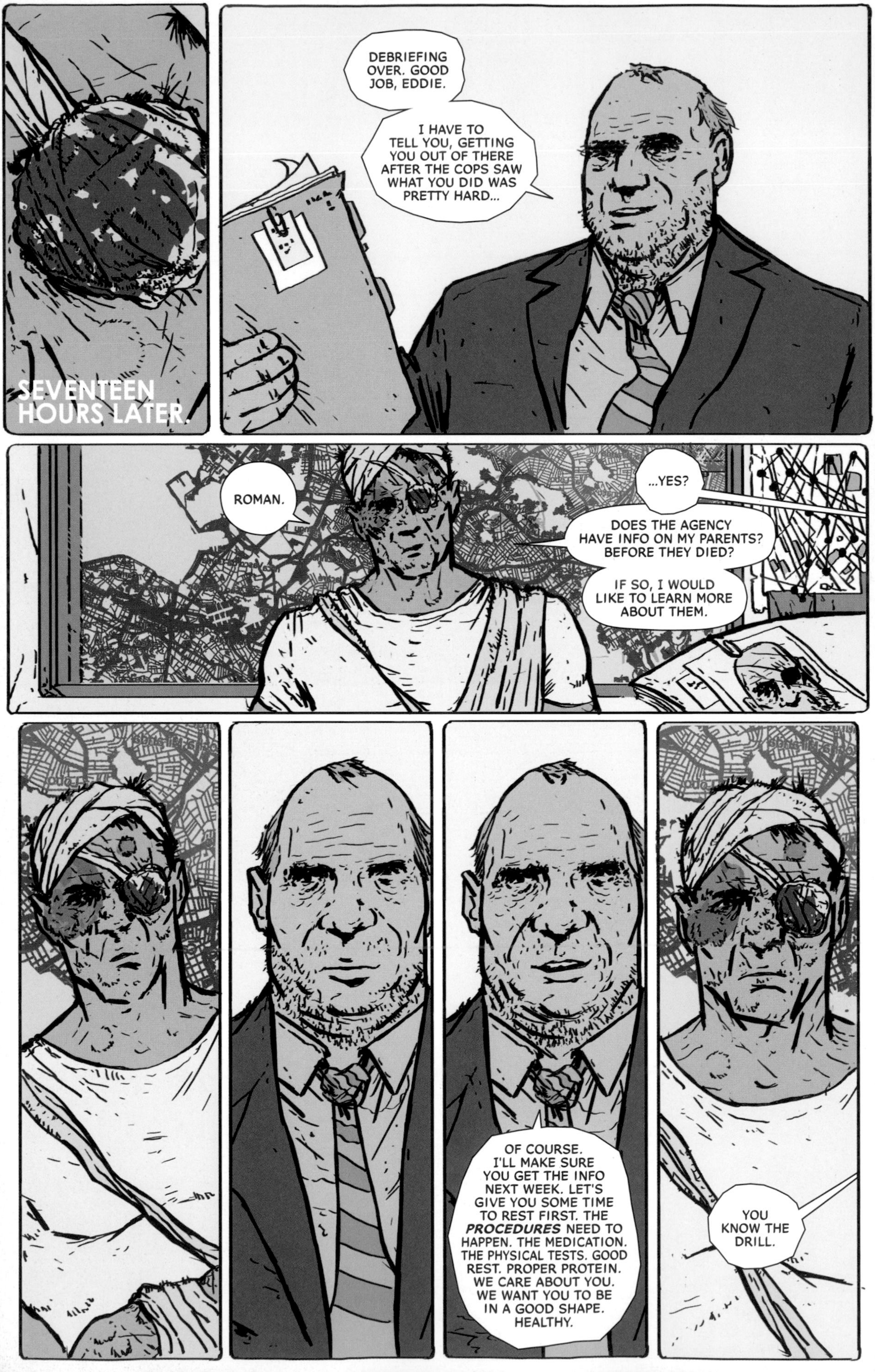
SEVENTEEN HOURS LATER.
DEBRIEFING OVER. GOOD JOB, EDDIE.
I HAVE TO TELL YOU, GETTING YOU OUT OF THERE AFTER THE COPS SAW WHAT YOU DID WAS PRETTY HARD...
ROMAN.
...YES?
DOES THE AGENCY HAVE INFO ON MY PARENTS? BEFORE THEY DIED?
IF SO, I WOULD LIKE TO LEARN MORE ABOUT THEM.
OF COURSE. I'LL MAKE SURE YOU GET THE INFO NEXT WEEK. LET'S GIVE YOU SOME TIME TO REST FIRST. THE PROCEDURES NEED TO HAPPEN. THE MEDICATION. THE PHYSICAL TESTS. GOOD REST. PROPER PROTEIN. WE CARE ABOUT YOU. WE WANT YOU TO BE IN A GOOD SHAPE. HEALTHY.
YOU KNOW THE DRILL.

CHAPTER FOUR:
VISION IMPAIRMENT

ST. PETERSBURG, 2009.

WHO THE FUCK IS ROMAN.

ZIZEK SAYS IT LIKE ROMAN IS NOT HIS NAME. THE MAN CALLED HIM BY HIS REAL NAME. THE MAN SHOULD NOT KNOW THE NAME. HE SHOULD NOT KNOW ENOUGH TO TAKE OUT HIS GUN. HE SHOULD NOT KNOW ENOUGH TO KEEP ZIZEK SITTING IN THE CHAIR HE FREQUENTED AS MICHAEL STOIKOVIC, THE BULGARIAN DRUG DEALER INTERESTED IN EXPLOITING THE NEW MARKET IN HIS HOME COUNTRY.

I DON'T KNOW NO ROMAN.

IT'S YOUR NAME.

IT'S NOT.

ZIZEK KEEPS QUIET, EYE CONTACT INTACT. WHEN YOU SPEND A LIFETIME LYING, ONE MORE TIME IS NOTHING.

OKAY.

THEN TELL ME.

WHO IS THE RAT?

IS IT YOUR FRIEND WHO FOLLOWS YOU EVERYWHERE?

YOU TELL ME.

WE WORKED HIM OVER ALREADY. HE SAYS NOTHING EXCEPT A NAME AT ONE POINT, WHEN ASLEEP. SOUNDED IMPORTANT. ROMAN. WE ASK HIM IF HE GOT A BROTHER, HE SAYS FUCK YOU. WE ASK WHO ROMAN IS, HE STOPS FOR A SECOND, THEN SAYS FUCK YOU. SO ROMAN IS IMPORTANT.

THEY DRAG IN THE MAN. TWO MEN, BOTH TALL AND FULL OF SCARS, ONE LOCAL, THE OTHER WHITE, ONE WITH A SPLIT LIP THAT HEALED LIKE A CRACK IN THE WALL DOES OVER TIME, THE OTHER MISSING AN EYE. THE MAN THEY DRAG IN REMINDS ZIZEK OF THE BEET SALAD HIS MOTHER SERVED WITH LUNCH SOMETIMES. HE DIDN'T TOUCH IT UNTIL HIS FATHER PUNCHED HIM IN THE FACE ONE DAY. HE ATE THEM SINCE.

THE MAN WON'T EAT AGAIN. HIS FACE IS BASHED IN ENOUGH TO MAKE SURE OF THAT. HE WILL SPEAK THOUGH, AT LEAST BY USING THE BROKEN FINGERS, BLINKS OF HIS BLOOD VIOLET SWOLLEN EYELIDS.

YOU KNOW WHAT WE DID? HE DOESN'T WAIT FOR THE ANSWER. WE GIVE HIM KROKODIL. KROKODIL MIGHT BE A GOOD EXPORT FOR YOU.

WHAT'S KROKODIL?

IT'S THE THING YOU SELL TO THE JUNKIES WHO DON'T HAVE ENOUGH MONEY TO BUY ANYTHING ELSE. THEY NEVER WILL. SO YOU KILL THEM, GET THEM OFF THE MARKET. BUT FIRST YOU SELL THEM KROKODIL, COLLECT THE LAST CASH.

WHAT DOES IT DO? IT GETS YOU HIGH?

I NEVER TRIED. I'M NOT INSANE. I GOT WHORES AND CARS. AND CHAMPAGNE. AND COCAINE. KROKODIL IS FOR...HOW DO YOU SAY IT? PISSANTS. WE THROW EVERYTHING IN. COOKING OIL. FLOUR. CLEANER. SHIT BITS OF DOPE. SOMETIMES WE PISS INTO IT FOR FUN. FUCK THEM. IT'S ALL SHIT.

THE MAN ON THE FLOOR TRIES TO SAY SOMETHING. A BUBBLE COMES OUT OF HIS MOUTH, OUT OF SYNC WITH THE GASP OF A FISH SLAPPED ON A WOODEN FLOOR, OUT OF THE AQUARIUM, WET WITH ITS OWN BLOOD, BITTER AIR FILLED WITH IRON. THE MEN ARE NEAR THE DOOR, SILENT.

THE MAN'S GUN IS ON THE TABLE NOW. CARLYLE COULD KILL BOTH MEN BEFORE ZIZEK MOVES; ZIZEK KNOWS THAT. HE DOESN'T NEED TO TURN AROUND TO KNOW THAT CARLYLE IS READY, STANDING ON THE LEFT SIDE OF THE DOOR, THE MAN WITH THE HARELIP ON THE RIGHT SIDE OF THE DOOR, NOT PAYING ATTENTION TO THE MAN HE WORKED WITH FOR THE PAST SEVEN MONTHS, THE MAN WHO BROUGHT IN HIS ENTIRE FABRICATED HISTORY. HE DOESN'T NEED TO TURN AROUND TO KNOW CARLYLE IS PERFECTLY RELAXED. HE DOESN'T NEED TO TURN AROUND TO KNOW HE'S PREPARED. ALL ZIZEK NEEDS TO DO IS KEEP EYE CONTACT WITH YIEVGENYI.

ADD SOME TEST SAMPLES TO THE PRODUCT. I THROW IT AROUND AT SOME PEOPLE, SEE IF IT SOLVES MY PROBLEMS. THEN WE CAN MOVE IT AROUND A BIT MORE.

YOU WANT TEST SAMPLES, SURE. YOU WANT TO SEE WHAT IT DOES, I CAN SHOW YOU CORPSES. OR YOU MAKE YOUR OWN. I DON'T CARE.

BUT I CARE ABOUT THE RAT. WHAT DO WE DO WITH THE RAT?

ARE YOU A RAT?

THE MAN LOOKS AT ZIZEK. THE MAN IS A DEEP COVER AGENT. HE WAS A DISPOSABLE AGENT FROM THE START, A GIVEAWAY SO CARLYLE CAN STAY EMBEDDED DEEP IN.

THE SORE EYE LEAKING THROUGH THE SWOLLEN GRAPES OF THE LIDS. THE MAN STILL BELIEVES THERE IS A PLAN TO SAVE HIM. THERE MUST BE. ZIZEK MUST HAVE PLANNED IT ALL SINCE THE BEGINNING.

THEIR EYES MEET AND THE MAN KNOWS IT IS NOT TO BE, KNOWS IT WAS NEVER TO BE.

A SLOW FILM MOVEMENT OF HIS HEAD DOWN AS HE ACCEPTS THE INEVITABLE. NOT BECAUSE HE AGREES, BUT BECAUSE HE COUNTS THE POSSIBLE MOVES AND THE CURRENT ABILITIES OF HIS BROKEN BODY AND HE BELIEVES THERE IS ONLY ONE UNIVERSE NOW, ONLY ONE WAY THE UNIVERSE GOES FORWARD.

MAYBE HE SOBS. MAYBE IT'S JUST A SOUND OF HIM GULPING DOWN BLOOD AND TEETH. NO LONGER LOOKING AT ZIZEK, HE LOOKS AT THE WOODEN FLOOR. CARLYLE STANDS, LOOKING AT HIM, NO EMOTION. YIEVGENIY SHOOTS THE MAN. THE DEAL IS MADE. ALL MEN WALK THEIR WAYS.

CHAPTER 5

THE MAP AND THE TERRITORY
Illustrated by Will Tempest

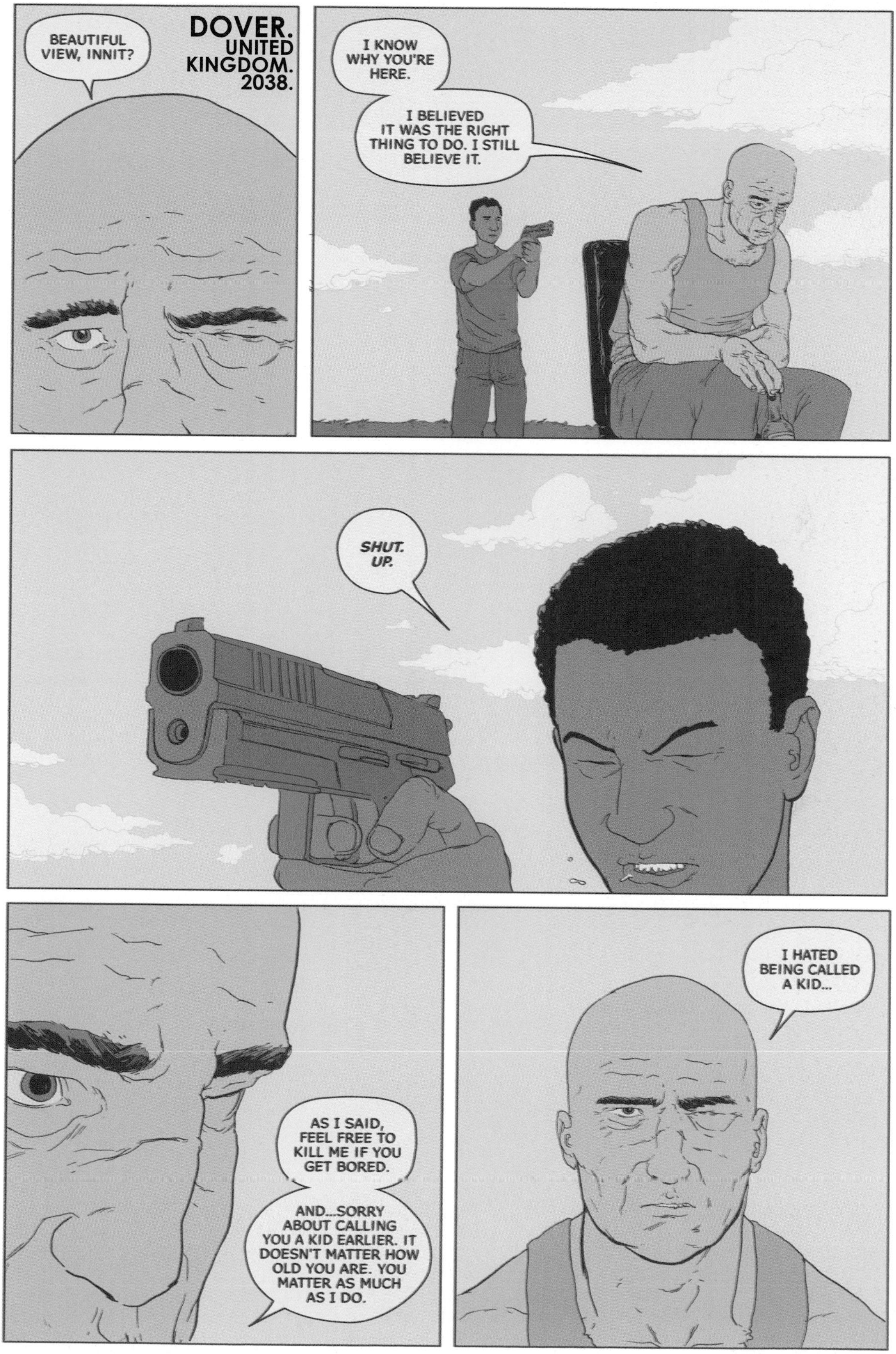
BEAUTIFUL VIEW, INNIT?
DOVER. UNITED KINGDOM. 2038.
I KNOW WHY YOU'RE HERE.
I BELIEVED IT WAS THE RIGHT THING TO DO. I STILL BELIEVE IT.
SHUT. UP.
AS I SAID, FEEL FREE TO KILL ME IF YOU GET BORED.
AND...SORRY ABOUT CALLING YOU A KID EARLIER. IT DOESN'T MATTER HOW OLD YOU ARE. YOU MATTER AS MUCH AS I DO.
I HATED BEING CALLED A KID...

WHY WOULD YOU ASK ME THAT?

THE UNITED KINGDOM, NOVEMBER 2019.

I WAS THINKING ABOUT MY PARENTS.

DO YOU REMEMBER THE DETAILS? HOW DID THEY DIE?

I DON'T THINK I EVER ASKED. WHY DID I NEVER ASK?

NOT REALLY. WE WEREN'T CONCERNED WITH THAT TOO MUCH.

DO YOU REMEMBER WHEN THESE THOUGHTS CAME? THE FIRST TIME, I MEAN.

AFTER MINA DIED.

OH.

DID YOU HAVE...DID YOU FEEL...

NO. I HAD NO FEELINGS FOR HER. BUT HER DEATH WAS A MISTAKE THAT COULD HAVE BEEN AVOIDED.

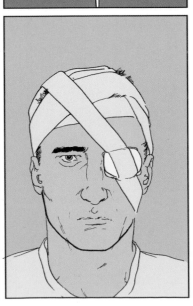

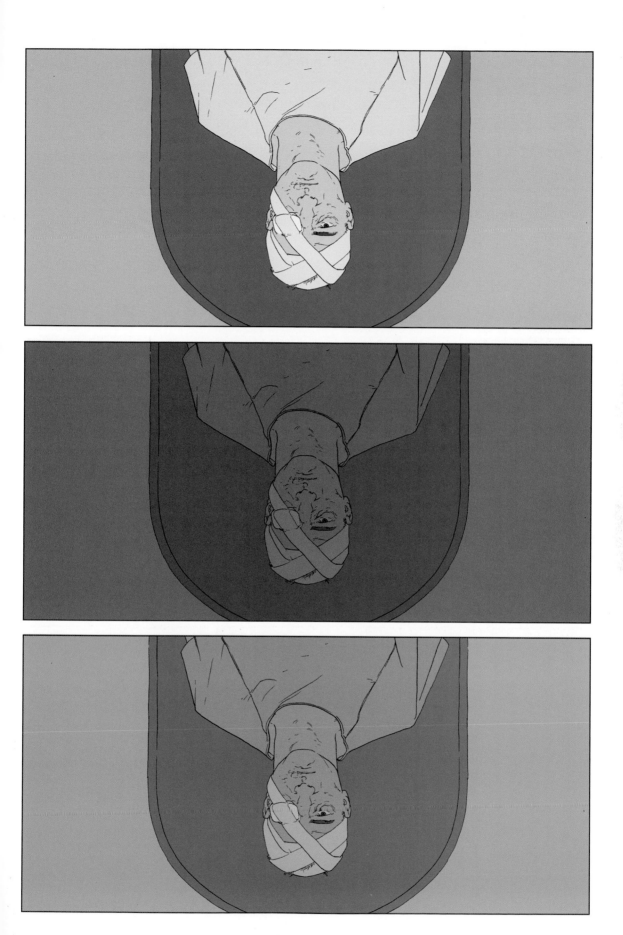

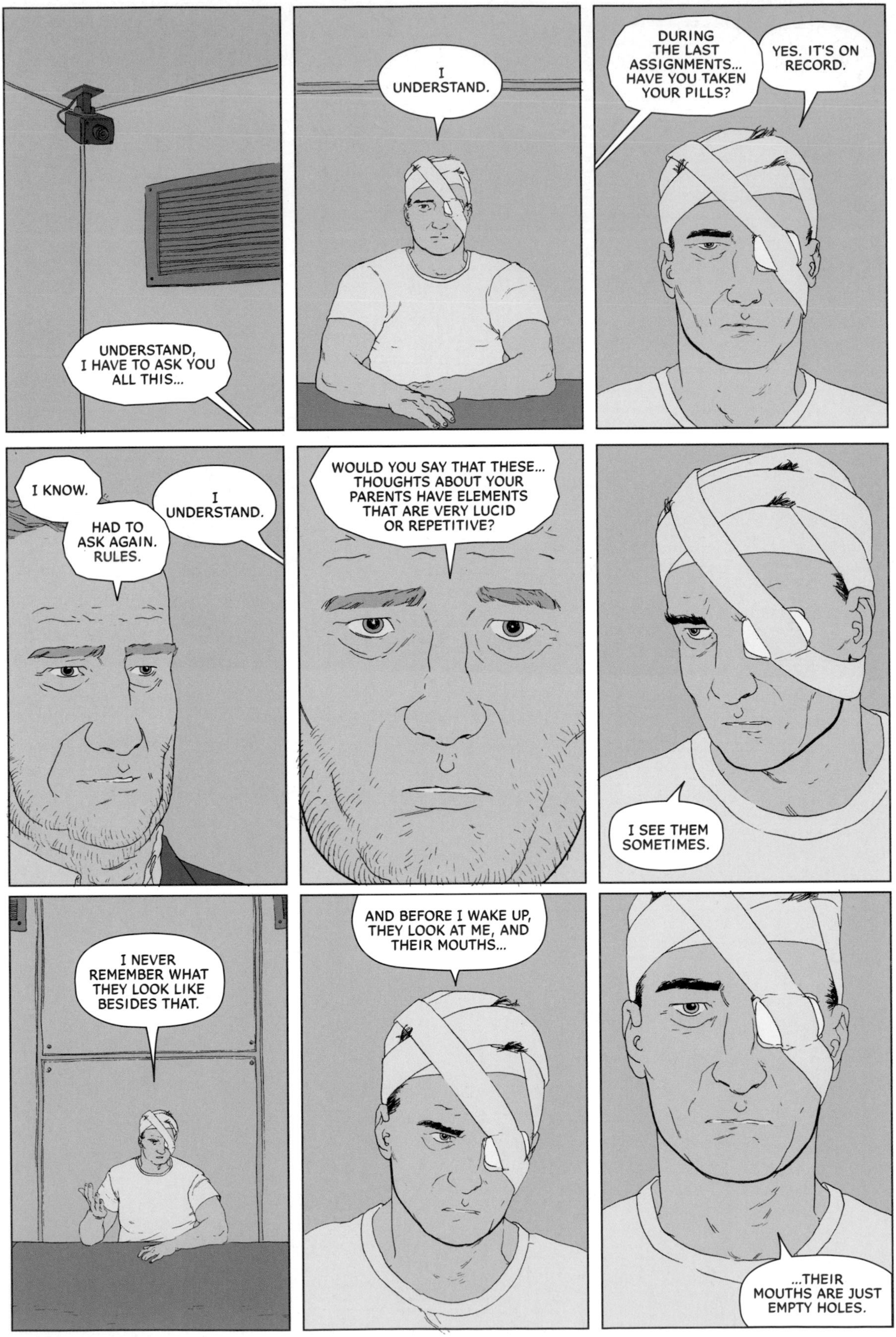
UNDERSTAND, I HAVE TO ASK YOU ALL THIS...
I UNDERSTAND.
DURING THE LAST ASSIGNMENTS... HAVE YOU TAKEN YOUR PILLS?
YES. IT'S ON RECORD.
I KNOW.
HAD TO ASK AGAIN. RULES.
I UNDERSTAND.
WOULD YOU SAY THAT THESE... THOUGHTS ABOUT YOUR PARENTS HAVE ELEMENTS THAT ARE VERY LUCID OR REPETITIVE?
I SEE THEM SOMETIMES.
I NEVER REMEMBER WHAT THEY LOOK LIKE BESIDES THAT.
AND BEFORE I WAKE UP, THEY LOOK AT ME, AND THEIR MOUTHS...
...THEIR MOUTHS ARE JUST EMPTY HOLES.

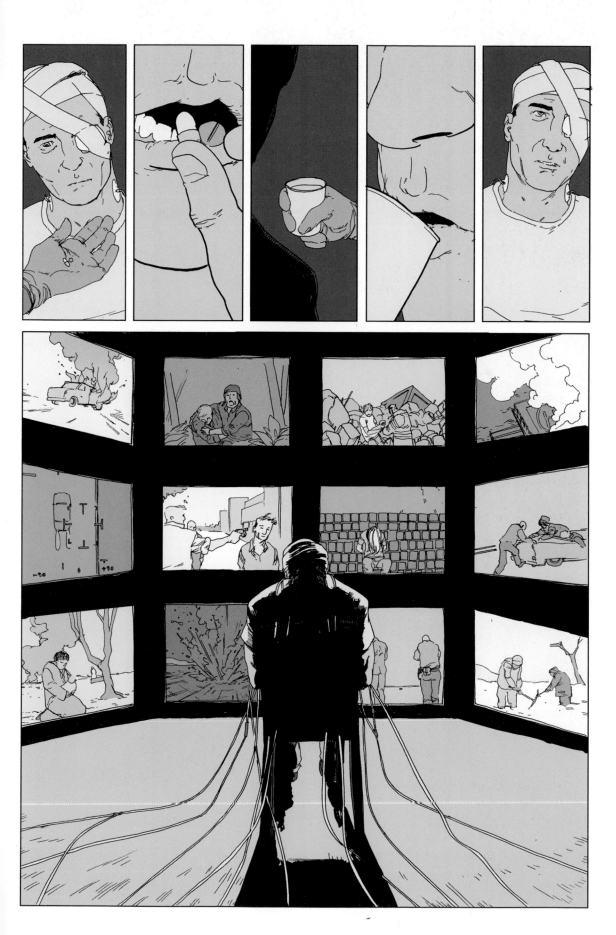

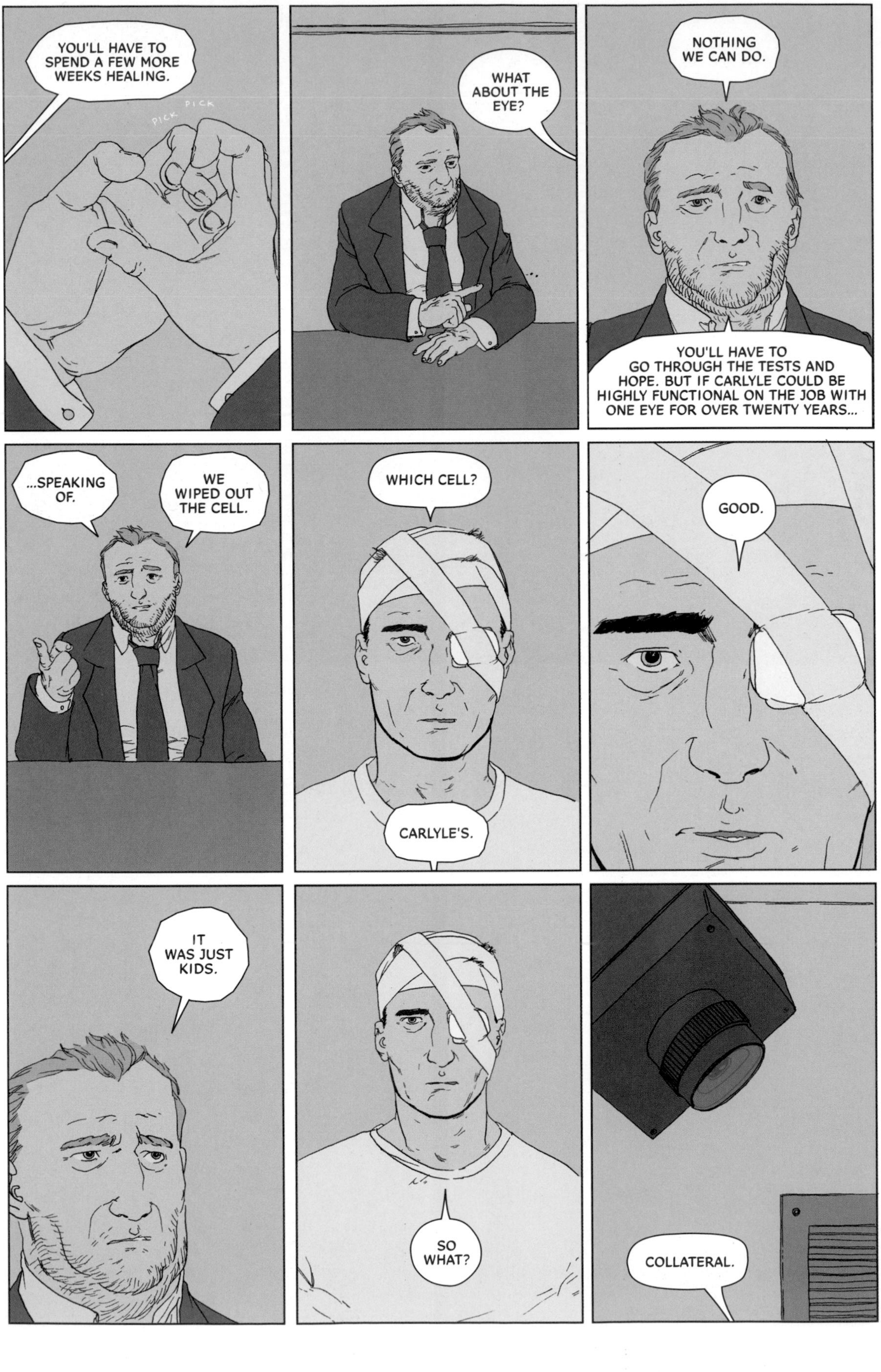
YOU'LL HAVE TO SPEND A FEW MORE WEEKS HEALING.
PICK PICK
WHAT ABOUT THE EYE?
NOTHING WE CAN DO.
YOU'LL HAVE TO GO THROUGH THE TESTS AND HOPE. BUT IF CARLYLE COULD BE HIGHLY FUNCTIONAL ON THE JOB WITH ONE EYE FOR OVER TWENTY YEARS...
...SPEAKING OF.
WE WIPED OUT THE CELL.
WHICH CELL?
CARLYLE'S.
GOOD.
IT WAS JUST KIDS.
SO WHAT?
COLLATERAL.

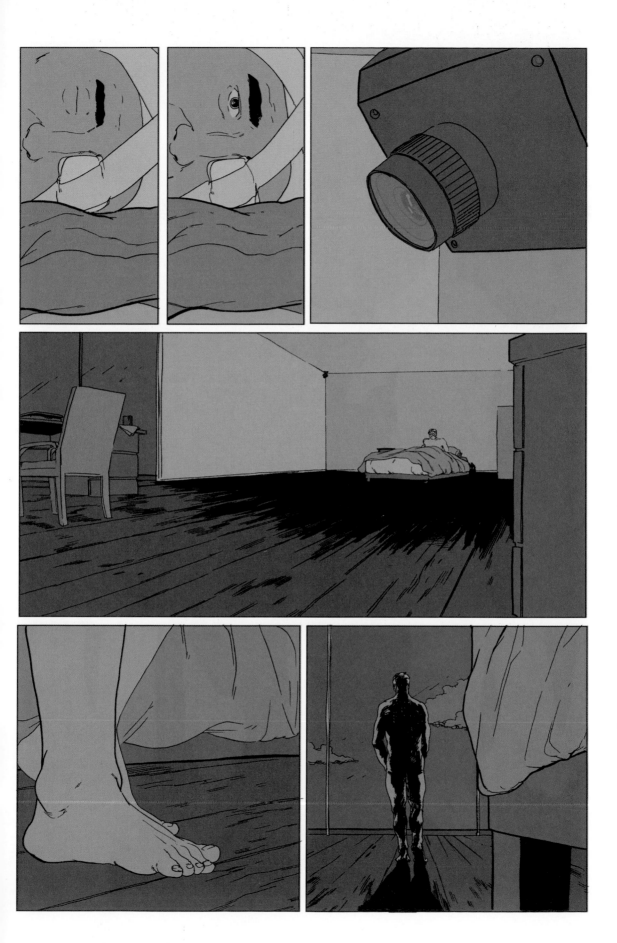

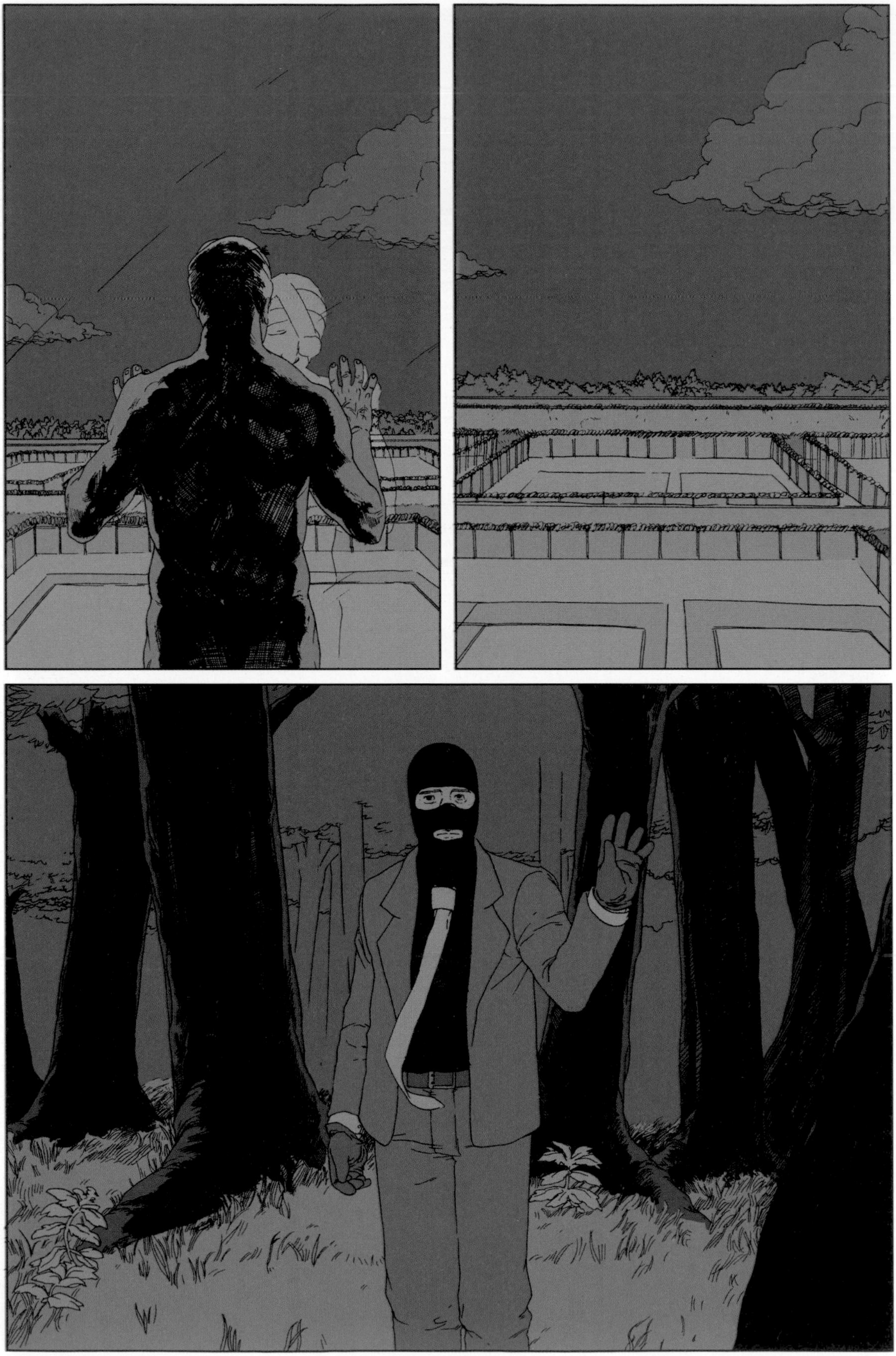

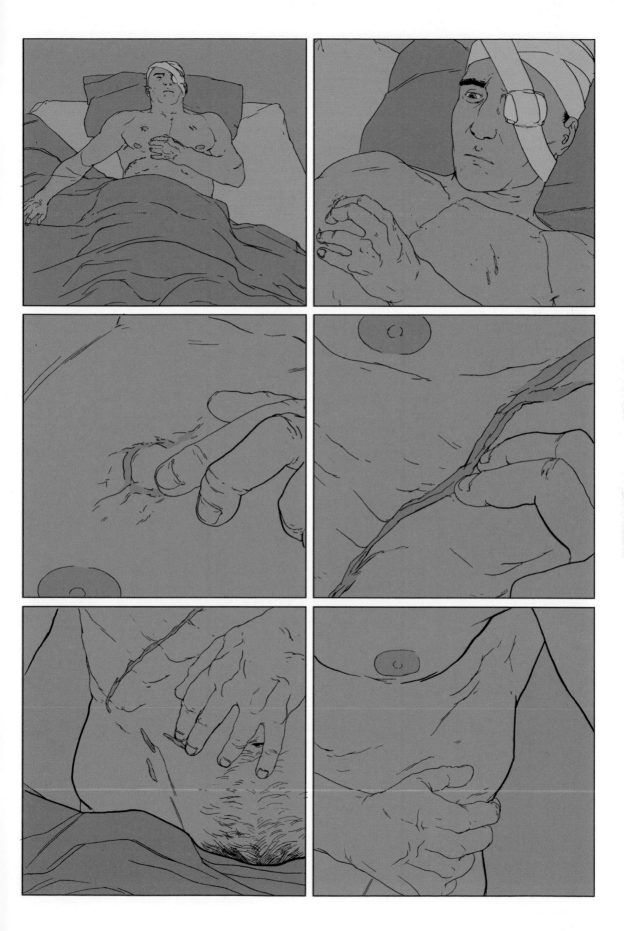

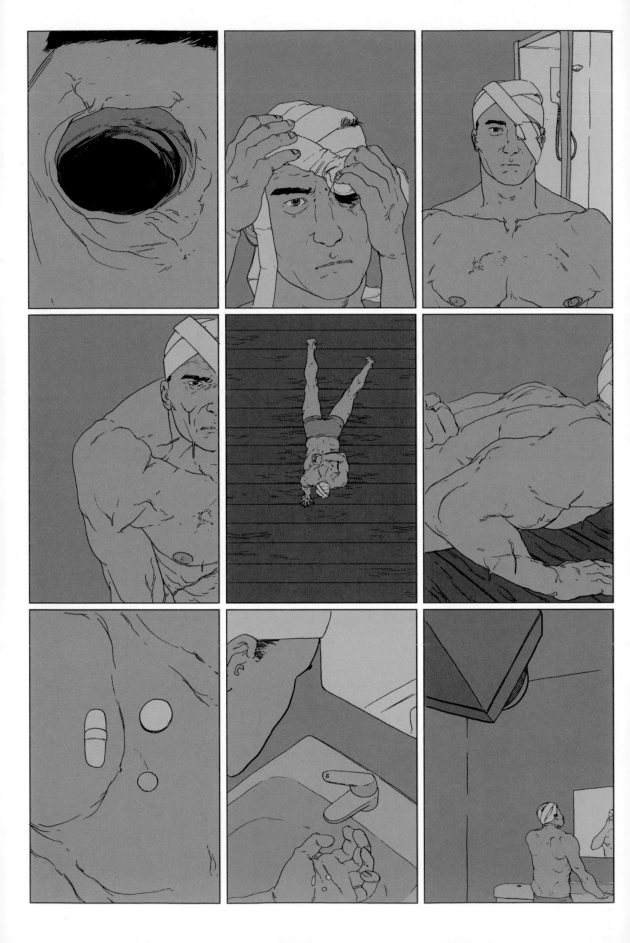

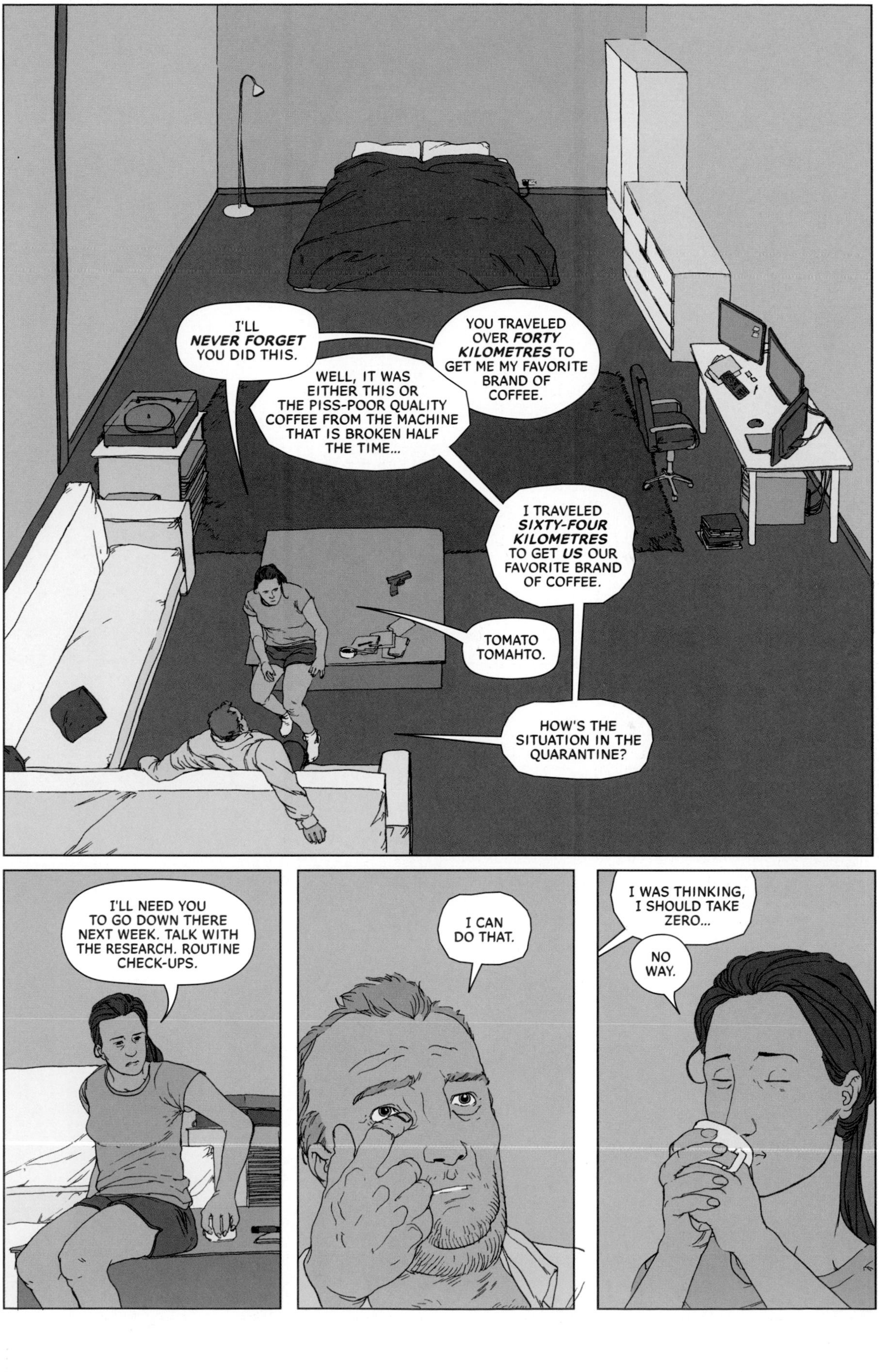
YOU TRAVELED OVER FORTY KILOMETRES TO GET ME MY FAVORITE BRAND OF COFFEE.
I'LL NEVER FORGET YOU DID THIS.
WELL, IT WAS EITHER THIS OR THE PISS-POOR QUALITY COFFEE FROM THE MACHINE THAT IS BROKEN HALF THE TIME...
I TRAVELED SIXTY-FOUR KILOMETRES TO GET US OUR FAVORITE BRAND OF COFFEE.
TOMATO TOMAHTO.
HOW'S THE SITUATION IN THE QUARANTINE?
I'LL NEED YOU TO GO DOWN THERE NEXT WEEK. TALK WITH THE RESEARCH. ROUTINE CHECK-UPS.
I CAN DO THAT.
I WAS THINKING, I SHOULD TAKE ZERO...
NO WAY.

HE WOULD LOSE HIS SHIT COMPLETELY.

I THINK IT WOULD GIVE HIM A SENSE OF PURPOSE.

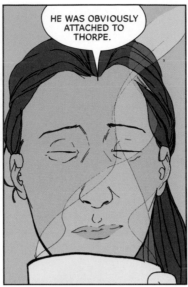

HE WAS OBVIOUSLY ATTACHED TO THORPE.

YOU COULD HARDLY CALL THAT AN ATTACHMENT. THEY NEVER SHOWED ANY SERIOUS SIGNS OF...

...OF WHAT?

...OF ANYTHING OUT OF ORDINARY, REALLY.

I DISAGREE.

BUT I'LL THINK ABOUT THE CAMP THING.

THANK YOU.

I'LL NEED TO TALK TO HIM FIRST.

WHY?

I WANT TO DISSECT HIM A BIT. SEE WHAT MAKES HIM TICK FROM UP CLOSE.

HE NEEDS REST.

I'M NOT ASKING.

PLEASE STATE YOUR NAME AND CODE.

EDWARD ZERO. UR-15.

DO YOU KNOW WHY WE'RE HERE TODAY?

NO.

WE'RE HERE BECAUSE I WANT TO UNDERSTAND IF YOU ARE STILL CAPABLE ENOUGH TO EXECUTE PROPERLY IN THE FIELD.

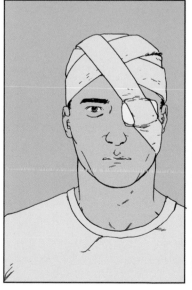

NO REACTION. NOTED.

I'LL ASK YOU A SERIES OF QUESTIONS. IF I LIKE THE ANSWERS, YOU STAY IN THE FIELD.

IF I DON'T...

...WELL, YOU KNOW HOW IT GOES.

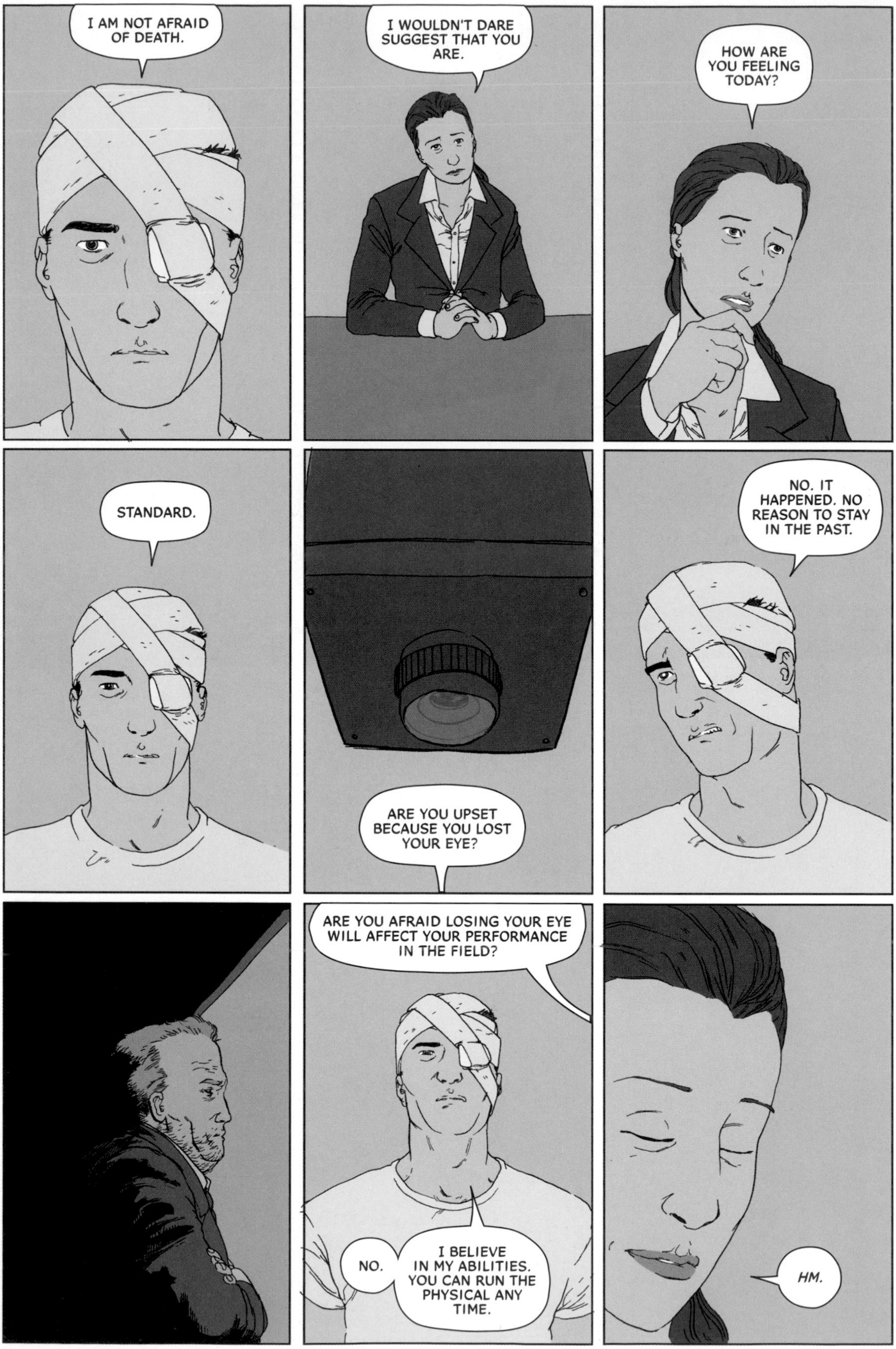
I AM NOT AFRAID OF DEATH.
I WOULDN'T DARE SUGGEST THAT YOU ARE.
HOW ARE YOU FEELING TODAY?
STANDARD.
ARE YOU UPSET BECAUSE YOU LOST YOUR EYE?
NO. IT HAPPENED. NO REASON TO STAY IN THE PAST.
ARE YOU AFRAID LOSING YOUR EYE WILL AFFECT YOUR PERFORMANCE IN THE FIELD?
NO.
I BELIEVE IN MY ABILITIES. YOU CAN RUN THE PHYSICAL ANY TIME.
HM.

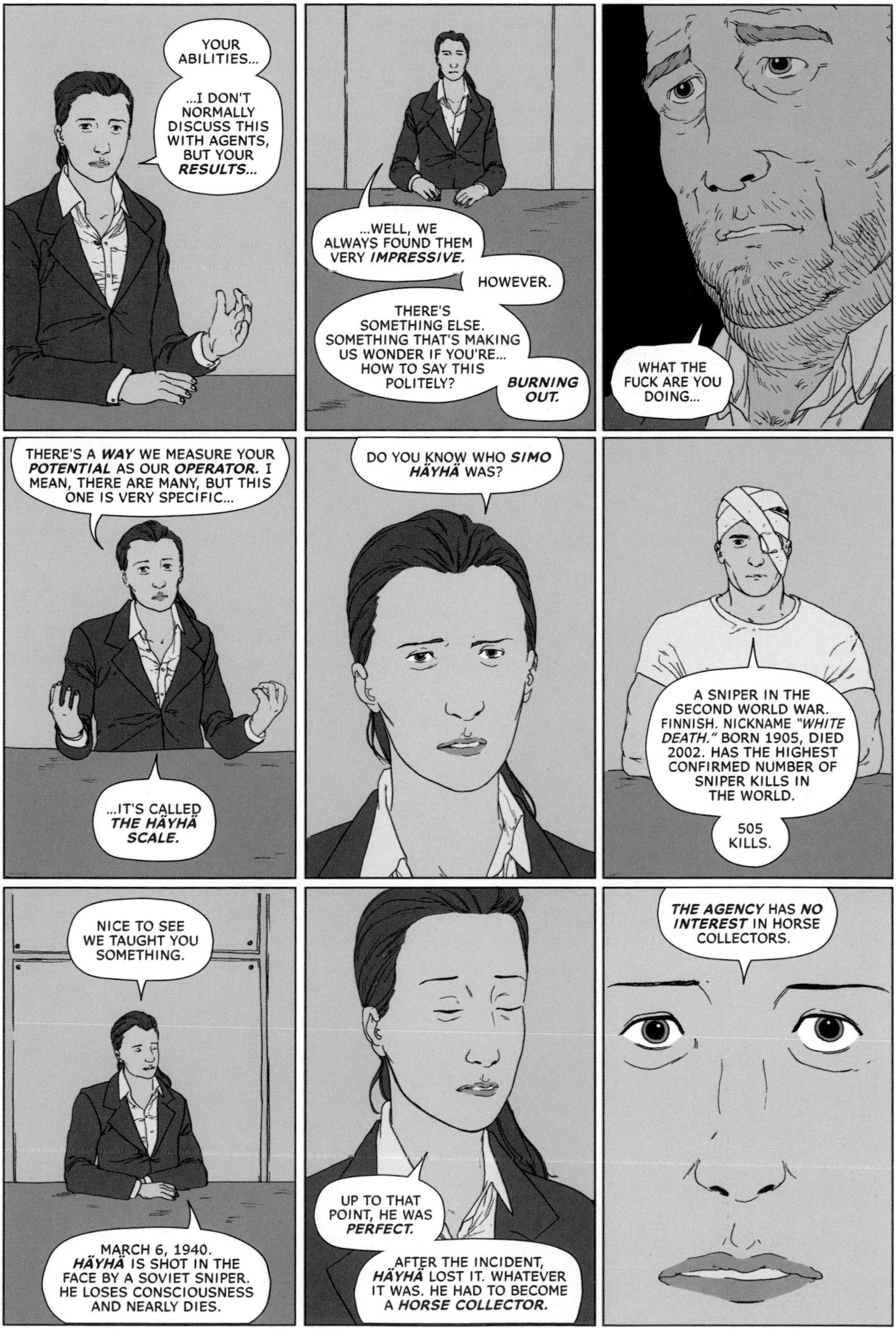
YOUR ABILITIES...
...I DON'T NORMALLY DISCUSS THIS WITH AGENTS, BUT YOUR *RESULTS...*
...WELL, WE ALWAYS FOUND THEM VERY *IMPRESSIVE.*
HOWEVER.
THERE'S SOMETHING ELSE. SOMETHING THAT'S MAKING US WONDER IF YOU'RE... HOW TO SAY THIS POLITELY?
BURNING OUT.
WHAT THE FUCK ARE YOU DOING...
THERE'S A *WAY* WE MEASURE YOUR *POTENTIAL* AS OUR *OPERATOR.* I MEAN, THERE ARE MANY, BUT THIS ONE IS VERY SPECIFIC...
...IT'S CALLED *THE HÄYHÄ SCALE.*
DO YOU KNOW WHO *SIMO HÄYHÄ* WAS?
A SNIPER IN THE SECOND WORLD WAR. FINNISH. NICKNAME *"WHITE DEATH."* BORN 1905, DIED 2002. HAS THE HIGHEST CONFIRMED NUMBER OF SNIPER KILLS IN THE WORLD.
505 KILLS.
NICE TO SEE WE TAUGHT YOU SOMETHING.
MARCH 6, 1940. *HÄYHÄ* IS SHOT IN THE FACE BY A SOVIET SNIPER. HE LOSES CONSCIOUSNESS AND NEARLY DIES.
UP TO THAT POINT, HE WAS *PERFECT.*
AFTER THE INCIDENT, *HÄYHÄ* LOST IT. WHATEVER IT WAS. HE HAD TO BECOME A *HORSE COLLECTOR.*
THE AGENCY HAS *NO INTEREST* IN HORSE COLLECTORS.

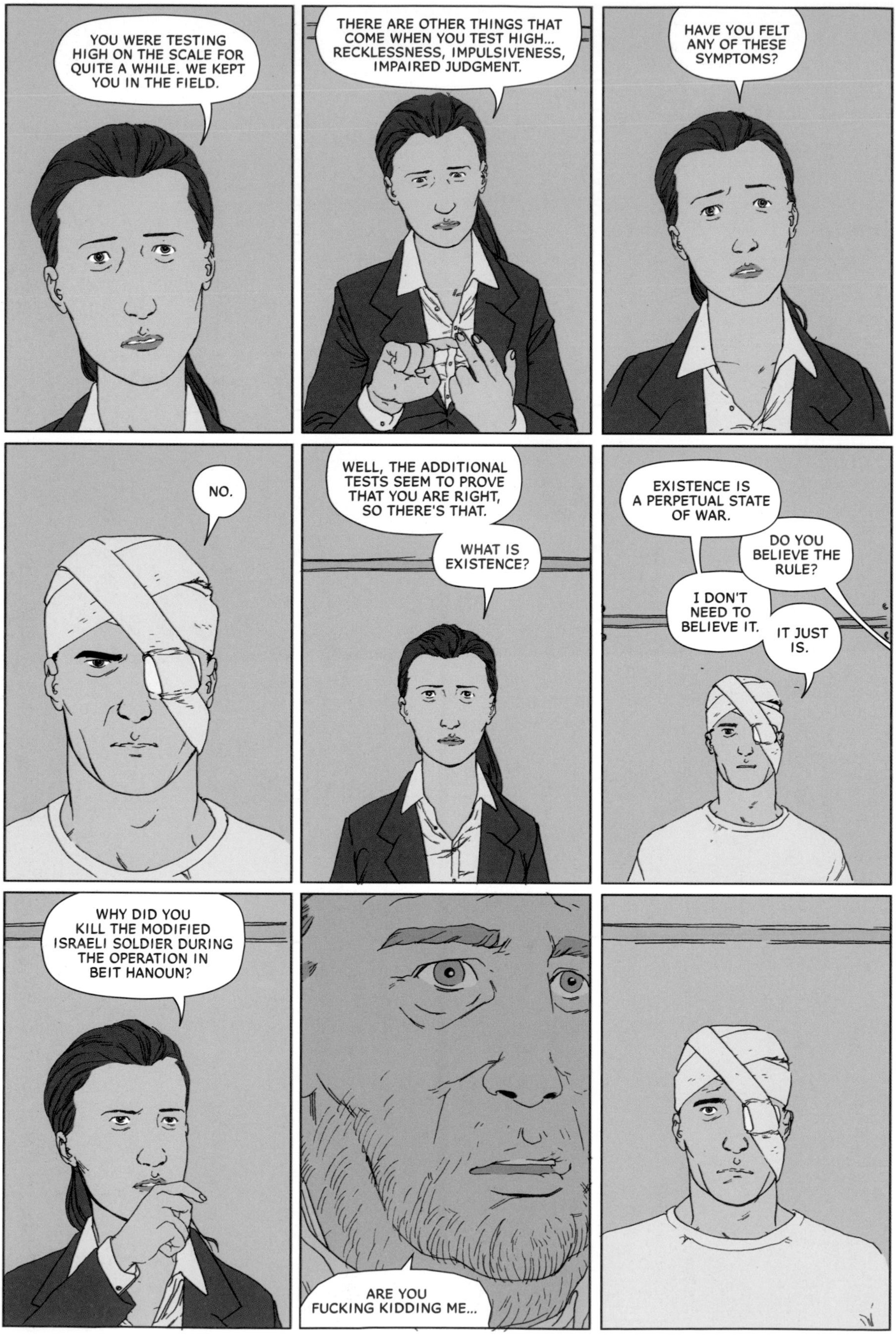
YOU WERE TESTING HIGH ON THE SCALE FOR QUITE A WHILE. WE KEPT YOU IN THE FIELD.
THERE ARE OTHER THINGS THAT COME WHEN YOU TEST HIGH... RECKLESSNESS, IMPULSIVENESS, IMPAIRED JUDGMENT.
HAVE YOU FELT ANY OF THESE SYMPTOMS?
NO.
WELL, THE ADDITIONAL TESTS SEEM TO PROVE THAT YOU ARE RIGHT, SO THERE'S THAT.
WHAT IS EXISTENCE?
EXISTENCE IS A PERPETUAL STATE OF WAR.
DO YOU BELIEVE THE RULE?
I DON'T NEED TO BELIEVE IT.
IT JUST IS.
WHY DID YOU KILL THE MODIFIED ISRAELI SOLDIER DURING THE OPERATION IN BEIT HANOUN?
ARE YOU FUCKING KIDDING ME...

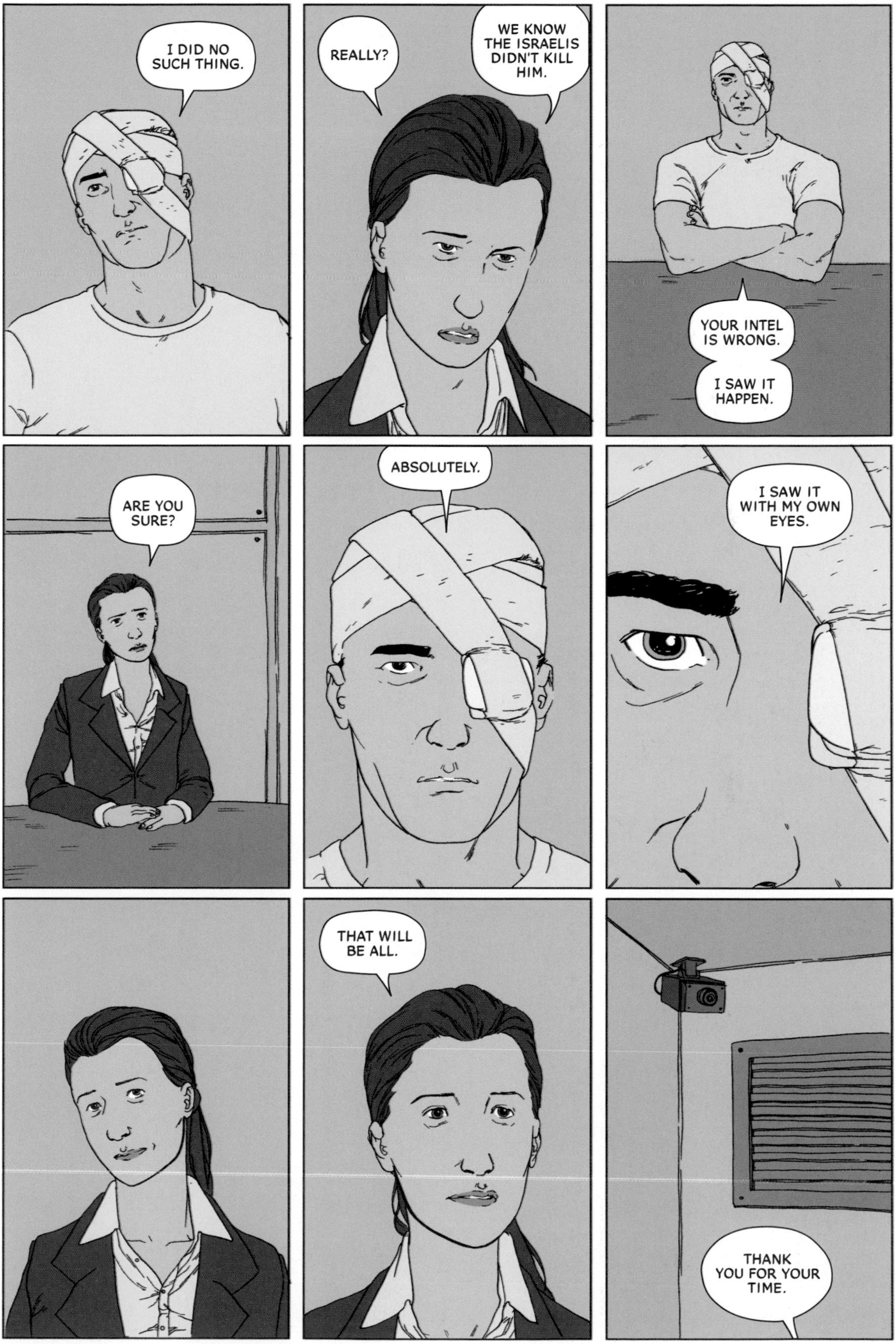
I DID NO SUCH THING.
REALLY?
WE KNOW THE ISRAELIS DIDN'T KILL HIM.
YOUR INTEL IS WRONG.
I SAW IT HAPPEN.
ARE YOU SURE?
ABSOLUTELY.
I SAW IT WITH MY OWN EYES.
THAT WILL BE ALL.
THANK YOU FOR YOUR TIME.

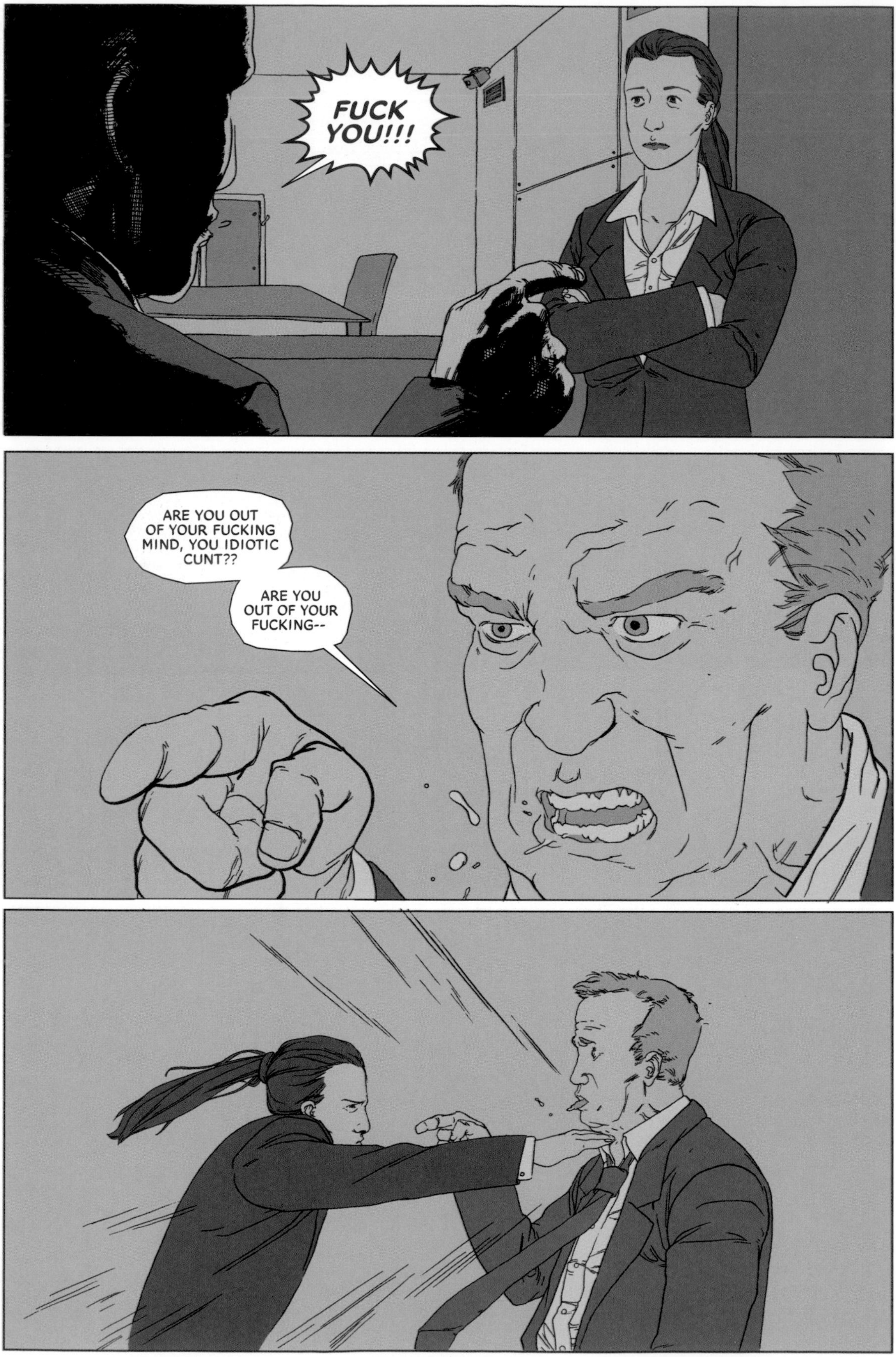
FUCK YOU!!!
ARE YOU OUT OF YOUR FUCKING MIND, YOU IDIOTIC CUNT??
ARE YOU OUT OF YOUR FUCKING--

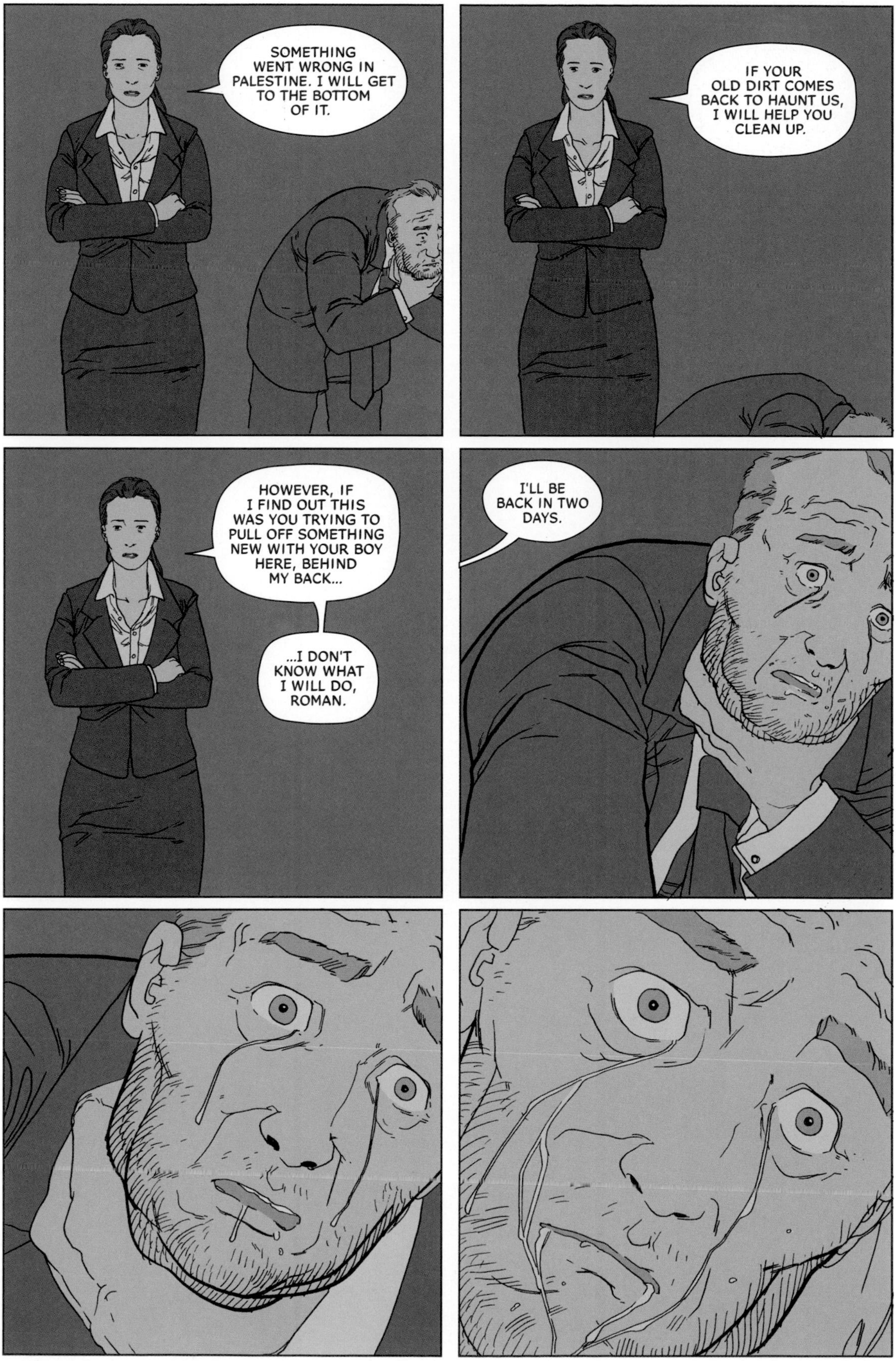
SOMETHING WENT WRONG IN PALESTINE. I WILL GET TO THE BOTTOM OF IT.
IF YOUR OLD DIRT COMES BACK TO HAUNT US, I WILL HELP YOU CLEAN UP.
HOWEVER, IF I FIND OUT THIS WAS YOU TRYING TO PULL OFF SOMETHING NEW WITH YOUR BOY HERE, BEHIND MY BACK...
...I DON'T KNOW WHAT I WILL DO, ROMAN.
I'LL BE BACK IN TWO DAYS.

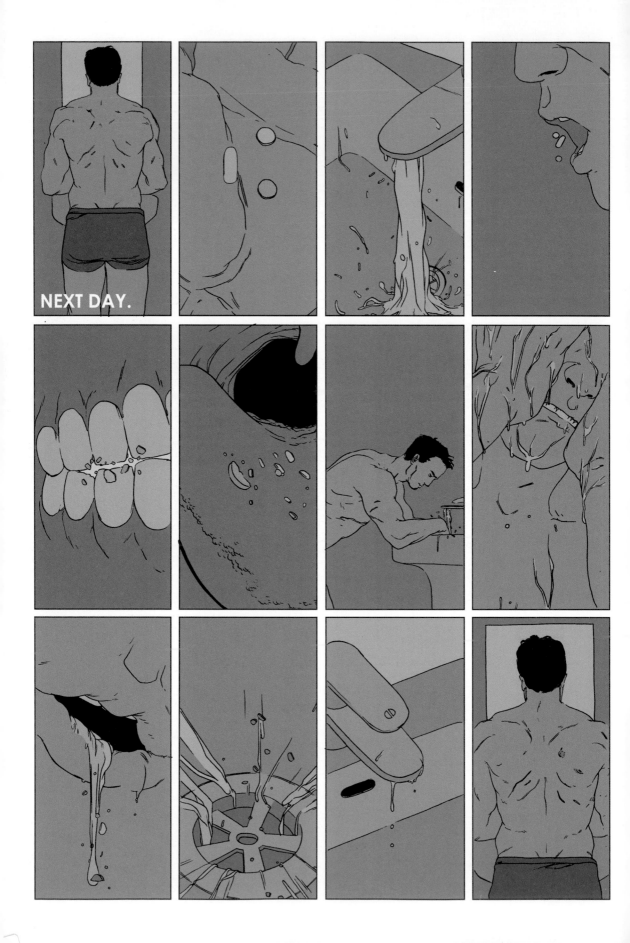

NEXT DAY.

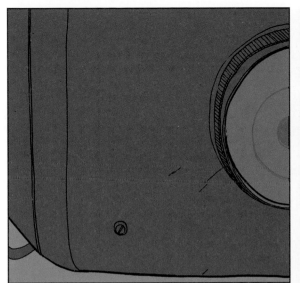

HEY.

HEY.

GET DRESSED.

GOT SOMETHING TO SHOW YOU.

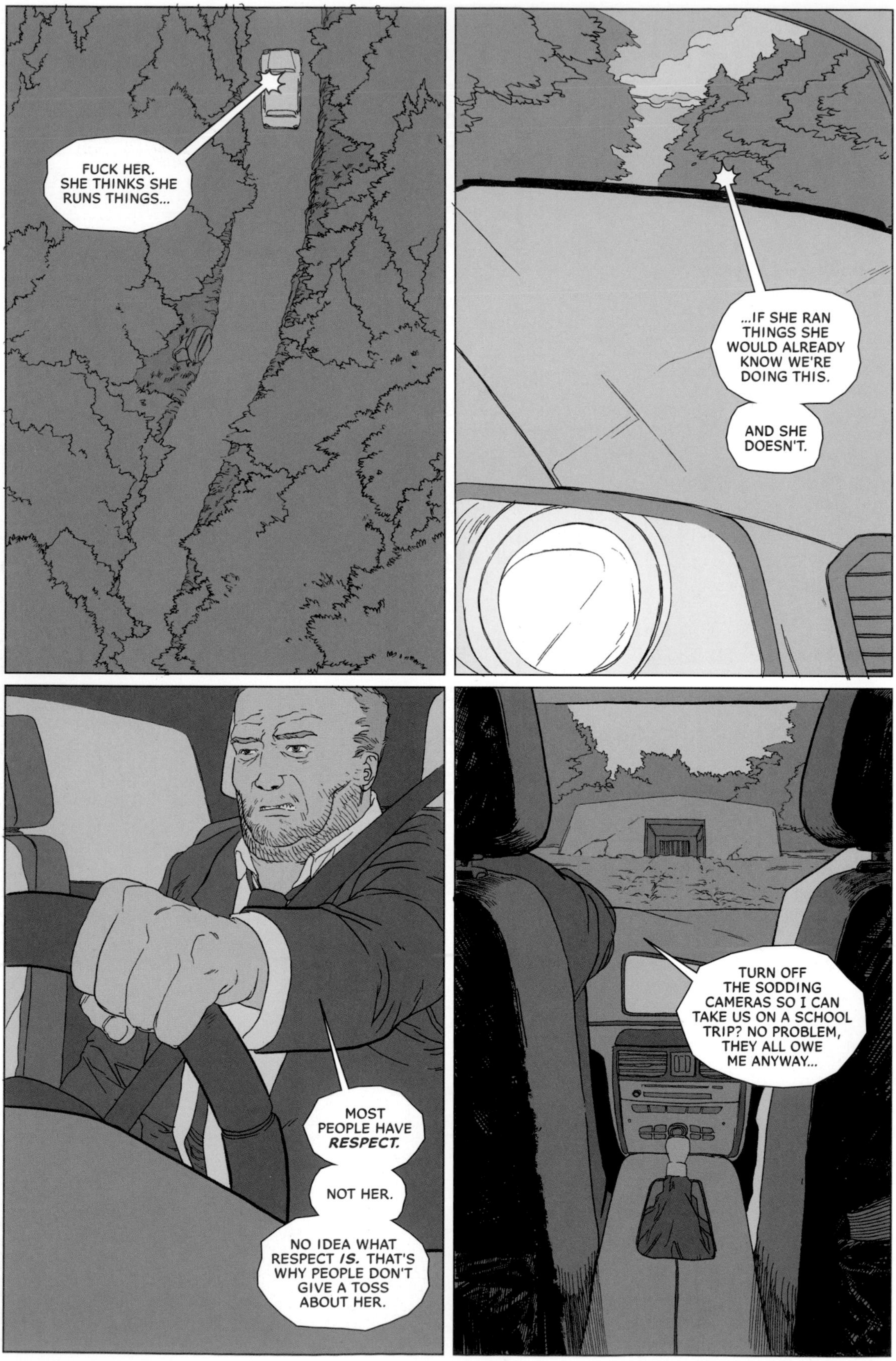
FUCK HER.
SHE THINKS SHE RUNS THINGS...
...IF SHE RAN THINGS SHE WOULD ALREADY KNOW WE'RE DOING THIS.
AND SHE DOESN'T.
MOST PEOPLE HAVE *RESPECT.*
NOT HER.
NO IDEA WHAT RESPECT *IS.* THAT'S WHY PEOPLE DON'T GIVE A TOSS ABOUT HER.
TURN OFF THE SODDING CAMERAS SO I CAN TAKE US ON A SCHOOL TRIP? NO PROBLEM, THEY ALL OWE ME ANYWAY...

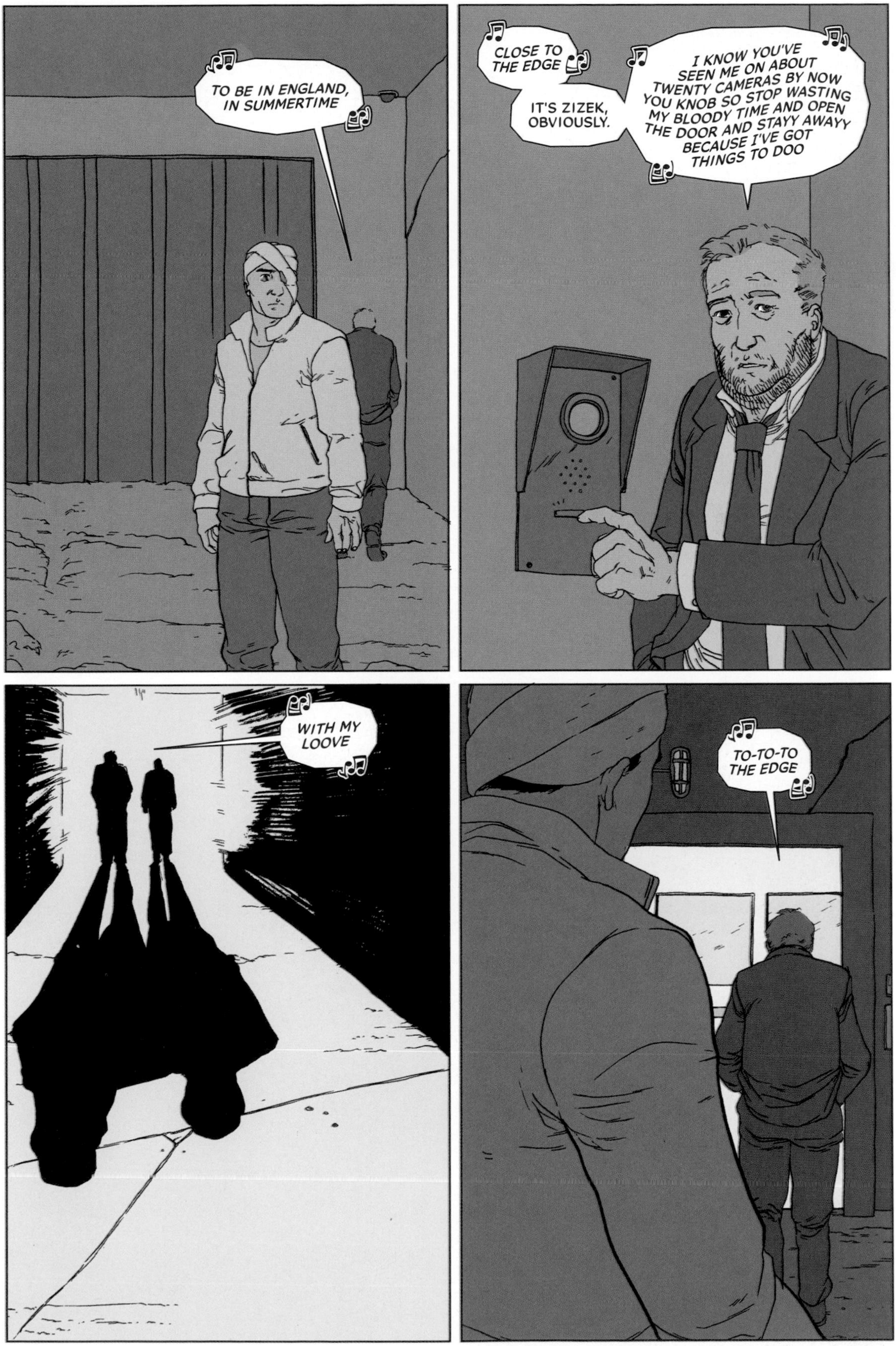
TO BE IN ENGLAND, IN SUMMERTIME
CLOSE TO THE EDGE
IT'S ZIZEK, OBVIOUSLY.
I KNOW YOU'VE SEEN ME ON ABOUT TWENTY CAMERAS BY NOW YOU KNOB SO STOP WASTING MY BLOODY TIME AND OPEN THE DOOR AND STAYY AWAYY BECAUSE I'VE GOT THINGS TO DOO
WITH MY LOOVE
TO-TO-TO THE EDGE

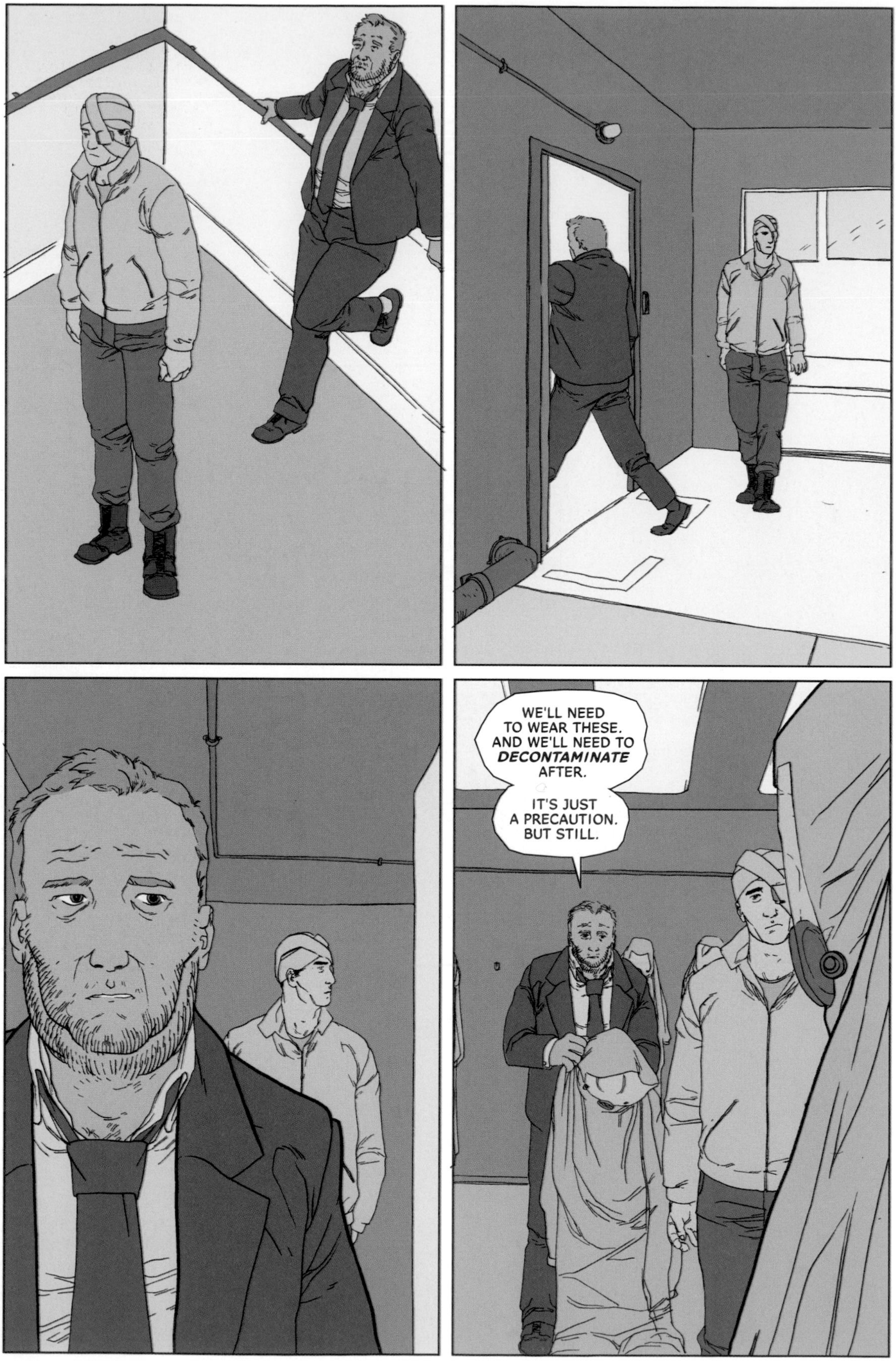
WE'LL NEED TO WEAR THESE. AND WE'LL NEED TO DECONTAMINATE AFTER.
IT'S JUST A PRECAUTION. BUT STILL.

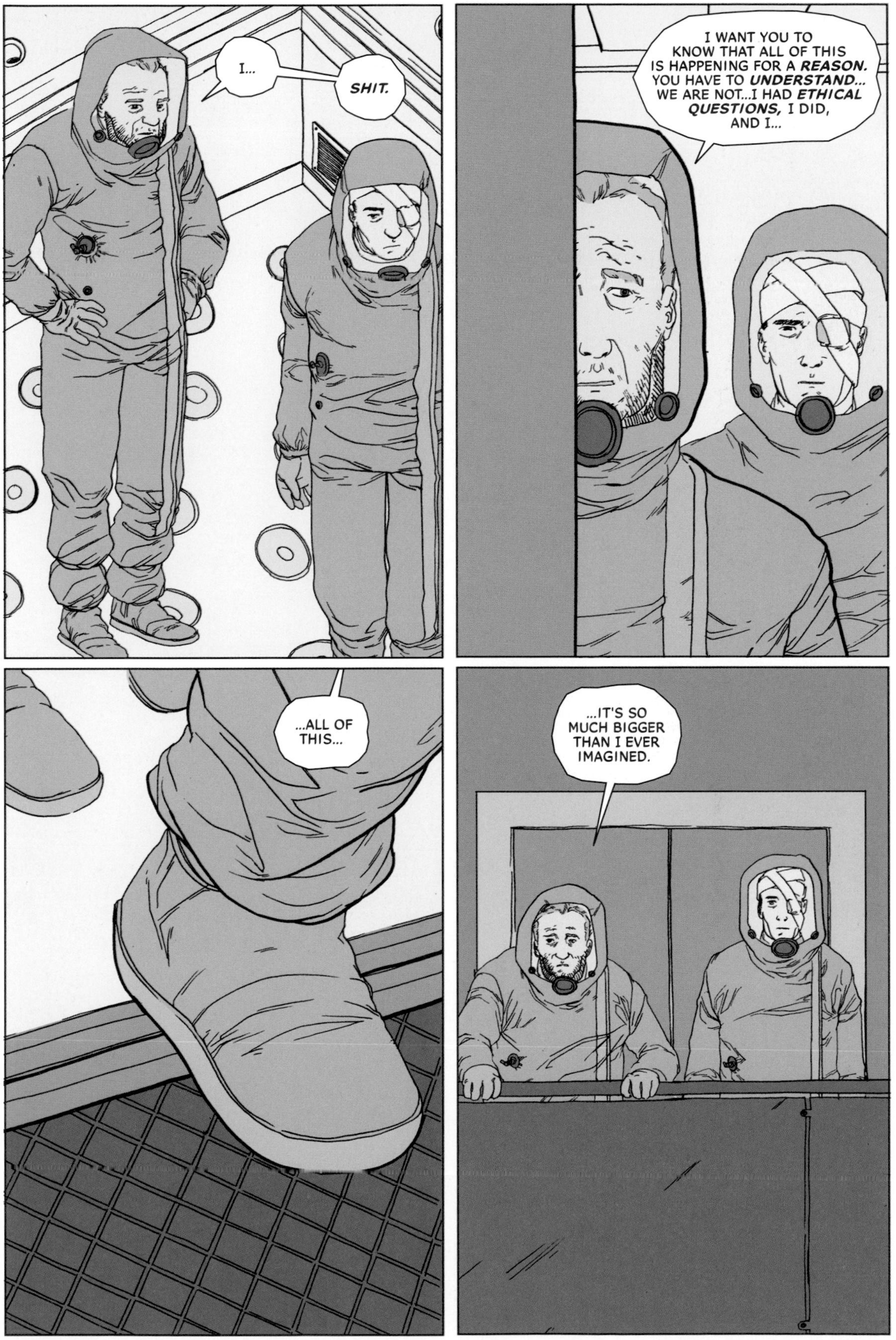
I...
SHIT.
I WANT YOU TO KNOW THAT ALL OF THIS IS HAPPENING FOR A REASON. YOU HAVE TO UNDERSTAND... WE ARE NOT...I HAD ETHICAL QUESTIONS, I DID, AND I...
...ALL OF THIS...
...IT'S SO MUCH BIGGER THAN I EVER IMAGINED.

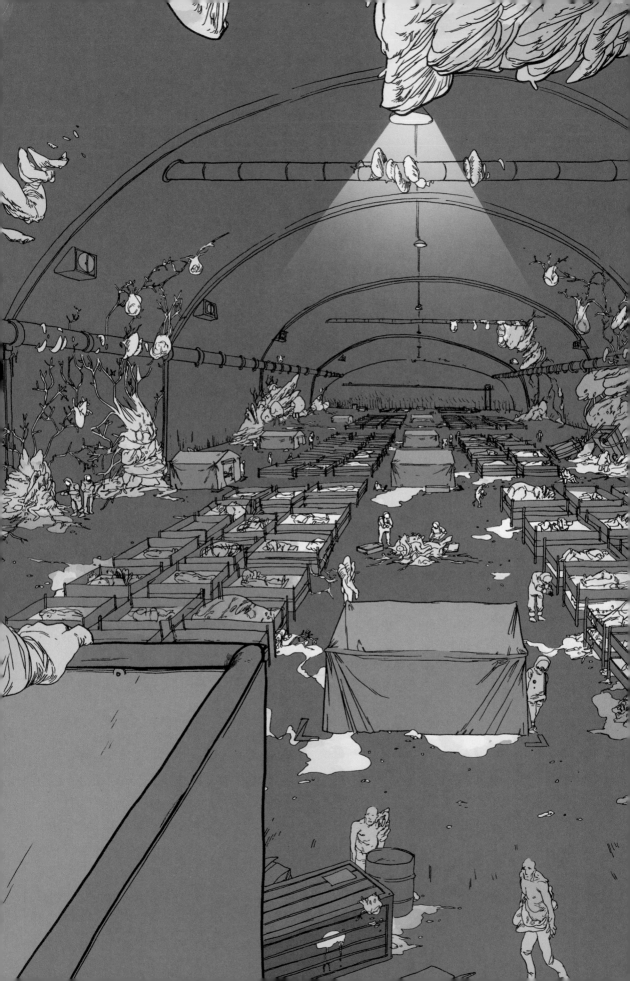

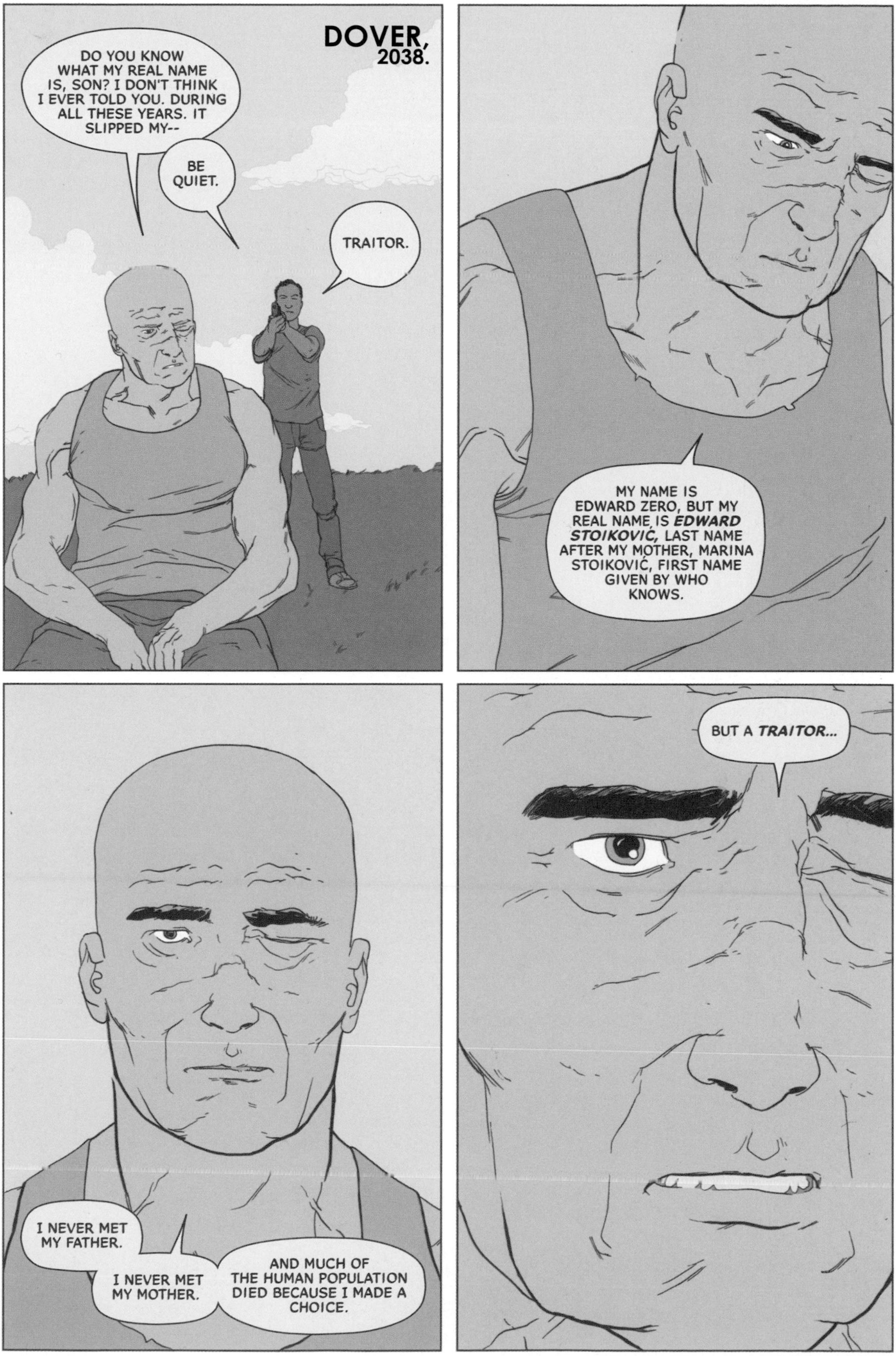
DOVER, 2038.
DO YOU KNOW WHAT MY REAL NAME IS, SON? I DON'T THINK I EVER TOLD YOU. DURING ALL THESE YEARS. IT SLIPPED MY--
BE QUIET.
TRAITOR.
MY NAME IS EDWARD ZERO, BUT MY REAL NAME IS *EDWARD STOIKOVIĆ,* LAST NAME AFTER MY MOTHER, MARINA STOIKOVIĆ, FIRST NAME GIVEN BY WHO KNOWS.
I NEVER MET MY FATHER.
I NEVER MET MY MOTHER.
AND MUCH OF THE HUMAN POPULATION DIED BECAUSE I MADE A CHOICE.
BUT A *TRAITOR...*

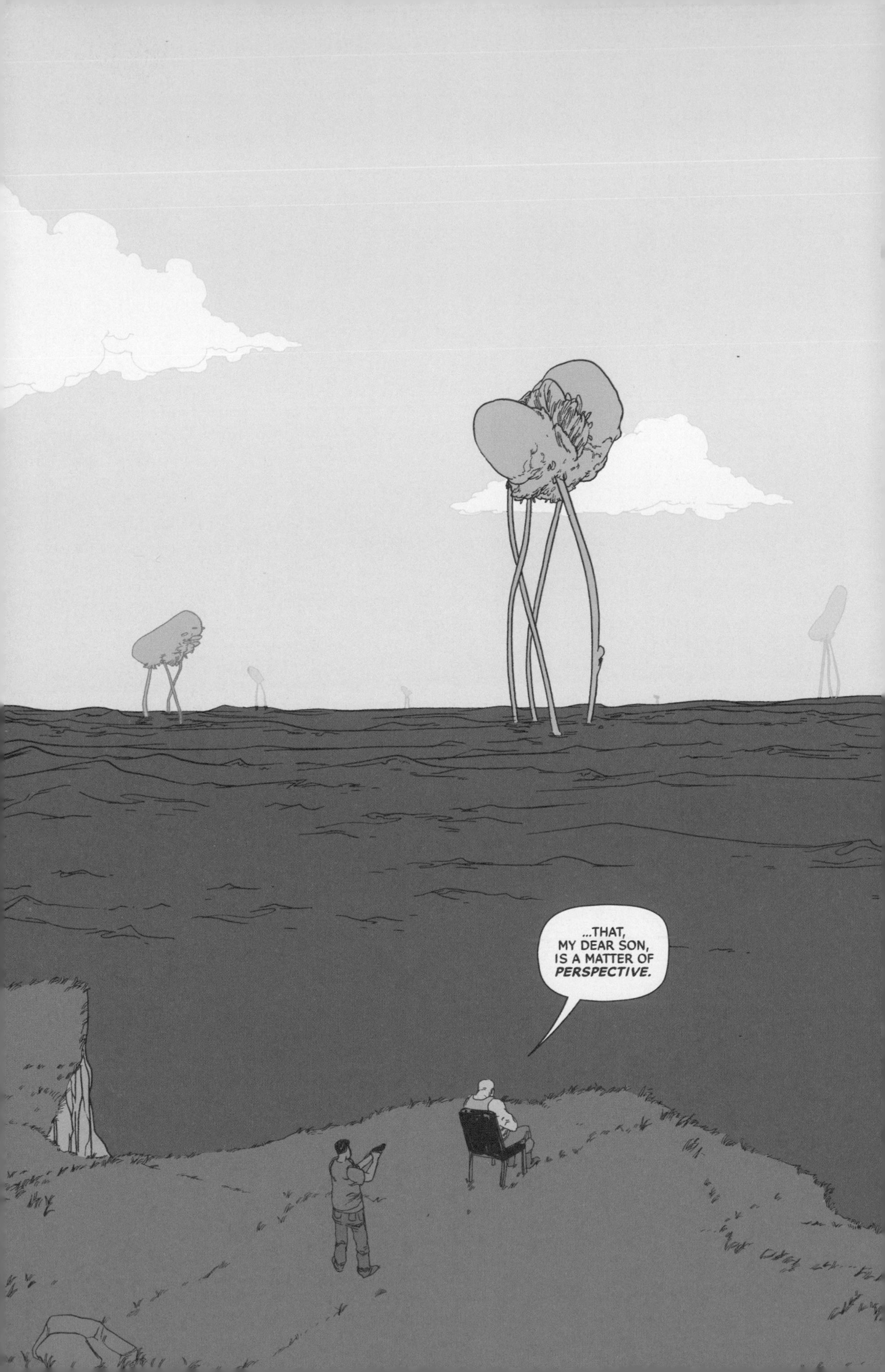
...THAT, MY DEAR SON, IS A MATTER OF *PERSPECTIVE.*

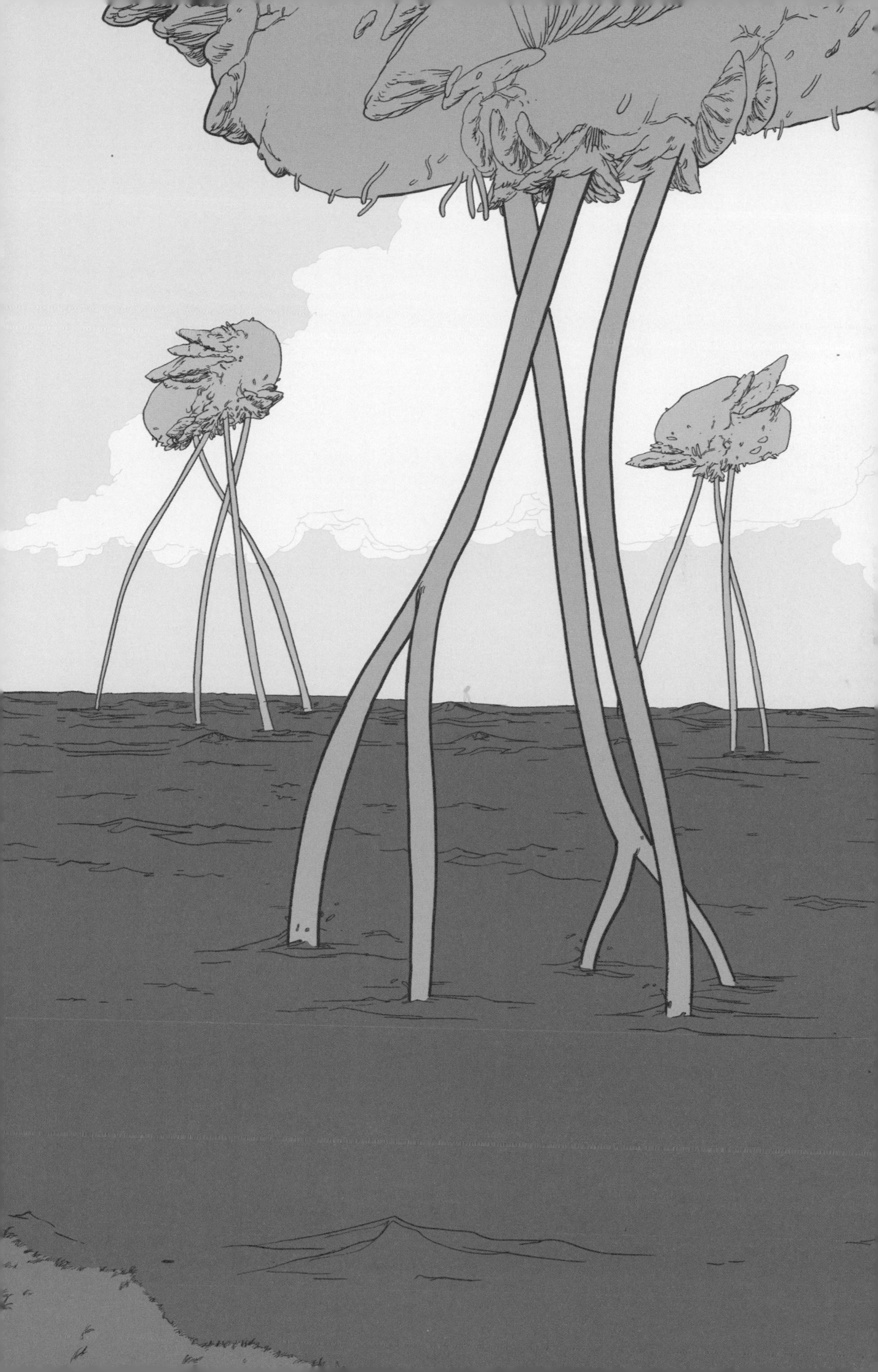

1   —   5

PUBLICATION   DESIGN

The original ZERO single issue publication designs by Tom Muller, with key art from series artists Michael Walsh, Tradd Moore, Mateus Santolouco, Morgan Jeske, and Will Tempest — and variant cover art from Becky Cloonan, Chris Burnham, Paul Pope, Tradd Moore and Christian Ward.

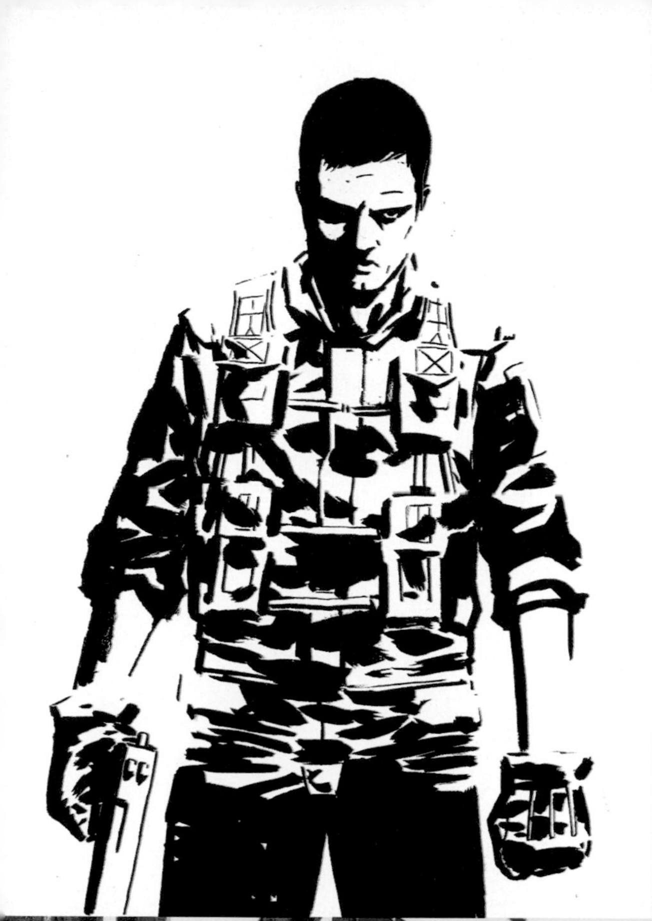

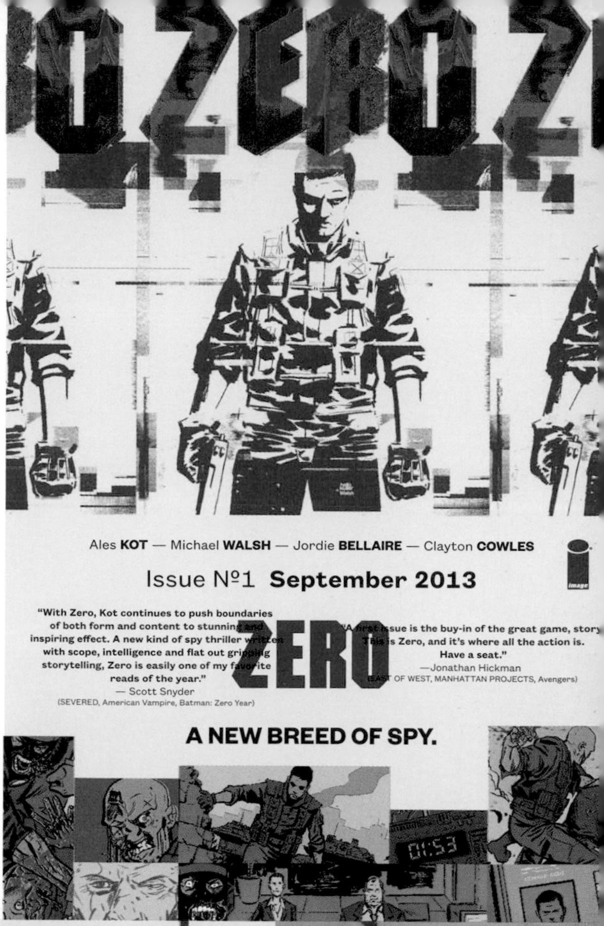
ZERO
Ales KOT — Michael WALSH — Jordie BELLAIRE — Clayton COWLES
Issue №1 September 2013
"With Zero, Kot continues to push boundaries of both form and content to stunning and inspiring effect. A new kind of spy thriller written with scope, intelligence and flat out gripping storytelling, Zero is easily one of my favorite reads of the year."
— Scott Snyder
(SEVERED, American Vampire, Batman: Zero Year)
ZERO
"A first issue is the buy-in of the great game, story. This is Zero, and it's where all the action is. Have a seat."
—Jonathan Hickman
(EAST OF WEST, MANHATTAN PROJECTS, Avengers)
A NEW BREED OF SPY.

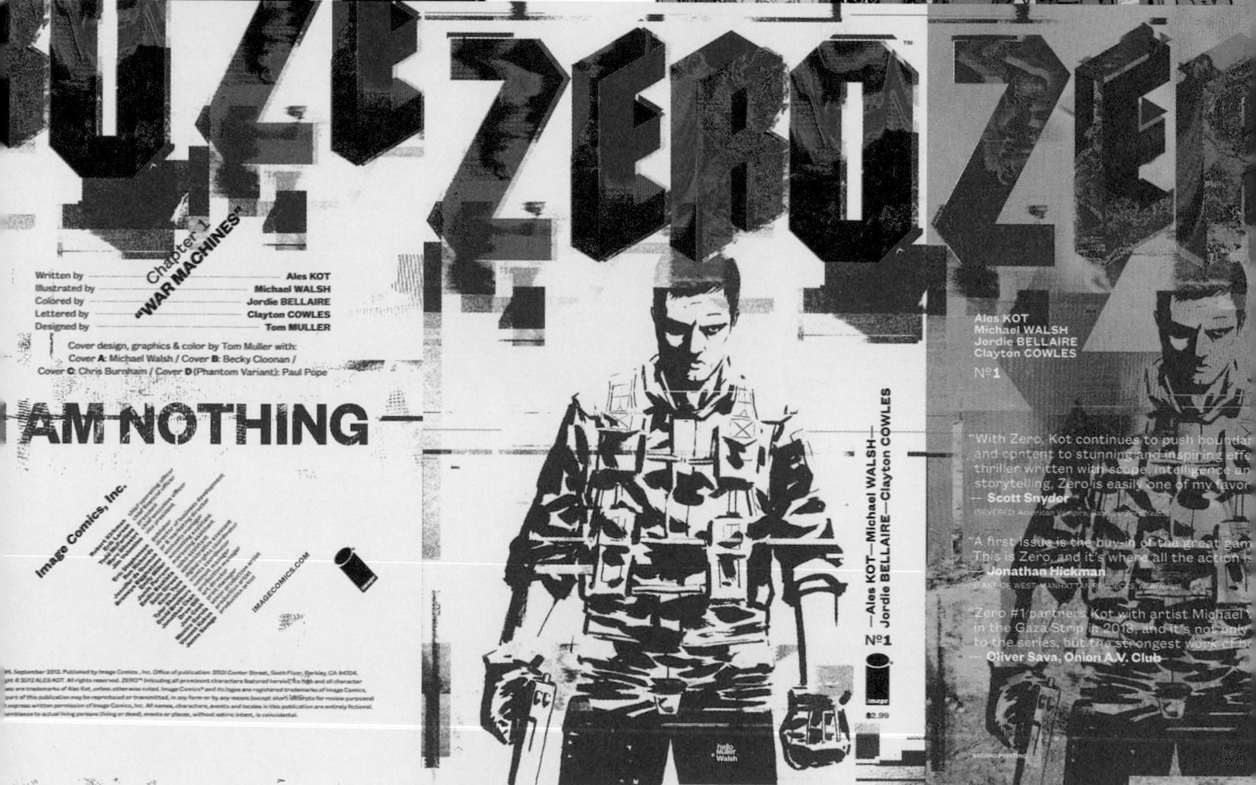
Chapter 1
"WAR MACHINES"
Written by Ales KOT
Illustrated by Michael WALSH
Colored by Jordie BELLAIRE
Lettered by Clayton COWLES
Designed by Tom MULLER
Cover design, graphics & color by Tom Muller with:
Cover A: Michael Walsh / Cover B: Becky Cloonan /
Cover C: Chris Burnham / Cover D (Phantom Variant): Paul Pope
I AM NOTHING
Image Comics, Inc.
IMAGECOMICS.COM
ZERO
—Ales KOT—Michael WALSH—
Jordie BELLAIRE—Clayton COWLES
№1
$2.99
Ales KOT
Michael WALSH
Jordie BELLAIRE
Clayton COWLES
№1
— Scott Snyder
— Jonathan Hickman
— Oliver Sava, Onion A.V. Club

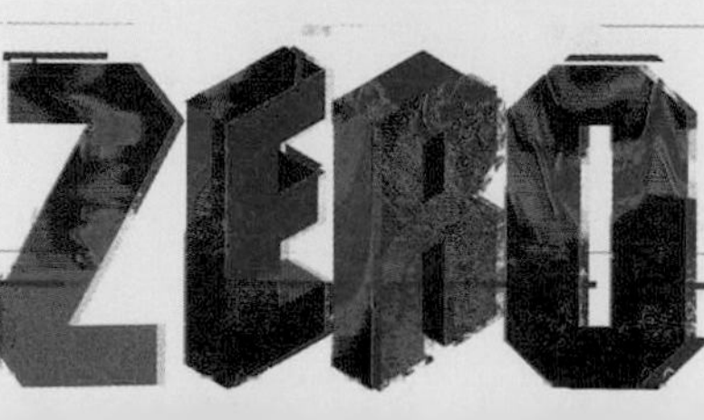
ZERO

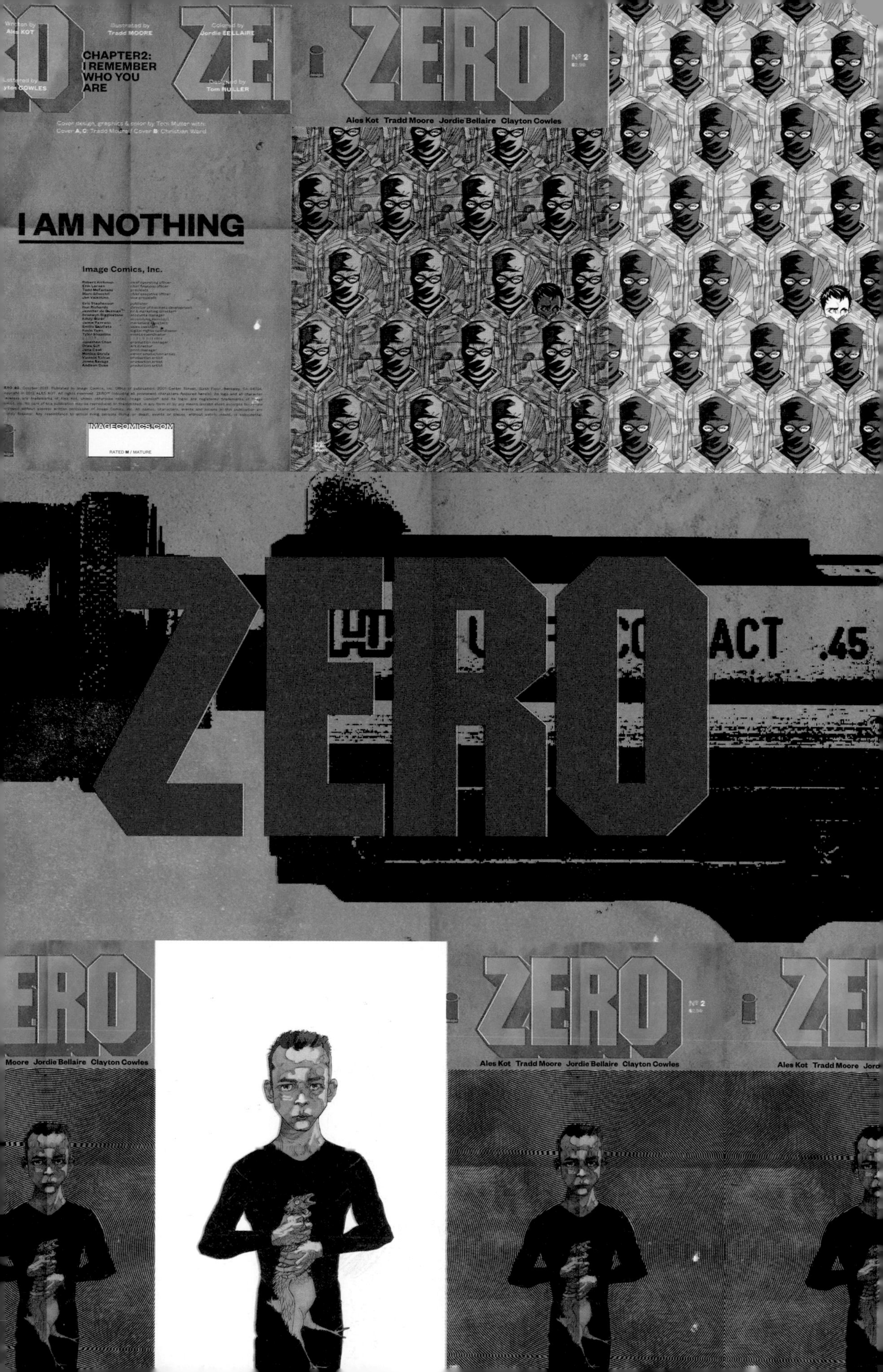
Written by
Ales KOT
Illustrated by
Tradd MOORE
Colored by
Jordie BELLAIRE
CHAPTER2:
I REMEMBER
WHO YOU
ARE
Lettered by
yton COWLES
Designed by
Tom MULLER
ZERO
Nº 2
Ales Kot Tradd Moore Jordie Bellaire Clayton Cowles
I AM NOTHING
Image Comics, Inc.
IMAGECOMICS.COM
RATED M / MATURE
ZERO
ACT .45
ZERO
Moore Jordie Bellaire Clayton Cowles
ZERO
Nº 2
Ales Kot Tradd Moore Jordie Bellaire Clayton Cowles
Ales Kot Tradd Moore

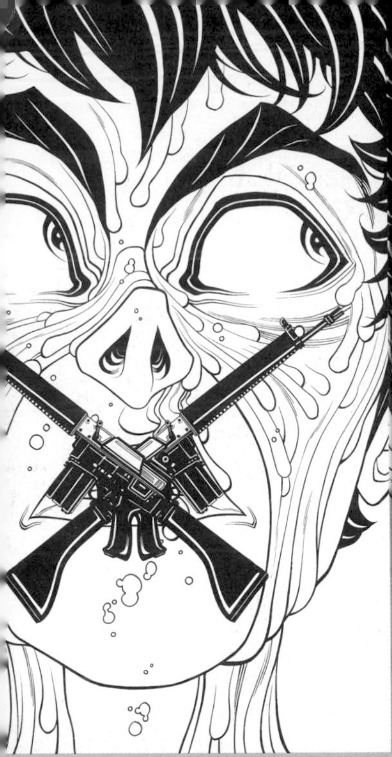

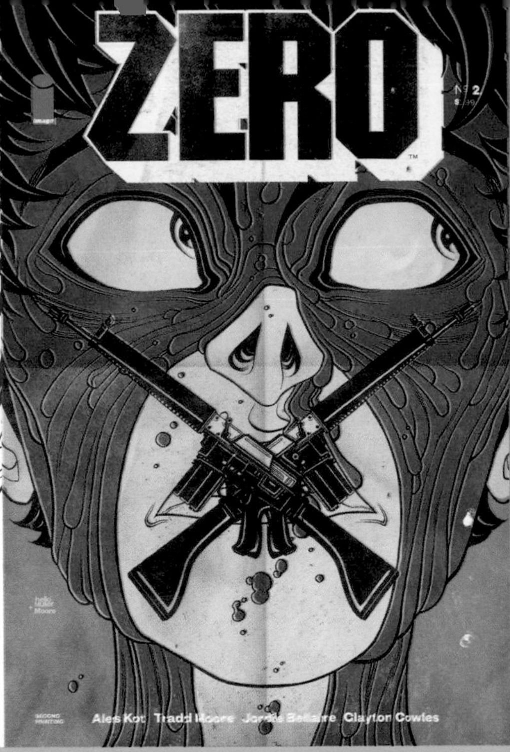
ZERO™
Nº 2
SECOND PRINTING
Ales Kot Tradd Moore Jordie Bellaire Clayton Cowles

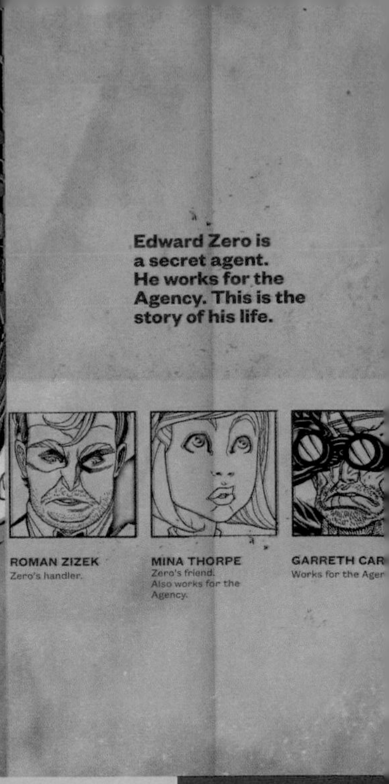
Edward Zero is a secret agent. He works for the Agency. This is the story of his life.
ROMAN ZIZEK
Zero's handler.
MINA THORPE
Zero's friend. Also works for the Agency.
GARRETH CAR
Works for the Ager

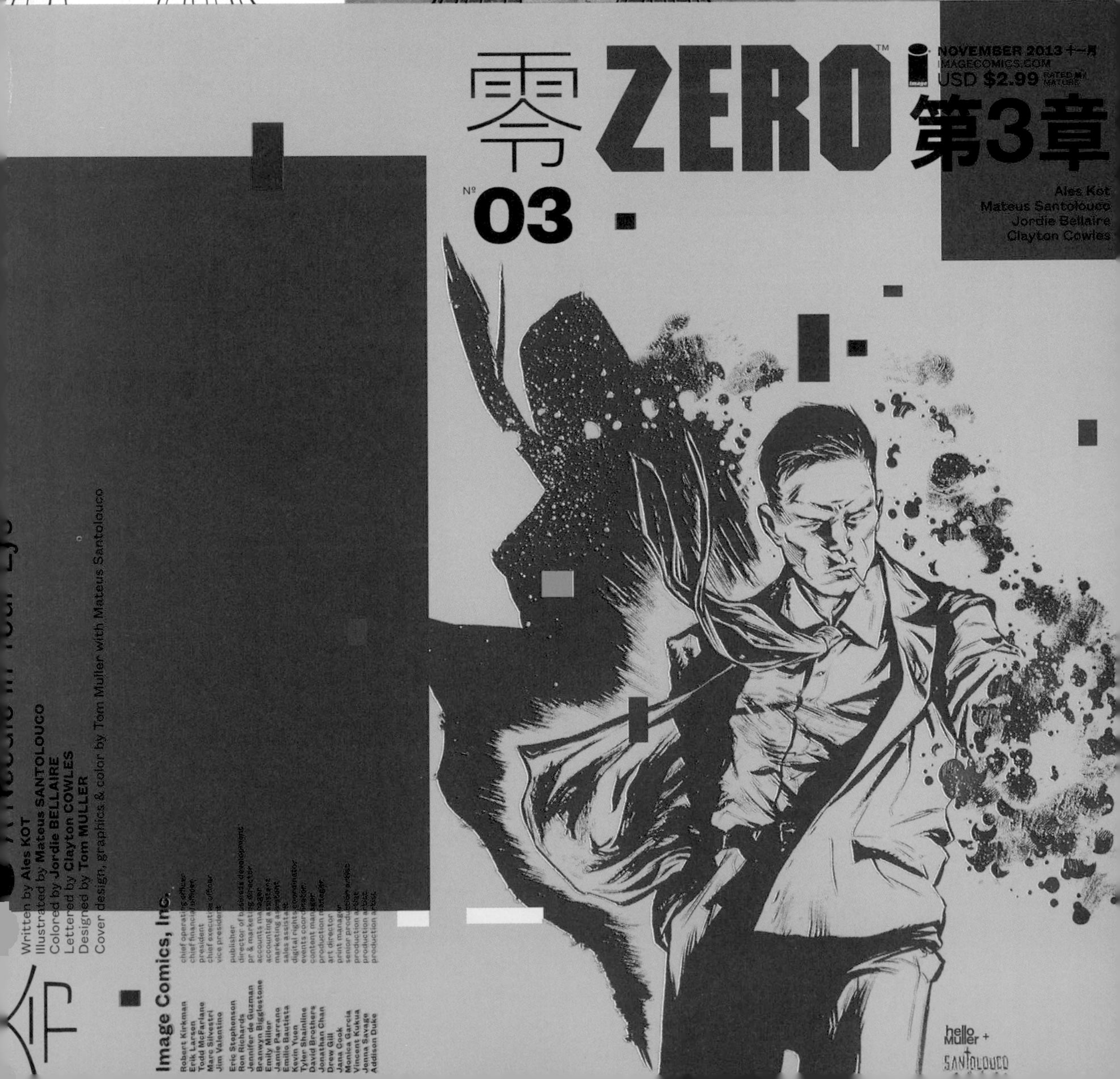
零 ZERO™
Nº 03
NOVEMBER 2013 十一月
IMAGECOMICS.COM
USD $2.99
第3章
Ales Kot
Mateus Santolouco
Jordie Bellaire
Clayton Cowles
Written by Ales KOT
Illustrated by Mateus SANTOLOUCO
Colored by Jordie BELLAIRE
Lettered by Clayton COWLES
Designed by Tom MULLER
Cover design, graphics & color by Tom Muller with Mateus Santolouco
Image Comics, Inc.
Robert Kirkman chief operating officer
Erik Larsen chief financial officer
Todd McFarlane president
Marc Silvestri chief executive officer
Jim Valentino vice president
Eric Stephenson publisher
Ron Richards director of business development
Jennifer de Guzman pr & marketing director
Branwyn Bigglestone accounts manager
Emily Miller accounting assistant
Jamie Parreno marketing assistant
Emilio Bautista sales assistant
Kevin Yuen digital rights coordinator
Tyler Shainline events coordinator
David Brothers content manager
Jonathan Chan production manager
Drew Gill art director
Jana Cook print manager
Monica Garcia senior production artist
Vincent Kukua production artist
Jenna Savage production artist
Addison Duke production artist
hello Muller + SANTOLOUCO

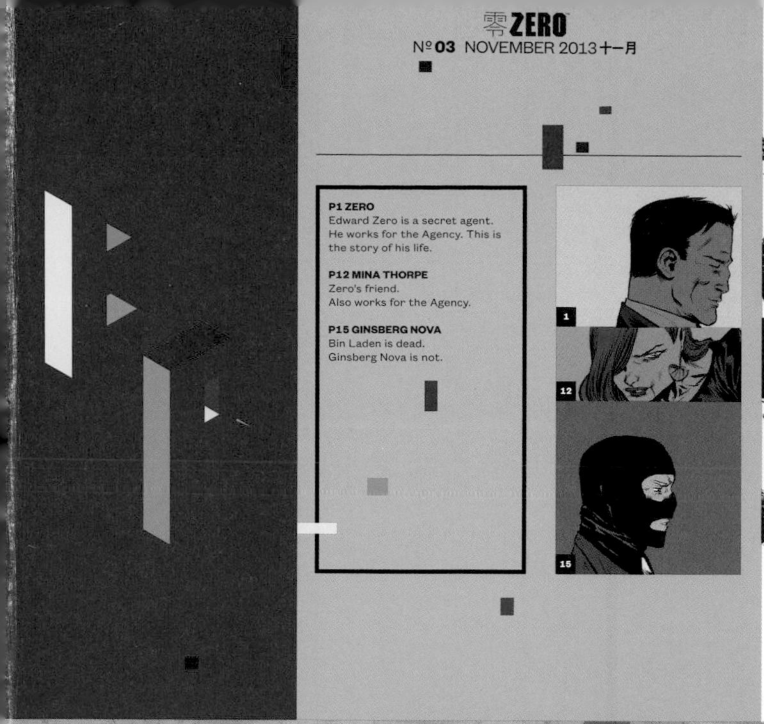
零 ZERO
Nº03 NOVEMBER 2013 十一月
P1 ZERO
Edward Zero is a secret agent. He works for the Agency. This is the story of his life.
P12 MINA THORPE
Zero's friend.
Also works for the Agency.
P15 GINSBERG NOVA
Bin Laden is dead.
Ginsberg Nova is not.
1
12
15

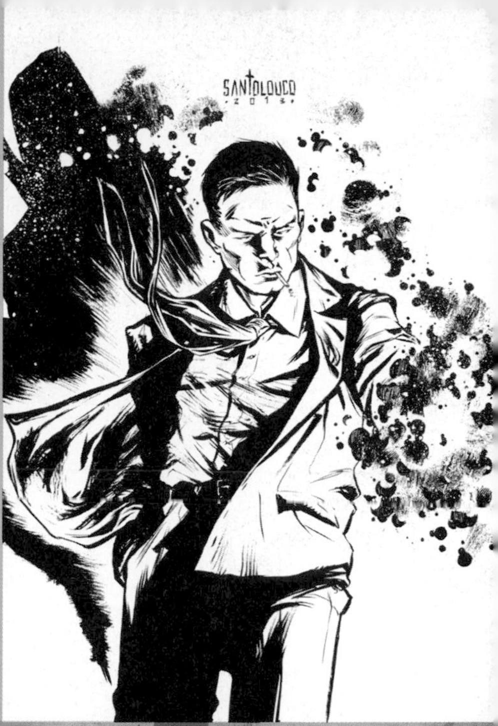
SANTOLOUCO

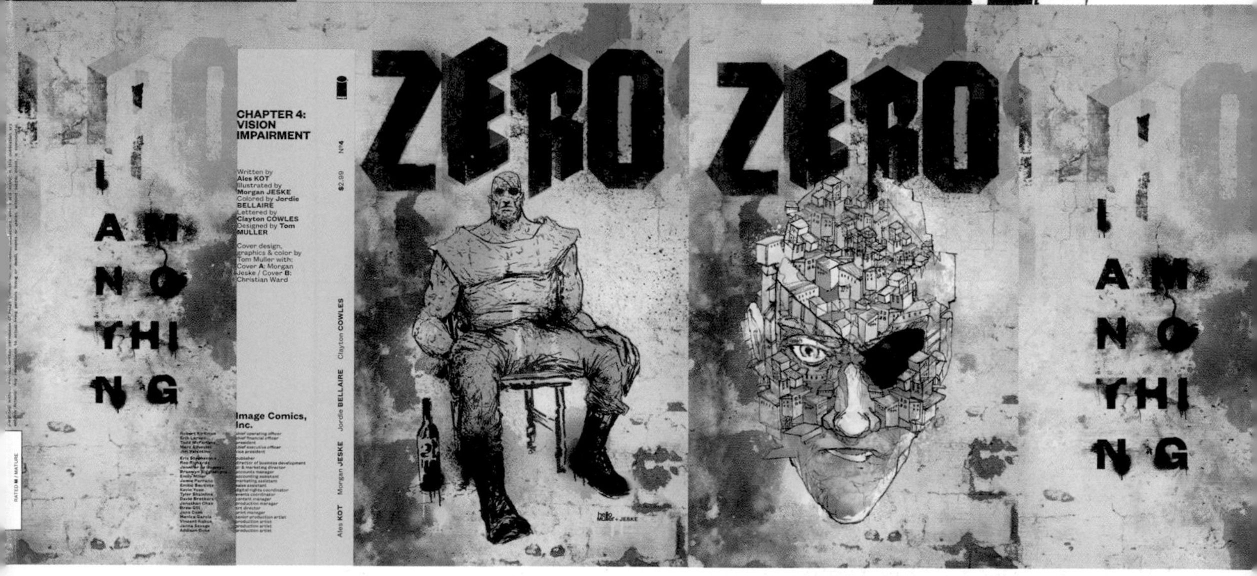
I AM NOTHING
CHAPTER 4: VISION IMPAIRMENT
Written by Ales KOT
Illustrated by Morgan JESKE
Colored by Jordie BELLAIRE
Lettered by Clayton COWLES
Designed by Tom MULLER
Cover design, graphics & color by Tom Muller with: Cover A: Morgan Jeske / Cover B: Christian Ward
Image Comics, Inc.
Nº4
$2.99
Ales KOT Morgan JESKE Jordie BELLAIRE Clayton COWLES
ZERO
ZERO
I AM NOTHING
RATED M / MATURE

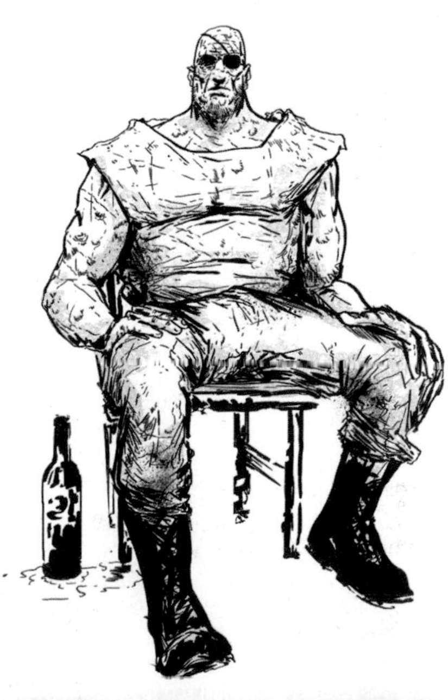

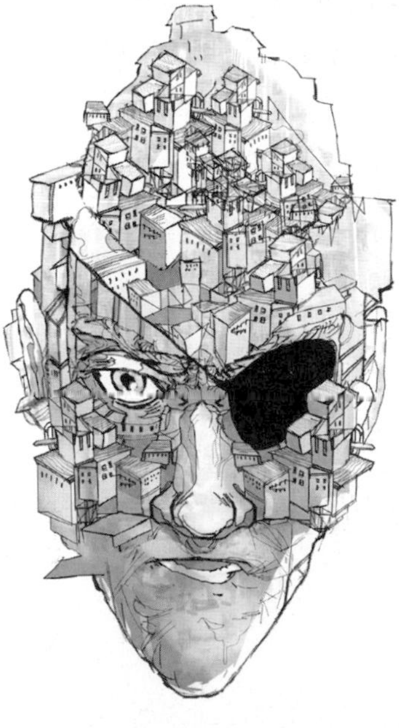

CHAPTER 5: THE MAP AND THE TERRITORY

WRITTEN BY ALES KOT
ILLUSTRATED BY WILL TEMPEST
COLORED BY JORDIE BELLAIRE
LETTERED BY CLAYTON COWLES
DESIGNED BY TOM MULLER

COVER DESIGN, GRAPHICS & COLOR BY TOM MULLER WITH WILL TEMPEST

IMAGE COMICS, INC.

ROBERT KIRKMAN — CHIEF OPERATING OFFICER
ERIK LARSEN — CHIEF FINANCIAL OFFICER
TODD MCFARLANE — PRESIDENT
MARC SILVESTRI — CHIEF EXECUTIVE OFFICER
JIM VALENTINO — VICE PRESIDENT

ERIC STEPHENSON — PUBLISHER
RON RICHARDS — DIRECTOR OF BUSINESS DEVELOPMENT
JENNIFER DE GUZMAN — PR & MARKETING DIRECTOR
BRANWYN BIGGLESTONE — ACCOUNTS MANAGER
EMILY MILLER — ACCOUNTING ASSISTANT
JAMIE PARRENO — MARKETING ASSISTANT
EMILIO BAUTISTA — SALES ASSISTANT
KEVIN YUEN — DIGITAL RIGHTS COORDINATOR
TYLER SHAINLINE — EVENTS COORDINATOR
DAVID BROTHERS — CONTENT MANAGER
JONATHAN CHAN — PRODUCTION MANAGER
DREW GILL — ART DIRECTOR
JANA COOK — PRINT MANAGER
MONICA GARCIA — SENIOR PRODUCTION ARTIST
VINCENT KUKUA — PRODUCTION ARTIST
JENNA SAVAGE — PRODUCTION ARTIST
ADDISON DUKE — PRODUCTION ARTIST

I AM NOTHING I AM NOTHING I AM NOTHING I AM NOTHING

ZERO #5. JANUARY 2014. PUBLISHED BY IMAGE COMICS, INC. OFFICE OF PUBLICATION: 2001 CENTER STREET, SIXTH FLOOR, BERKELEY, CA 94704. COPYRIGHT © 2013 ALES KOT. ALL RIGHTS RESERVED. ZERO™ (INCLUDING ALL PROMINENT CHARACTERS FEATURED HEREIN), ITS LOGO AND ALL CHARACTER LIKENESSES ARE TRADEMARKS OF ALES KOT, UNLESS OTHERWISE NOTED. IMAGE COMICS® AND ITS LOGOS ARE REGISTERED TRADEMARKS OF IMAGE COMICS, INC. NO PART OF THIS PUBLICATION MAY BE REPRODUCED OR TRANSMITTED IN ANY FORM OR BY ANY MEANS (EXCEPT SHORT EXCERPTS FOR REVIEW PURPOSES) WITHOUT EXPRESS WRITTEN PERMISSION OF IMAGE COMICS, INC. ALL NAMES, CHARACTERS, EVENTS AND LOCALES IN THIS PUBLICATION ARE ENTIRELY FICTIONAL. ANY RESEMBLANCE TO ACTUAL LIVING PERSONS (LIVING OR DEAD), EVENTS OR PLACES, WITHOUT SATIRIC INTENT, IS COINCIDENTAL.

IMAGECOMICS.COM

RATED M / MATURE

ALES KOT
WILL TEMPEST
JORDIE BELLAIRE
CLAYTON COWLES
NR: 05
RRP: $2.99

ZERO
EDWARD ZERO IS A SECRET AGENT.
HE WORKS FOR THE AGENCY.
THIS IS THE STORY OF HIS LIFE.

ROMAN ZIZEK
ZERO'S HANDLER.

SARAH COOKE
ZIZEK'S SUPERIOR.

GINSBERG NOVA
BIN LADEN IS DEAD.
GINSBERG NOVA IS...?